Assessment in Scho

THEORY AND PRACTICE IN EDUCATION

General Editor: Dennis Child

Assessment in Schools
Second Edition

David Satterly

BASIL BLACKWELL

First published 1981
Reprinted 1985, 1986
Second edition published 1989

Basil Blackwell Ltd
108 Cowley Road, Oxford, OX4 1JF, UK

Basil Blackwell Inc.
432 Park Avenue South, Suite 1503
New York, NY 10016, USA

British Library Cataloguing in Publication Data

A CIP catalogue record for this book is available from the British Library.

Library of Congress Cataloging in Publication Data
Satterly, David.
    Assessment in schools / David Satterly. – 2nd ed.
       p.   cm. – (Theory and practice in education: 1)
    Bibliography: p.
    Includes index.
    ISBN 0–631–16982–2
    1. Educational tests and measurements – Great Britain.
    2. Grading and marking (Students) – Great Britain.
    I. Title.   II. Series.
    LB3056.G7S28   1989
    371.2′64 – dc19   89–94
                                                                    CIP

Typeset in 10 on 12pt Times by Vera-Reyes, Inc.
Printed in Great Britain by Billing & Sons Ltd., Worcester

Contents

Editor's Preface to the Second Edition

In my preface to the first edition, I was hopeful that students and teachers would find this book sound, comprehensive and readable. Clearly from the feedback we have received and the requests for up-dating, this was the case. So much has happened in assessment in education by way of innovation (and renovation) since the book was first published that a revision has become inevitable. The introduction of a core curriculum, performance measures at regular intervals in the school-life of children, and a GCSE to replace the O and CSE level exam are but a few of the changes.

With these and other changes in mind, David Satterly has substantially revised parts of his first edition. Some of the first edition has been removed to make way for more recent developments. For example, the early work of the APU and the arguments surrounding the use of the Rasch model have been pruned back to make room for recent growth areas such as the development, construction and validation of criterion-referenced tests, profiling and records of achievement. As expected, David Satterly presents this new material in his usual cogent, readable style, which teachers have found refreshing in this difficult technical subject.

Dennis Child
University of Leeds

Acknowledgements

It is impossible to acknowledge all the writers to whom I am indebted for the following pages. However, I am particularly grateful to Robert Ebel, Lee Cronbach, Louis and Marylin Karmel, William Mehrens, Irvin Lehmann, David Payne, Derek Rowntree, Gareth Lewis, Patricia Broadfoot, Desmond Nuttall, Harry Black and W. B. Dockrell, among others who have written extensively on assessment topics. To Frederic Lord and Melvin Novick whose work on statistical theories in testing is a classic in the field, to Robert Thorndike for his collection of some of the best writing on educational measurement and to numerous other writers whose original cointributions to the literature on assessment are to be found in the pages of the relevant journals. A number of publishers have kindly given permission for me to include their material and these are acknowledged at the appropriate points in the text.

I also wish to thank colleagues and students in the Division of Advanced Studies who have helped in too many ways to enumerate. I owe a great deal to Beryl Collins, Beryl Wells, Val Maine and Margaret Battson for the careful typing of chapters presented to them in varying degrees of legibility and stages of development. I am grateful, too, to Dennis Child for many helpful comments and suggestions which have always been toward the improvement of the book. My thanks are also due to the editorial staff of Basil Blackwell Limited, for their friendly support and attention to the minutiae. Finally, I wish to thank the Publications Fund of the University of Bristol for a loan towards the costs of typing the manuscript.

1

The Nature of Educational Assessment

Writers of 'academic' books frequently begin by demonstrating their knowledge of the etymology of keywords in their title. For those bereft of a classical education, however, recourse to the dictionary is the only substitute. Nevertheless, the outcome is frequently informative. The word 'assessment' is from the Latin *assidere* to sit beside. Sitting beside children suggests a close relationship and a sharing of experience. It is ironic, therefore (with due allowance for the ways in which the meaning of words changes with time), to find that educational assessment is associated in many people's minds with one of two contrasting interpretations. First there is a hard-nosed objectivity, an obsession with the measurement of performances (many of which are assumed to be relatively trivial) and an increasingly technical vocabulary which defies most teachers save for the determined few with time on their hands. Secondly, and to many others, assessment presents a very different face as the means by which schools and teachers – wittingly or unwittingly – sort out children for occupations of different status and remuneration in a hierarchically ordered society.

Yet the act of assessing others is deeply embedded in the way we come to terms with our environment. We constantly appraise a child's performance, criticize our own (or others') teaching, try to find out the nature of John's reading difficulty or the reason why many are so disruptive, examine a syllabus for its relevance to the lives and prospects of children or search for words to describe a person. In so doing we are, of course, the inheritors of a tradition which influences our judgement as to what is important. In making an assessment, whether informal or formal, we make a great many assumptions about the nature of human ability, its distribution and needs of society and insofar as these often go unexamined and remain accepted by a majority of self-evidently true they constitute an ideology.

We shall look briefly in chapter 2 at some of the contemporary controversies in assessment since all practices have unintended or hidden consequences. Ostensibly, assessment in schools is undertaken largely in the search for relatively unbiased and fair ways of arbitrating intellectual or other merit. In due course, those judged most deserving of the higher positions in the social order are thus identified and the potential of the educational process for ensuring the equal distribution of opportunity realized. Recent sociological analysis has reinterpreted the practices of assessment, however, and argues that they function as 'subtle and complex agencies of social reproduction and control' (Broadfoot, 1979, 85). Briefly, the argument holds that schools socialize children and prepare them to fill particular occupational roles in an hierarchical social order. According to this perspective it is those in elite positions who organize an education which emphasizes teaching, acquisition and assessment of skills representative of their own culture rather than those which are useful in later life. This group not only has the most vested interests in the maintenance of capitalism but so dominates that its view-points of the social order have been accepted as common sense. This idea is expressed through the Marxist concept of hegemony; the ascendancy and domination of the social order by one social class. The consequences for assessment are that the criteria for distinguishing and evaluating individuals native to that class become the dimensions along which all children are to be assessed. This, in its turn, reinforces the elite culture enabling its members to reproduce, in successive generations, their own positions most easily. Nevertheless, the public face of assessment is of a fair and objective process whereby those most able to profit from education are identified. This acts to legitimate both methods and outcomes in the eyes of most participants, dulling the sensibilities even of those whose 'failure' is most obvious and effectively disguising the class bias of the educational system as a whole (Broadfoot, 1979).

WHAT IS EDUCATIONAL ASSESSMENT?

Educational assessment is an omnibus term which includes all the processes and products which describe the nature and extent of children's learning, its degree of correspondence with the aims and objectives of teaching and its relationship with the environments which are designed to facilitate learning. The overall goal is not to stop at the description (whether quantitative or qualitative) but to provide information to be used in decision making. Some writers on assessment imply that the decisions to be made are those which concern either placement or matching. Typical results of an assessment might be: (a) the matching of a child's characteristics to an educational alternative such as a particular teaching method or materials; (b) a decision to allow or encourage a child to tackle a particular topic having identifiable pre-requisites; (c) a decision to place him or her in a group of similar learners; (d) the selection of one or another educational environment such as type of school or in the case of assessment of a 'young offender', placement in a community home which offers a regime or treatment held to be suitable for youngsters of specified characteristics. Many other examples of assessment for placement could be given. A diagnostic assessment often implies the existence of a suitable remedial strategy, and assessment in career guidance – although specially vulnerable to the arguments about certification of pupils for social roles – could be seen as an attempt to match the demands of particular careers (or at least of those who control entry to them) to the features of a child's educational achievement or personal characteristics.

Quite obviously, assessment for placement involves the integration of the information obtained from a variety of techniques, instruments and types of judgement. Information may be acquired by formal and systematic methods (such as regular testing) and by impromptu means (such as the judgements made by teachers as experience of a child's performance accumulates in informal classroom observation). The information, though, is always subject to error, especially where teachers' subjective judgements are made and great care must be exercised in interpretation where no corroborative evidence is available. In addition, the information may be required for a number of different purposes and communication to a variety of audiences, and the great variety of techniques which have been developed vary in their degree of acceptability to the public at large. External examinations tend to be held in higher esteem than internal examinations, but the new GCSE incorporates internal assessment of course work alongside external assessment of papers in the award of the final grade in some subjects. Though varied, all these practices have the common feature of data collection and interpretation in order to provide information for making decisions or in an evaluation for the purposes of certification.

The most common arguments for assessment can be classified using three broad categories: effects on teaching, effects on pupils, needs of society.

Effects on Teaching

Arguments put forward in favour of assessment understandably stress the beneficial consequences of the practices adopted. As always, there is 'another side to the coin' which will be examined more fully in chapter 2 but hinted at here.

Teaching and evaluation

Assessment is indispensable for teachers for without it there would be no evaluation of their own effectiveness. Knowledge of the results of pupils' performance provides information which is potentially capable of improving teaching. Where teachers are clear as to the aims and objectives of their instruction and are able to state in advance the criteria by which children may be said to have attained those objectives, assessment is seen not as a time-wasting appendage to classroom practice but as an integral part of planning of effective instruction. Note, however, that the goals of teaching are almost always set by the teacher who is in turn consciously or unconsciously constrained by a view of the function of education which has been transmitted by social processes. Thus there is a danger that other goals may be downgraded especially those in which criteria of attainment cannot easily be set in advance. Nevertheless, whatever is being taught or whatever child-centred activities are being organized, teachers require some sort of information on which to evaluate their own practices whether or not they have to account to some other body for the outcomes which result.

Teaching and setting objectives

Few teachers will be happy to enter a classroom on a purely empirical basis; that is without intention or plan and simply to 'see what happens'. Nevertheless, preliminary objectives may, on evaluation, prove not to have been attained by any pupils. Given this possibility teachers are faced with a dilemma: might those objectives have been attained with more effective teaching or are those objectives unrealistic for the children? There is no easy way of resolving this problem, however. Teaching, like any other human activity is often motivated by a set of ideals and some teachers may constantly strive to enable pupils to reach heights of attainment held by others to be fanciful. Nevertheless, and assuming that the teacher has done all he or she can to teach more effectively towards an objective, there are good grounds in psychological theory for arguing that unrelieved exposure to failure will be deleterious for *all* pupils. Assessment, then, potentially equips teachers to define and teach for objectives which are suitably poised for the abilities and aptitudes of the pupils in question.

Teaching and diagnosis

Assessment of individual progress will take place continuously and teachers will constantly be appraising their methods in the light of indications received from pupil response. This form of assessment can have constructive or unconstructive consequences. We are all too familiar with the essentially unproductive use of assessment data: it stops at the classification of pupils as 'dull', 'disruptive', 'lazy' and so on. Scarcely less unproductive, although more welcome, are 'bright', 'imaginative' or 'budding genius'. Nonetheless such acts of classification are of little value unless they are followed by an intelligent attempt to modify or to adapt the features of the educational environment to individual characteristics of children. Thus assessment aimed to diagnose does not stop at application of labels. It aims to identify a child's learning needs and to develop a remedial strategy if necessary. By contrast, assessment can equally lead to the recognition that the school is failing to set an appropriate challenge to a pupil whose ability exceeds that of his or her teacher. If one's concept of effective teaching incorporates adaptation to individual children based on their strengths and weaknesses rather than the treatment of the class as a unit, some form of assessment is required if this is to be accomplished. Not only is this process one of assessment of the pupil but it also involves assessment of the objectives and strategies of the teacher.

Effects on Pupils

The effects of assessment on the pupil are far more contentious. By and large the chief influences seem to be motivational. If we think of motivation as states of the learner which activate, direct and sustain his or her attention and efforts towards the achievement of goals, assessment can serve three chief functions: goal setting, formative feedback and summative feedback.

Goal setting

Setting goals helps clarify what it is that the learner's efforts are being harnessed to bring about. Goals can be intrinsic (that is, they can be inherent in the competence acquired) or extrinsic (they can indicate the reward to be attained by 'good performance'). We acknowledge, of course, that the rewards can be in the competence but make the distinction to acknowledge that teachers sometimes 'hold out carrots' to spur children on (privileges and prizes for good work) or even punish for poor performance, irrespective of whether the child has decided that the goal of learning is of intrinsic value to his or her own aspirations. Assessment and the knowledge that one is to be assessed at some future date provides one way by which children's attempts to learn can be given focus, for without such points of reference learning can be aimless or even a process of ferreting around to discern just what it is a teacher expects.

Formative feedback

This points to the positive effects of assessment *during* learning, unlike goal setting which is located at its *commencement*. All learners require signs which confirm they are on the right track or provide corrective information if they are not. There is little point in sending a child up a cul-de-sac in problem solving unless the teacher believes that it would be beneficial to do so, either to enhance curiosity or to keep a pupil humble. Positive signs during learning can serve to enhance motivation, negative signs to the need to correct errors or rectify a strategy. Such signs can be externally controlled by teachers or internally derived by the learners themselves. They are obtained largely through informal formative assessment although they may be summative (see below) where a discrete goal must be attained before a second major stage in the development of a skill or competence is attempted.

Summative feedback
This is differentiated from the previous type of feedback in that the assessment is of the end product rather than at an intermediate stage in learning. It can be the stage at which assessment becomes competitive, or at least comparative between pupils, and it supplies a sort of seal of approval (or disapproval) on the child's efforts. The assessment exerts a potentially powerful effect on the child's self-esteem and growing sense of identity as a learner in a particular subject area.

Teachers recognize the educational value of informal assessment in goal setting and formative feedback yet many are nevertheless aware of the dangers of summative evaluation. This is because of the potentially harmful effects on those whose results are insufficiently encouraging to motivate them to try harder or even sustain their efforts. New techniques which try to recognize only the positive achievements and use a variety of assessment tasks and response modes promise to remove the worst effects of failure. These are referred to in chapter 10. Records of achievement for all pupils may provide incentives for the 20% or so of children who left school with no acknowledgement or certificate under the old GCE and CSE system.

The 'Needs of Society'

Writers and people at large differ, often vehemently, on the extent to which education serves or ought to serve as an agent of social change. It is probably true to say, however, that the majority of educational sociologists are of the view that the practices of assessment in education function most effectively as instruments of social control and in perpetuating rather than revolutionizing the existing social order. It is hardly surprising, therefore, to find that the 'needs of society' which assessment is held to serve are threefold: certification of pupils, accountability to those who finance the system and maintenance of standards in teaching and learning.

Certification (sometimes known as 'accreditation')

Certification [writes Broadfoot] is indeed the epitome of the overtly meritocratic basis of our society since in theory it allows free competition based on academic ability and industry and thus is regarded as the fairest basis for the allocation of opportunities for high status or remunerative careers. (Broadfoot, 1979, 21–2).

This is obviously a simplification but it contains some truth. We need hardly pause to point out the relatively low status and low pay of teachers to realize that some are more fully accredited by academic success than others. At important stages in a child's educational career, in all formal educational systems throughout the world, pupils are afforded the opportunity to show their achievements in relation to those of others and certain levels are specified for admission to institutions of higher education (which have a clear pecking order easily recognized by the 'man in the street') or to different occupations. Many professions exercise tight control over entry in this way. Entry is often competitive and the methods are accepted by many as the fairest that can be devised. (In weak defence of the British system one could point out that selection is less draconian here than in certain other members of the European Economic Community.) Few can doubt that some occupations demand higher levels of academic competence than others. But many researchers have questioned the validity of academic assessment in the prediction of job performance or success in higher education, and have pointed out that even objective tests – whose scoring does not depend on a marker's idiosyncrasies – are less than totally reliable and accurate. This issue is discussed more fully in later chapters but whilst we acknowledge the role of assessment in the certification of performance to other teachers, to schools at the next 'level' of education, to the world of work and to parents, even the best assessments are rough approximations to the truth and other ways must be sought if the goal of fairness to all pupils is to be realized.

Accountability and the maintenance of standards

Traditionally schools in this country have done little by way of formal accountability to justify their expenditure of others' money. But, in practice, what goes on in schools is powerfully constrained by norms and expectancies in the community at large so that practices which depart significantly from mainstream are often viewed with suspicion. Accountability in the United States has been thought of as a negotiated relationship between participants who agree in advance to accept certain levels of support for schools, provided the attainment of specified goals is evaluated in a mutually acceptable way (Alkin, 1970). In this country little or no attempt has been made to negotiate the aims of schools with parents (who, ultimately, as tax payers determine the level of support the education system is to receive) although what actually goes on in schools is monitored by other officials such as local authority or HM inspectors. Only in relatively rare (though possibly increasing) cases are parents actually able to choose schools whose practices conform to their own preferences, however. (Unless of course they are wealthy enough to opt for independent schooling.)

It is not the purpose of this section to examine the principle of accountability nor to identify the problems involved. But in the USA over thirty states have already introduced some form of testing basic skills in all their schools and in this country a step seems to have been taken in this direction by the setting of targets within the national curriculum and the testing of all children at ages 7, 11, 14 and 16 in England and Wales.

This section of the chapter can be summed up as follows: assessment in education can be justified by the need to evaluate the effectiveness of teaching, to provide incentive and feedback information to children, to certificate performance, to obtain the data for accountability and to ensure the maintenance of educational standards. In all these uses, however, assessment has certain potentially damaging side-effects. Some of these are examined in chapter 2.

A PRELIMINARY CLASSIFICATION OF CLASSROOM ASSESSMENT PRACTICE

The purpose of this section is to provide working definitions of a few central terms to be used throughout the book. A glossary of terms is provided as an appendix so only those necessary to organize the preliminary discussion will be examined here. First, a

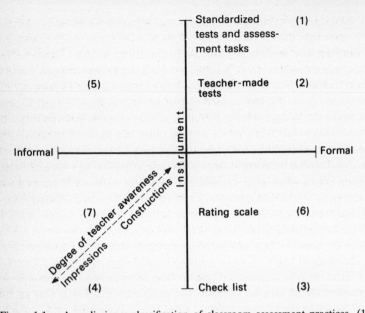

Figure 1.1   A preliminary classification of classroom assessment practices. (1) Standardized testing of ability or attainment in the national curriculum attainment testing programme; (2) teacher-made tests administered under exam conditions; (3) check list used in assessing practical work under exam conditions; (4) check list used to assess performance during normal class learning activities; (5) assessing performance during pupils' use of text book and work cards; (6) rating scale used under exam conditions; (7) rating scale to assess performance during normal classroom learning activities.

preliminary and schematic map of the field will be provided (figure 1.1)

Educational assessment takes place in many ways using a variety of instruments designed for the purpose. Many teachers believe, however, that much assessment is antithetical to the education of pupils. There are indeed strong grounds for regretting an ubiquitous pre-disposition to assess children. The argument stems from the belief that they should be afforded maximal opportunity to discover or to experiment – indeed to learn – unencumbered by the constraints imposed by the knowledge that they are being assessed. But even though the requirement to assess and formally to record the results can be minimized, teachers will inevitably form and accumulate impressions from a child's behaviour in a variety of day-to-day circumstances, even when they have not set out to do so. For this reason figure 1.1 incorporates a dimension labelled *impressions versus constructions*. The choice of terms is designed to distinguish an assessment which results from features of a child's performance which – loosely speaking – 'leave their mark on the teacher's mind' yet which lack conscious organization or interpretation until a situation arises in which the teacher is pressed to make a verbal report from those in which the teacher deliberately uses pre-set criteria and where he or she is explicitly aware of what he or she was 'looking for'. Quite obviously the formal record of the former kind of assessment turns it into a 'construction'. Although this dimension may appear to be similar to the distinction usually drawn between *subjective* and *objective* assessment this is not the case. 'Subjective' usually describes those assessments which originate in the mind of the thinker (teacher) and not from an examination of the performance being assessed. Results are, therefore, potentially variable from assessor to assessor. 'Objectivity' of a result (a test score, for example) is not distorted by any personal bias of the assessor and any number of markers are expected to reach agreement by using the same set of clearly defined criteria (as would happen if an objective marking scheme were adopted). This distinction is made again in relation to scoring of essay type tests in chapter 6.

The second dimension in our model is labelled *informal versus formal*. It distinguishes an assessment made during the child's normal learning activities from those made during periods set aside for the purpose. A good deal of the information obtained by teachers and later used in reports and comments is obtained in situations of the former kind. It represents the teachers' interpretation of observations made in the context of everyday classroom activity (working with other children, working alone in problem solving, carrying out a scientific experiment and so on) and most kinds of process assessment as discussed in chapter 3. Formal assessment takes place when settings are organized – critics might say contrived – with the specific aim of evaluating the child's performance. As Rowntree (1977, 119) points out, this difference may in practice correspond with unobtrusive versus obtrusive assessment or even with the covert versus overt distinction. This last-named dimension contrasts assessment made without, or with the child's awareness, respectively. Rowntree remarks that teachers may justifiably have ethical twinges about covert assessment especially where downright deception (as has been known in some experiments by social psychologists) is involved. This kind of deception seems highly undesirable in schools, to say the least. But the justification for carrying out informal assessment is that it can obtain information about children's performance in the 'real' context in which it is normally learned and exercised. This can mean that it is more representative of the strengths and weaknesses of children in normal activity, especially for those anxiety-prone in test situations.

The question as to whether children ought always to be aware that they are being assessed is more difficult to answer than whether they should at times be deceived in their own interests. The answer to the latter is an uncompromising 'no', to the former 'maybe', if by assessing without the child's knowledge teachers are enabled to acquire information ultimately helpful to the child which would be less easily obtained if he or she were aware of the assessment taking place. Impression formation (discussed in the previous section) may well have gone on without the awareness by the teacher, of course!

The third dimension of our model is the *instrument* dimension, that is the nature of the tools used to obtain the information. At one extreme (the testing and measuring pole) we have located the formal standardized test of ability or attainment. It is usually a test which has high reliability (chapter 7), makes explicit claims and presents evidence as to its validity (chapter 8), gives norms for interpretation and results in the measurement of the attribute in question, usually on an interval scale (that is where adjacent points on a scale are at equal intervals). Teacher-made tests normally lack some of these properties. Teachers do not commonly estimate reliability and are in no position to carry out validation studies for their tests. The results are probably best thought of as placing children in rank order. This is a 'weaker' form of measurement than interval scales but is itself 'stronger' than rating scales. A rating scale is a method of collecting data using a continuum with points along it, marked by numbers or descriptive phrases, and sometimes by both. Each child is then classified by the number or phrase held to be most applicable to him/her. Although many rating scales are graphic, essentially the same information can be presented in other ways. In general, respondents seem able to cope most easily with a five-point scale.

A fourth type of instrument, which does not involve the use of numbers and cannot, therefore, be thought of as a form of measurement is the check list. Check lists can be used to assess pupils' behaviour in a variety of settings or to record which instructional objectives have been mastered. The usefulness of a check list, however, is proportional to the precision with which the categories can be described. We shall see later that check lists do not preclude a form of scoring which can be achieved if desired by summing the number of items checked. Similarly, check lists overlap in content with criterion-referenced tests (chapters 3 and 5).

We have tried to 'locate' many of the methods of educational assessment using three simple dimensions of classification: instruments (ranging from check lists to standardized tests), the degree of formality of the test setting, and a dimension which contrasts teachers' impressions with their structured search for specific kinds of information about performance. These dimensions are not independent, of course. It would be hard to envisage a standardized test being used informally, since, by definition, it is not an assessment made during the child's normal classroom learning activities. In figure 1.1 some of the most common types of assessment are placed according to their position on these dimensions. Chapter 3, however, presents an alternative classification which draws on labels more common in assessment literature.

EVALUATION AND MONITORING

The chapter concludes with a brief examination of the meaning of two other terms frequently encountered in assessment. *Evaluation* refers to the processes by which the worth of something is judged. In assessment terms it is usually applied to the attempts to find out how effectively a teaching programme has achieved its objectives or more especially to its degree of effectiveness in relation to the costs of and effort involved in a curriculum experiment or innovation. It does not apply to the assessment or measurement of children's performances alone, although these may be factors in the overall programme. A curriculum would normally be evaluated in, say, seven essential steps:

(1) specifying goals and objectives;
(2) planning a programme to achieve them;
(3) selecting methods of data collection and developing new ones if necessary;
(4) collection of data, including children's performance if necessary;
(5) processing, summarizing and analysing data;
(6) comparing results of (5) with content of (1);
(7) reporting results.

Notice that in evaluation attention is directed to the effectiveness of the programme.

Monitoring is the name given to a programme of testing designed to check or to keep a continual record of performance over a period of time. This will be accomplished by regular testing of the attainment targets in the new national curriculum.

2

Against Assessment

Theories, assumptions and practices of assessment are deservedly
subject to continuous critical scrutiny by professionals and lay-
people alike. Although the day-to-day routine of schools prohibits
detailed discussion of assessment, many teachers question its
necessity whilst others are implacably opposed to all forms of
'labelling'. There are, of course, many problems with educational
testing, but although some observers have seen it as indispensable
to the maintenance of standards others regard it as tyrannical and
antithetical to the process of education itself. As examples of the
latter view readers should refer to the widely quoted writings of
Hoffman (1962) and Black (1962) which are extremes of their
kind.

The purpose of this chapter is to introduce the reader to some
of the most common arguments against assessment and to sketch
out the kinds of rejoinder that can be made to them. The issues are
varied. Arguments by sociologists have highlighted certain social
and political consequences of assessment practices. Ethical objections have also been raised. Other arguments point to the undesirable side-effects of testing on children and teachers and further
objections are rooted in an examination of the technical defects of
current methods at our disposal. Still more critics have argued the
potential danger of forms of assessment which inhibit educational
change, control the curriculum and emphasize those objectives of
education which are most easily measurable at the expense
of equally legitimate (some would say more important) aims of
education which are difficult to evaluate, at least in the short term.

Neither the objections nor the replies do full justice to the
arguments which are, in any case, likely to be reinterpreted in the
light of contemporary social and political circumstances. In
indicating the concerns, however, it is hoped to keep teachers
aware of the ways in which assessment (which may have become

routine and be taken for granted) can have adverse effects on the individual, the institution and on society at large.

ASSESSMENT: A POLITICAL ACTIVITY

An objection often raised is that:

> Assessment is a political activity which preserves the social order in society.

Though teachers are often heard to say that education should be 'kept out of' politics, their actions, particularly when assessing pupils, are inescapably political in the sense that Jencks et al. (1973, 135) have described:

> . . . schools serve primarily as selection and certification agencies, whose job is to measure and label people, and only secondarily as socialization agencies, whose job is to change people. This implies that schools serve primarily to legitimize inequality, not to create it.

According to this argument, which we have already met in chapter 1, assessment is part of the apparatus by which schools perpetuate the existing hierarchical structure of society, for it results in the application of labels which determine children's opportunities in further education and life itself, their social status, privilege and power, and even their 'worth'. A capitalist society such as ours has an authority structure which depends for its continued existence on the identification of an elite to occupy its most influential positions.

It is a convenient assumption for those who would perpetuate this structure that human ability, and the achievement to which it is assumed to give rise, is normally distributed with only a comparative few of sufficiently high potential to profit to any great extent from the opportunities which schools provide. Thus tests which are constructed to produce such a distribution provide a spurious scientific validation that the hierarchical organization of society reflects a law of nature. In concentrating upon the differentiation of individuals, assessments and the schools which perform them make little impact on our society for they fit pupils to existing opportunities. Inevitably, therefore, raising standards of achievement for some pupils can be accomplished only at the expense of others: society has only so much room for success. In short, assessment furthers an unjust process for it is the method of 'sorting children' in ways which serve only to strengthen a bourgeois bureaucratic order.

However, assessment does not act only as an instrument in the reproduction of inequality (which is the opposite of its ostensible function in equalizing opportunity) but that which is assessed is itself biased towards the cultural traditions of the dominant social groups (see next objection). More insidiously, pupils and others come to accept the system of assessment as 'fair' and as a legitimate means by which they are selected to occupy a particular slot in the occupational hierarchy. The result, for many, is a sense of alienation from schooling which increasing attention to examinations at 16+ does little to repair.

Reply

It is obvious that this argument refers to the part played by assessment in the reinforcement of a model of society which is held to be objectionable by the kinds of thought which characterize so much of contemporary sociological writing. Though it cannot be denied that assessment fulfils some of the functions described above it would be an oversimplification to argue that it is a fundamental cause of the value system itself or to suppose that an overnight and permanent union ban on all assessment by teachers would do more than dent the structure!

In addition, this objection refers chiefly to the part played by assessment in the selection of children through norm-referenced testing (i.e. that in which the placement of pupils relative to one another is the principal goal) but with considerably less force to the practices of criterion-referenced assessment (to be described in chapters 3 and 5) where no implication of comparison with the performance of other children need be drawn. Thirdly, this objection rests upon the assumption that if schools and teachers were to give up their practices of assessment it would help to pave the way for a better form of order than exists in society at present. Even there, some assessment of competence would presumably be required if only to protect the public from the practice of professions which require special skill and knowledge by those unfitted by lack of training if not by aptitude to perform them. Fourthly, it is difficult to envisage a planned educational programme which has to justify its existence to those who will eventually determine its support without at least some form of assessment, even if this is of the system itself rather than of the individual within it. Many teachers can, and do, refuse to make assessments which, directly or indirectly, compare one child with another. Nevertheless they do appraise their pupils as individuals in informal ways. It could be argued that it is only where the processes of such assessment are open to scrutiny that their excesses and lack of fairness may be identified, for rational discussion of the means as well as the ends of assessment requires that the participants possess the ideas and information for doing so – as well as the conditions under which thought may be exchanged.

To charge schools exclusively with the responsibility for bringing about changes in society at large at the expense of overlooking the paradoxical demand that they maintain and transmit what is held by consensus to be worthwhile is to deny an aspect of reality. It is only in totalitarian states that an educational system is explicitly harnessed to bring about changes required by a single ideology. As the movement towards the accountability of schools gains momentum, practices of assessment will continue only as long as they serve functions required by the majority view, as this is determined by democratic process.

Critics of assessment have not always maintained the distinction between the assessment itself and the uses to which the results are put. The prime purpose of an assessment is to obtain information but one may distinguish those who use it to classify pupils on behalf of others from those who use it to help pupils learn. That the result of an assessment *could* be used to help perpetuate a model of society which a teacher holds to be undesirable is not an argument against the positive use of that same result to inform both teachers' and pupils' efforts to learn. Arguments which help to raise the consciousness of teachers regarding some of the unintended consequences of assessment are a necessary step in the evolution of an improved philosophy and practice of assessment and in a recognition that human ability takes many more forms than those prized most highly by dominant social groups.

ASSESSMENT AND CLASS

The second objection can be stated as:

> Assessment favours children of the middle class, is to the disadvantage of other groups, and is too often interpreted as the result of differences in innate potential.

The processes of education and of assessment are often criticized for being oriented towards the middle class. What teachers assess, whether formally or informally, is the attainment of 'middle class concepts', using 'middle class language' and on the assumption that all children have been exposed to 'middle class experiences'. Tests, in particular, are heavily culture-loaded. Since the development of 'culture-free' or 'culture-fair' tests is a chimera their results are inevitably biased in favour of one rather than another culture or social class group. (Piaget's tests and the inferences he has drawn from them, for example, have often been criticized for his insufficient attention to cultural influences on performance.) As a consequence of this kind of bias, teachers and psychologists will underestimate the capabilities of working class and minority group children. Given circumstances with which such children are familiar, differences in problem solving are no longer apparent. The task of the teacher, therefore, is to devise situations and an assessment idiom which favour those who at present under-perform in the middle class milieu.

It would, admittedly, be difficult to construct a test whose results failed to differentiate groups of pupils and yet which was, at the same time, capable of predicting effective functioning within a complex industrial society. Since the ability to learn something new depends upon what pupils already know and what they know is in part a consequence of their previous learning experiences and environment, different types of experience differentially prepare children to profit from teaching. These may be reflected in test scores or other results of assessment; for example, in infant teachers' perception of readiness for school. It seems almost certain that the cultural experiences of some groups in society are more congruous with the assumptions made by schools than others but it is the assumptions of schools rather than those of other cultures which should be changed.

These kinds of criticisms have found American educators more sensitive than their British counterparts. In 1957, for example, the American Psychological Association appointed groups to investigate and clarify the degree of fairness of tests used in education with so-called 'disadvantaged pupils' (Clearly et al., 1975). Cultural bias does undoubtedly exist, and it is doubtful whether it could ever be removed. Too often, however, it can be easily overlooked. The writer recently taught an American student in a group of teachers who were examining the structure and content of an intelligence test used extensively in Britain. The student was defeated by the requirement to supply the 'next but one' in a given series of numbers not through his lack of mathematical competence but because of his unfamiliarity with the phrase itself.

The argument in this second objection applies with greatest force to intelligence testing and the reply which follows will be constructed with special reference to that type of test (including 'verbal reasoning tests').

Reply

The apparent inability of children from minority groups, especially those of varying ethnic origins, to perform well on tests which assess and predict effectiveness in our culture continues to cause anxiety. This is an extremely complex issue and cannot be dismissed as a mere artefact of an 'unfair' or 'biased' system of assessment but it is worth pointing out that it is only through an assessment that the presence of children unable to make extensive profit from the opportunities currently provided by schools (whatever the reason) can be identified.

Those who are most critical of assessment for its discrimination against certain groups have tended to generalize their conclusions from the effects of intelligence testing on teachers' beliefs about learning potential. Some influential psychologists in Britain (e.g. Eysenck) and the USA (e.g. Jensen) have calculated that the variation in intelligence test scores is predominantly inherited. This has often been mistakenly taken to mean that an individual's intelligence is inherited and subject only to minor changes, and that differences in mean score between certain racial, ethnic and social groups are themselves attributable to biological factors. This view has been savagely attacked and many people believe it should be suppressed. In a counter attack, in 1972, the *American Psycho-*

logist published a strongly worded resolution from fifty scientists in a variety of fields which reasserted, amongst other things, the strength of hereditary influences in human ability (*American Psychologist*, 1972, 660). The issues are obviously 'hot' in both science and politics (Kamin, 1974), and Block and Dworkin (1976) argue that there are few issues in the history of science that present such a complex mingling of conceptual, methodological, psychological, ethical, political and sociological questions.

Several commonly held views on the relationship of intelligence test scores to school achievement can be identified:

(1)   That intelligence and differences in IQ are largely inherited and determine a child's potential for a wide range of learning demands.

(2)   That the IQ reflects the result of highly complex interactions between heredity and experience but their relative effects remain unidentified. Nevertheless IQ scores do predict scholastic differences with some accuracy and the results of the assessment of intelligence are therefore useful to teachers in the placement and selection of pupils for educational alternatives, in the diagnosis of educational disadvantage and in the explanation of differential performance.

(3)   That the IQ, within the biological limitations common to all members of the species, reflects chiefly differences in experience: it is therefore largely the result of the environment in which children are conceived, nurtured and reared.

All these views are represented within a typical group of teachers. Whatever the truth of this complex matter, however, certain conclusions, encouraging to teachers, may be drawn. In the first place, even though the results of the IQ assessment do correlate with school achievement, correlations typically range from 0.4 to 0.6. The measurement of correlation will be discussed more fully in chapter 6, but from these figures it can be calculated that only between 16% and 36% of the differences in achievement in a group of pupils can be predicted from differences in their IQ. Or, to put it another way: between 64% and 84% of differences in achievement are predicted by factors *other than* those measured by intelligence tests.

Secondly, the results of an intelligence test, like all others, are at best only error-ridden approximations to true scores (see chapter 7 on reliability) and like other achievements of children they change in favourable environments. More importantly, if the dependability (the results of two intelligence tests taken close together) and the stability (the agreement between two testings two or three months apart) of IQ are measured for children who have had no marked change in environment, it can be shown that the constancy of the attribute is considerably lower than many studies of intelligence have assumed. Further details of this procedure are described with reference to the work of Cattell (1973) in chapter 7 on test–retest reliability.

Thirdly, any conclusion that potential for learning, insofar as this may be reflected in the IQ, is distributed co-extensively with either social class or ethnic origin depends for its validity on technical arguments and assumptions which are open to a great deal of criticism (Block and Dworkin, 1976). Even so, the cultural bias of tests is not quite so pronounced as is sometimes assumed. For example, the children of high-scoring parents on intelligence tests will, on average, have lower scores than their parents (this is known as 'regression to the mean') but the variation about this mean is almost as large as the variation in scores by children in general (Clearly et al., 1975). This is even more pronounced in scores on achievement tests.

Fourthly, the arguments against the usefulness of intelligence test scores do not apply to criterion-referenced assessment nor to most educational tests, where no implication of the measurement of an innate characteristic is made. This problem will be taken up more fully in the discussion of validity (finding out what tests do actually measure) in chapter 8. It is, of course, quite meaningful to speak of the heritability of any characteristic (that is, the proportion of the variation in individual differences in that trait predictable from genes) but no one, as Jensen himself has admitted, is in any position to state the causal links which constitute the chain from genes to mental test or achievement test scores (Jensen, 1972, 5) except in the case of relatively rare and pathological conditions such as phenylketonuria or in chromosomal abnormalities (e.g. trisomy in Down's syndrome) which are always accompanied by some deficiency in test scores. It seems safe to say that the heritability of scores in achievement tests is far lower than that claimed for IQ scores.

Cronbach (1975) has described the changes that have taken place in the interpretation of test scores and has demonstrated the relationship between prevailing social conditions and the acceptability of differing emphases. Assessment indicates, not that some children are born inferior, but that culture exerts a powerful effect – positive or negative – on the performance of children. The tasks which comprise an assessment must reflect the skills and objectives required for effective functioning in our society but the principle of equality of opportunity demands that groups or individuals who have been deprived of the chance to learn fundamental skills and concepts are identified, and remedial action undertaken. Any assessment which is to further this aim must be capable of identifying cultural handicaps. As Wesman (1972) has argued, the remedy is to provide educational opportunity not to do away with the assessment which is the source of the information.

ASSESSMENT: MEASUREMENT OF THE TRIVIAL

The third objection to assessment can be stated as:

> Assessment is limited to relatively trivial educational objectives whilst the most important aims of schooling are inaccessible to testing.

Critics have often seen assessment as a relatively mechanical activity of measurement of the trivial and have pointed out that the achievements of schools and pupils which fall into the affective domain are often overlooked because they are particularly difficult – if not impossible – to assess. The affective domain is a little difficult to define but most educators follow Krathwohl et al. (1964, 8) in their definition as those objectives which 'emphasize a feeling tone, an emotion, or a degree of acceptance or rejection'. The affective aims of teachers are often phrased as a set of abstract virtues which emphasize teaching for attitudes, values, interests and appreciation. It is a perfectly proper aim for a teacher to teach for 'awareness' of literary features, for the 'development of a value system', for 'moral sensitivity' and so on, but rephrasing these aims in terms of observable pupil behaviour trivializes them. Their assessment presents difficulties absent from the assessment of attainment in areas of the curriculum which have a recognizable logical or hierarchical structure or factual basis. Mehrens and Lehmann (1978) suggest that many teachers believe that the attainment of a cognitive objective is accompanied by a corresponding change in the affective domain and that the latter is a by-product of the former. Other people have suggested that teachers lack feelings of personal responsibility or accountability for the general non-cognitive aims of schools. The essence of this third objection, therefore, is that the comparative ease of assessment of the cognitive objectives (those associated with remembering, reproduction of material and with the solution of problems) leads to a lack of attention to the more important objectives which are much more difficult to evaluate.

Reply

Inspection of some attempts to assess affective outcomes reveals some justification for this argument. Those who have tried to establish objective methods for the assessment of affect hold that the first stage is a more careful and detailed specification of objectives in terms of what pupils who exhibit the desired attribute would be able to do by way of demonstration that they had achieved that objective. A typical illustration is provided by Mehrens and Lehmann (1978) who cite as an example of good practice the attempt by Fraenkel (1969) to specify the assessable behaviour which would demonstrate that a learner has 'recognized the dignity and worth of others' as follows:

(1) waits till others have finished speaking before speaking himself;
(2) encourages everyone involved in a discussion to offer his opinions;
(3) revises his own opinions in the light of those of others;
(4) makes statements in support of others no matter what their social status.

One cannot help but sympathize with Fraenkel who admits that these statements do not totally capture the essence of the more general goal! We also note how all these behaviours could be easily faked. In short, not only is the objective difficult to define in terms which permit its assessment, but it may also be simulated by any learner to a far greater extent than would be possible with any corresponding objective in the cognitive domain. In general, the more abstract the objective the more difficult it will be to assess.

The argument, therefore, has some validity. It is often difficult to get agreement as to how affective objectives should be phrased but considerable progress has been made in their assessment (see, for example, Payne, 1974). Secondly, if schools and teachers are to be held accountable for their effectiveness in the affective development of pupils what evidence are they to present to justify continued support for their endeavours except by a more determined effort to assess the less tangible than British schools have attempted to date? There is certainly no shortage of types of behaviour that critical outside observers of schools have held to be relevant: truancy, vandalism of school and community property, delinquency, out of school demeanour, reputation of the school and so on. This type of assessment requires a change of focus from the individual pupil to the school as a system. It involves a variety of information acquired by objective testing, as well as informal observation. That it can be integrated into an account of the effectiveness of schools as institutions in the affective domain has recently been demonstrated by Rutter et al. (1979). Although several quite serious difficulties inherent in the methodology have been pointed out by critics, this research suggests that schools can encourage less tangible pupil development and that assessment plays an indispensable part in the demonstration of this claim.

Finally, because some types of aim and objective of teaching are difficult to assess this is irrelevant to the assessment of a great variety and range of cognitive objectives with which this book is principally concerned. Attention to the assessment of attainment in the cognitive domain need not be to the detriment of concern for the affective. Faced with the great demands upon their competence it is understandable to find teachers who emphasize exclusive concern for one or other set of objectives: this remains, nevertheless, a defensive reaction.

ASSESSMENT AND EXPECTANCY

The fourth objection can be stated as:

> The results of assessment have an uncanny knack of being self-fulfilling.

Assessment has an effect on two important expectancies: the teacher's expectancy of pupils and pupils' expectancies of their future performance. To take the latter first. Once an assessment has been made it may be incorporated by pupils into the concepts they are developing of themselves as learners in a particular discipline or area of skill and knowledge. In particular, pupils come to see themselves as – to simplify matters – successes or failures as mathematicians, or whatever. Repeated experience of success or failure (even though the assessment may not actually employ these terms) gradually develops into an expectancy for the results of future attempts to learn. The child who has predominantly 'succeeded', especially if he or she believes this to be the result of ability and effort, anticipates future success; the child who has chiefly failed may, in extreme cases, even withdraw from further attempts to learn.

Assessment can codify and reinforce a pupil's picture of self, but early in his or her development it plays an important part in its formation. From the early days of a child's schooling, teachers are not disinterested observers of all the abilities and performances of pupils but only of selected abilities in contexts defined by teachers. Although human ability expresses itself in a great variety of forms only comparatively few are judged to be sufficiently worthwhile to constitute the school curriculum. Fortunately, though recent attempts to establish the content of a core curriculum have made some progress beyond the stage of political rhetoric, there is agreement that this should include the elements of literacy and numeracy. But the children who come fresh to any academic activity at whatever level have little or no idea whether they are any good at it but wait instead for the teacher to assess their attempts to learn or they make their own comparisons with other pupils. Thus assessment which is essentially common to all pupils in a class can lead to levels of expectancy which, in turn, themselves direct future effort, affect performance and powerfully influence the pupil's self-concept of ability. Readers interested in the ways in which children's expectancies of self can be incorporated into personality structure and influence achievement could refer to an article by Bar-Tal (1978).

Teachers also build up expectancies about pupils. These accumulate as a result of informal assessment of pupil and home background and by formal and standardized assessment where used. The teachers' predictions then interact in complex ways with actual classroom behaviour. Difficult and challenging tasks are set for some children, low-level demands for others: there may be prolonged interaction with one child because it is mutually satisfying whilst another is left to get on by himself because little can be expected of him, and so on. The theory holds that children can also detect the more covert ways in which expectation is transmitted. But the overall result of a teacher's assessment can be detrimental for those children who are set low expectations and correspondingly damaging for those, who because of an unreliably optimistic assessment, are set levels they are quite unable to fulfil. The term 'self-fulfilling prophecy' has been coined to describe the state of affairs in which children perform the way we expect them to perform. The mere fact that an assessment has been made is held to be sufficient to influence children's self-concepts, their expectations of their own performance and their motivation. An interesting collection of articles on this topic is presented by Sperry (1972).

Reply

A reply must acknowledge the possibilities outlined by this criticism of assessment. But it has already been said that attempts to predict eventual success in achievement leave a great deal of scope for surprise and teachers must be alert to the many unconscious ways in which their expectancies constrain a child's opportunities to learn. A number of everyday classroom observations indicate these expectations at work. When a child has received a favourable assessment or has made a favourable impression in one context (perhaps because she is assessed as being 'nicely spoken' or 'from a good home') a 'halo effect' can operate. By this is meant that the residual effects of the early assessment can 'spread over' into the later assessment or that the teachers can search for confirmation that the original assessment was correct. No name has been given to its converse but the 'horn effect' seems an apt description in which 'giving a dog a bad assessment' prevents objectivity in later appraisals.

That teachers do indeed have differential expectations arising from the earlier assessments has been amply demonstrated by Hargreaves (1967) who also showed that these were clearly perceived by pupils of secondary school age, and by Nash (1972). Attempts to demonstrate the size of the expectancy effect have, however, failed to come up with clear results. One very well known study is apparently thought by many to have provided such a demonstration (Rosenthal and Jacobson, 1968) but its methodology was clumsy and its statistical analysis inept (see, for example, Thorndike, 1968). In spite of the lack of hard experimental data, the intuition of teachers and a wealth of sociological theory (Merton, 1957) points to the possible ways in which the results of assessment can influence the outcome of children's future learning attempts. A clearer realization that no test predicts with other than relatively poor accuracy but that children's performances change in favourable environments, and a movement towards greater use of criterion-referenced assessment (see chapters 3 and 5) can help to neutralize the potential effects of the self-fulfilling prophecy.

ASSESSMENT AND SCHOOL CURRICULA

The fifth objection can be stated as:

Published forms of assessment – such as standardized tests – mould school curricula and inhibit new developments.

There are two strands to this objection. In the first place there is the influence on the school curriculum of the adoption of tests which define the objectives of teaching. Secondly, there is the presence of an external assessment programme in which the teacher is not free to decide whether or not pupils take the tests: these are then marked outside the school, and only the overall result is communicated. As an example of the former one could cite the case of teachers who, having used only teacher-made tests for some time, wish to see how well their pupils compare with others in different schools. Our teachers choose a standardized test available from a publisher's catalogue but, on inspection, realize that it includes several topics which they have not 'covered'. In order to make time for this teaching, they jettison several topics in the existing syllabus which has been devised on educational principles. In this way the original curriculum designed to meet local needs is shaped by the form of assessment adopted. An obvious example of the second type is the 11+ examination (where held), a GCSE syllabus or, in the case of many independent schools, the Common Entrance Examination. It remains to be seen how far the testing programme in the national curriculum will force schools to 'teach for the targets' at the expense of other goals.

Reply

Domination of the school curriculum by the content of tests reflects their misuse. Where the school decides that the objectives of its curriculum are adequately evaluated by an existing test and this test reflects aims and objectives common to other schools, then the assessment can provide a valuable basis for examinations of the goals of the teaching and a relevant comparison with the achievements of similar children elsewhere. Some critics of the amount of freedom allowed to English schools to determine in detail the aims and objectives of their teaching would, of course, see the control of the curriculum by this use of testing as beneficial.

If teachers develop their assessment skills and use only those tests which are congruent with their own objectives, this fifth objection becomes a minor one. If, however, the content of the assessment – especially where it is determined by and carried out for persons other than the pupils and teacher – is allowed to become the determining criterion, then the assessment tail will be wagging the educational dog to the conceivable detriment of the latter.

The second point implied by this objection is potentially more serious, however. It is acknowledged that the teachers have an obligation to cover enough of an external syllabus to ensure a reasonable chance of their pupils' success. This is most certainly a powerful parental expectation of schools, yet concentration on the coverage of content can work against the development of pupils' abilities to learn such that memorization and storage of facts and routine operations for reproduction 'on the day' become the principal teaching goals. Historically, the pursuit of examination success has sometimes resulted in scant attention to the need to show pupils how to learn. New techniques of testing and examining – in the GCSE and standard assessment tasks – will, however, demand far more than recall from the examinees.

ASSESSMENT AND THE KNACK OF TAKING TESTS

The sixth objection can be stated as:

> Assessment encourages the pupil to develop the styles of
> thought or intellectual 'tricks' required by tests and, there-
> fore, inhibits the development of other skills.

This argument is usually levelled at those types of assessment which require the respondent to supply or to select the single correct answer to a test item. Such items encourage the production of convergent thinking or, in the case of multiple choice formats, favour certain types of examinees and penalize others for reasons which are unrelated to their knowledge of the material being assessed. Rowley (1974), for example, has shown that candidates who are prepared to take risks score higher than others whose knowledge and ability are equivalent. A related aspect of this objection is that pupils are quick to spot that certain sections of the work which is to be assessed provide the greatest payoff for their efforts and will consequently invest more time and resources in mastering these, whilst ignoring others. Overuse of multiple choice tests discourages the development by the pupil of oper-ations which require the organization of material demanded by essay and open-ended items and leads to a conception of the goal of learning as primarily reproductive memory of material acquired or the production of what Whitehead (1950) has called 'inert ideas'.

Reply

Most of these objections conceive of assessment narrowly and overlook the imaginative instruments for wide-ranging assessment of all types of learning now available (see, for example, Bloom et al., 1971). Secondly, although pupils may acquire the particular knack of being assessed or taking tests, there is no evidence that experience of particular types of test prevents the acquisition of other modes of thought or cramps an individual's style of thinking (Payne, 1974). But because 'test-wiseness' (skill in taking tests *per se*) is learnt, it will be necessary to ensure that all children are given practice in test-taking when (and these occasions need only be rare) norm-referenced assessment for comparative or merit purposes is undertaken. In short, a good deal of action can be taken by the teacher to minimize the force of this objection.

ASSESSMENT AND ROLE-RELATIONSHIP

This seventh objection is stated as:

> Assessment inevitably takes place in a role-relationship. This is antithetical to a truly educational setting where encounters between teachers and pupils are interpersonal.

This objection is implicit in the writings of 'humanistic psychology' (Schmuck and Schmuck, 1974). Any assessment is made *by* someone *about* someone. It is often a spurious attempt by a teacher to distance him- or herself from the object of study, the pupil. In so doing the child is placed in a position of inferiority and dependence; he plays, or fails to play, the rules dictated by the teacher. The constructs employed by teachers in making an assessment refer chiefly to the children's level of competence or motivation in relation to subject matter and lead to the application of labels familiar to readers of school reports, for example, 'hard worker', 'conscientious', 'average ability in this subject'. They result from the kind of transactions that Buber (1958) has referred to as 'I–It' transactions; those in which the goal of the teacher is to 'categorize and objectify' aspects of the pupil. By contrast, truly educational transactions occur when 'whole persons encounter one another on an equal basis, each with full respect for the array of qualities to be found in the other' and where each participant in this interaction recognizes, appreciates, respects and values the other as a total being (Schmuck and Schmuck, 1974, 6). These transactions or meetings, called 'I–Thou' transactions, are ruled out by much of the organizational features of schools and are prevented by the type of relationship native to the act of assessment.

Reply

Like the first objection, this involves fundamental criticisms of schooling which, whilst reflected in assessment, are not confined to it. But the objection contains its own reply. I–Thou transactions cannot be pre-meditated; planning an assessment involves attempts to control or manipulate, and requires prior decisions as to who should be assessed, by whom and in what areas of knowledge or competence. As Schmuck and Schmuck (1974, 7) themselves claim 'I–Thou transactions arise as unexpected gifts, the best we can do is to orient ourselves to be receptive to their occurrence'. There seems no reason why, given time, the teacher should be unable to participate in such a transaction when the results of an assessment are discussed with a child. Some teachers have been observed to supply the emotional support and encouragement which are the hallmarks of I–Thou transactions following the admission that they, too, face learning difficulties – even in some of the tasks they have required children to perform! This should not be taken to imply a recommendation for the 'cosy-huddle' model of education (Dearden, 1968) based on sentimentality, but a belief that there is nothing in assessment inherently inimical to the establishment of a teacher–pupil relationship of the type advocated by humanistic psychologists, where pupils have shared with teachers the experiences of learning and in which the assessment of the outcome has been used to promote the competence of the pupil.

ASSESSMENT: AN INVASION OF PRIVACY

This eighth objection can be stated as:

> Many types of assessment are an invasion of the privacy of the individual.

There are misuses of the results of educational assessment and tests. In the USA, Messick (1965) has pointed to the sensitivity of this issue but believes that there is inherent danger any time an assessment is made in academic selection or for employment, in diagnosis (especially of personality disorder) and guidance, or in research. So far as the writer is aware no legal action has been taken in respect of this kind of abuse in the UK but Payne (1974, 440–2) presents examples from the United States in which congressional hearings were held into the uses and interpretations of one widely used personality test. Amongst the charges was the claim that personality testing represented a form of 'searching the minds' of employees and applicants, that test records were not kept confidential and that once the assessment had been made it tended to follow people through their careers. Legal hearings were conducted into the discriminatory use of tests: these established that only those assessments which have 'a manifest relationship' to the employment in question should be used. The overall thrust of this argument is that the use of assessment should be pruned to retain only those instruments which result in information directly related to the criterion in question and one should not attempt to derive other kinds of data. In the educational context only those types of data which are of direct relevance to learning or later achievement or job performance would be permitted. Measures of personality, opinion, personal values and attitudes, and indices of family background would be excluded as not directly helpful to the teacher's task of fostering intellectual growth. Under certain circumstances – for example in the kinds of research designed to uncover causal relationships – these latter types of data would be acquired, but subject to strict controls and undertakings on the use and dissemination of the findings.

Reply

The onus is on the test user or the teacher making the assessment to demonstrate that the information gathered will be useful to the child from whom it is obtained. It is probably true that a good deal of the information obtained by teachers serves to reinforce their prejudices or theories of educational progress: there is no reason why any child should be required to state his father's or mother's occupation, for example. The argument does not arise in relation to criterion-referenced assessment (chapter 3) where what is assessed is directly related to the task being learnt. It is valid in the case of the results of intelligence tests if these follow the child throughout his or her school life or if the school is unable to demonstrate their adaptive usefulness in making decisions which benefit the child's education.

Teachers are unlikely to wish to use the results of personality tests: certainly their relationship to school learning is far too tenuous to make the results especially informative. Controls do exist over the use of those types of assessment whose interpretation is particularly difficult. The catalogue of the Test Division of the National Foundation for Educational Research makes clear the restrictions on the availability of these instruments.

Finally, we have already seen the removal from a British publisher's test list of one instrument designed to measure pupil interest on the grounds that it contained a sexist bias through its implicit acceptance of the suitability of different career options for boys and girls. With the increased potential of the computer for detailed record keeping, great attention must be maintained to ensure that only the information beneficial to pupils in their efforts to learn is stored if the charge of invasion of privacy is to be avoided. Questions of the validity of the results of an assessment are raised in chapter 8.

ASSESSMENT IS UNRELIABLE

The ninth objection may be stated as:

> All assessment – especially using tests – is unreliable and predicts imperfectly.

This objection highlights the accepted lack of reliability in test scores and their known inability to afford perfect prediction of criterion. If one cannot claim the dependability of a score on a given occasion but has, instead, to state an often large margin of error, then the test user is forced to question the cost-effectiveness of the assessment programme. Still further, and in the light of the dangers described by the fourth objection, if these error-ridden scores only marginally improve our predictions over chance prediction this calls into question the advisability of the demand for prediction itself. Instead teachers should adopt a 'teach' rather than 'test' philosophy.

Reply

Decades of work in measurement theory and test construction have sought to reduce the unreliability of tests and to provide better techniques for the estimation of true scores. It is preferable in many cases to use test scores and to quote the best estimate that can be given of the size of the error attached to them than it is to rely on the subjective judgements of teachers which make no pretence at the quantification of error. In the first case the test users do at least know what can and cannot be inferred from the result. Secondly, an assessment programme cannot live by tests alone: as Payne (1974, 438) says 'tests can do a very creditable job in combination with other kinds of information'. Thirdly, the less-than-perfect relationship between a test and a criterion which it seeks to predict indicates the difficulty of test validation, and is not a limitation of tests alone but of all kinds of assessment. There is no justification for the continued use of tests or other forms of assessment which are persistently found to lack validity.

A reply to this objection requires some knowledge of the topics of test reliability and validity: these are dealt with in some detail in chapters 7 and 8.

CONCLUSION

Those who have found learning to be a predominantly enjoyable experience have often assumed the value of school learning in its own right. Yet for what is probably the majority of pupils, and for a variety of reasons, learning is not easy and some form of assessment seems to be indispensable in the motivation of many learners especially those at secondary school.

Most people would probably comment unfavourably on the stress that accompanies knowledge that they are to be assessed. Certainly some of the most enjoyable experiences of learning are those associated with the intrinsic motivation of self-chosen study. Yet in school and colleges subjects often lack respectability until they have been assessed in conventional ways. In general, 'non-examination subjects' and 'non-examination children' lack status and reward. For example, teachers of liberal studies in technical colleges and colleges of further education frequently bemoan the low status of their work both within the hierarchy of the institution and in the attention of their students. In polytechnics – especially in faculties of education – teachers of art, physical education and movement studies have rewritten large portions of their syllabus to incorporate material suited to traditional forms of assessment. Students are quick to profit from the dilemma: even in universities (where our most successful learners are, presumably, to be found) it is common to find poor attendance at aspects of the course which are to be left unassessed.

Inevitably an enormous amount of time and effort has been expended in activities associated with assessing children. An industry has developed: hundreds of tests are available to add to the informal assessments which have become a regular feature of classroom practice. In the view of many people, there is far too much assessment. Questioning the practices and pointing out their consequences for pupils, teachers, institutions and society, is, therefore, worthy of disciplined scrutiny and rational discussion. Problems such as those examined in this chapter inevitably raise questions of the significance of education in contemporary society.

Of course, ideologies and the social contexts of the time influence the degree of acceptability of any theory or set of practices. Assessment is no exception to this rule. Readers will not require extensive analysis of the contemporary social and political concerns which have added impetus to the IQ debate. Much earlier, the economic motivation of men to exploit new lands gave added thrust to the development of astronomical and navigational aids to exploration. Many other examples could be given. Sometimes prevailing social influences inhibit or even suppress intellectual enquiry. 'Codex 1181' of 1633 prohibited teaching by Galileo of the Copernican model of the structure of the Universe. One is not, of course, implying that any of the aspects of assessment theory approach, even remotely, the intellectual status of Galileo's ideas nor that assessment theories can be suppressed only by threats of torture! The examples serve to illustrate the principle of the complex interaction of social as well as intellectual components in the determination of the degree of acceptability of practices and fields of study. One example within the sphere of assessment can be given. Intelligence testing in the 1940s and 1950s was widely hailed as the means whereby 'bright' children from working class homes could be identified and selected for 'grammar school education'. This was seen as furthering the basic principles of educational opportunity irrespective of parental income. More recently, a very different interpretation has been adopted. Intelligence tests unfairly discriminate against such pupils: a 'grammar school education' for a few means a 'secondary modern school education' for the majority. The intimate relationship between educational prescription and political alignment is too obvious to require further comment.

The problem of assessment is not only – nor even primarily –

one of the development of better techniques. Far more fundamental questions are involved (Rowntree, 1977). Many people have written of their concern for what they see as disturbing trends in modern industrialized society such as ours. Though the discussion is often superficial the worries and anxieties are profound. There is an increasing distrust of 'science', there are suspicions of the widespread use of computerized records and fears that human beings may be 'reduced to numbers' by tests and records. To many people these trends imply a reduction in human freedom. Others fear that too much attention is paid by the education system to only a small portion of the abilities of children – usually their quantitative and verbal skills – with the danger that the complexity of human potential is overlooked.

One response to this objection has been the introduction of profiles and records of achievement (chapter 10) where a range of attributes is assessed in an attempt to provide a much broader picture of a pupil's school career than narrowly defined examination success. Greater use of criterion-referenced tests and assessment tasks, which present worthwhile learning and problem solving demands, are also planned: these complement the limited picture of a pupil given by the traditional test and examination result. The introduction of the national curriculum with its testing of age cohorts 7, 11, 14 and 16 is certain to bring changes in the content and method of teaching. Working groups in mathematics and science have already reported, each with suggestions for the types of test item necessary to assess the attainment targets. A clear connection between objectives and testing is proposed and an enlightened diversity of instruments seems certain to be employed. Nevertheless, teachers will retain considerable freedom in deciding how they will assess. The next chapter outlines some of the options open to them.

3

Choosing the Mode of Assessment

Attempt is made in this chapter to indicate some of the options open to teachers on how to assess. It is a difficult task to choose which of several apparently conflicting modes of assessment best reflect the educational intentions of teachers and schools or which combination best serves the evaluation of the attainment of educational objectives. The term 'mode of assessment' concerns the way the practices are carried out, not the actual instruments employed. As we saw in the previous chapter, substantive objections to the effects of assessment have been advanced. But the increasing emphasis on the 'accountability' of schools seems likely to require at least as much attention as at present if we are to justify our activities.

We shall argue in the pages which follow that there are two dominant approaches to the assessment and testing of children and several ways of going about each. We shall begin by spending some space on a fundamental distinction between two types of practice which, though they overlap to a quite considerable extent, reflect different emphases in the measurement of performance and fulfil different assessment goals. These two approaches have come to be known as 'norm-referenced' and 'criterion-referenced' assessment and each is associated with a somewhat different type of measurement. Teachers have been carrying out both types of assessment for generations but it is only comparatively recently that a formal distinction has been drawn between them, and only in the last ten years that criterion-referenced assessment has become of much interest to psychometricians – those concerned with the measurement of individual differences.

The differences between norm- and criterion-referenced testing lie in the respective purposes, the types of score they derive and their interpretation, and the philosophies of education which they embody.

NORM-REFERENCED ASSESSMENT

When a school or teacher reports a child's progress or receives an
external evaluation of a pupil's performance in the cognitive
domain (as in the case of an internal or external exam result) a
norm-referenced approach is adopted. We shall consider more
fully in chapter 10 the teacher's responsibility to communicate an
interpretation of the results of an assessment but for present
purposes it is sufficient to identify – without evaluating them –
some of the most common techniques. In many schools, grades
(which may be numerical or literal) are reported and these are
often accompanied by labels or short verbal descriptions: these
labels or descriptions evaluate the children's performance in relation to the group to which they belong. Typically a grade 'A' might
be described as 'outstanding', 'C' as 'average', and so on. Thus the
norm is the group and the assessment refers to it. Take, as another
example, the report: 'John's reading age is 8 years and 9 months'.
Just as in our first example, the score acquires meaning, not as a
measure of the amount of anything, but only with reference to the
scores of a much larger group, from which the average has been
calculated. To take one final example, suppose a class of pupils
takes one of the tests developed by the National Foundation for
Educational Research (say the Basic Mathematics Test C, age
range 9.07 to 10.10 years, designed to assess the child's attainment
in area, graphs, symmetry and knowledge of sets, decimals and
fractions). From the test the teacher obtains the 'raw score' (the
number 'right'), refers this to a table of 'standardized scores' given
in the manual for the child's age and finds the standardized score
to be 115 (see chapter 6). This is interpreted to mean that, in a
very large group of children of that age the obtained raw score will
separate the 16% highest scores from the remaining 84%. (See
figure 6.11 which translates standardized scores into percentages.)
As before, the score can be interpreted only in relation to a large
number of scores obtained by other children who constitute the norm.

From these examples we can abstract one common feature: a
score or grade which has meaning only insofar as it is compared
with others which make up a group. The basic purpose of norm-
referenced testing, therefore, is to discriminate among individuals.
In the generalizable sense, a norm-referenced measurement has
the following logical form:

Individual i exhibits more (or less) of characteristic x than the mean amount of x in group y (the population).

Notice the importance of the reference point: 'mean amount of x in group y'. Parents who receive a school report which states that 'John is slightly above the average in French for the group' with no indication of the composition of the group and its average performance are told very little indeed about their son's achievement.

To summarize, norm-referenced testing:

(1) is carried out for the purposes of comparison and discrimination between individuals;
(2) aims at high variability among scores to maximize this discrimination;
(3) interprets scores in relation to those of a number (preferably large) of other individuals (norm groups);
(4) is indispensable on the relatively rare occasions in education where fixed quota selection decisions have to be taken, for example, when selecting from a larger pool of children for the distribution of limited resources as in the competition for places.

CRITERION-REFERENCED TESTS AND MASTERY LEARNING

Criterion-referenced tests have been developed in response to some of the limitations of norm-referenced testing, both practical and philosophical. Many teachers believe that drawing comparisons between individuals and providing scores which describe the child's standing in a group serve chiefly to foster a spirit of competition which is inimical to the maintenance of a climate for learning in which children are able to develop at their own pace. Certainly a score which describes only the standing of a child relative to a group is uninformative about the actual achievements made and tells the teacher only which pupils have made greatest, average, or least attainment. Because of this, attempts have been made to develop tests and other instruments which describe the achievements of children compared with the established standards. Moreover certain approaches to learning – for example, in programmed learning or computer-assisted instruction – have emphasized individual differences in rate of learning and have proposed that time taken to learn to a given standard is the most important and educationally relevant dimension on which children differ. Some researchers who have developed individualized systems for learning have claimed that an education which is truly oriented towards individual differences is one in which most children could master almost all the basic objectives in schooling if given time to do so. Norm-referenced test are obviously unable to provide much of the necessary information for a teacher who wants to give children as much time as is practicable to master a given objective, to monitor children's achievements while they are learning a sequence of clearly defined goals, and to provide other interested parties with as precise a description as possible of the actual features of a child's achievement. In short, objectors to exclusive reliance on norm-referenced testing have argued that knowledge of a child's standing relative to the achievements of others is of trivial interest compared with knowledge of the extent to which a learner's attainment approaches a given standard of performance. Any instrument which provides this latter type of information is known as 'criterion-referenced'.

To propose a simple example: a teacher has drawn up a list of objectives in elementary arithmetic. Four objectives in the sequence are as follows:

(1)   add two, two-digit numbers without carrying
(2)   add two, three-digit numbers without carrying
(3)   add two, two-digit numbers involving carrying
(4)   add two, three-digit numbers involving carrying

A number of items is drawn up for each objective: two per objective are given as examples, but a minimum of ten per objective would probably be required to established mastery of the objective.

Items for each objective are homogeneous, that is they are, on the face of it, of equal difficulty, and the objectives are organized hierarchically, that is later objectives build upon the knowledge and skills required by earlier objectives. These items are criterion-referenced when a criterion level or performance ('C') is specified. A frequently adopted criterion for these kinds of objec-

Objective	Items (a)	Items (b)	
(1)	$\begin{array}{r} 15 \\ +\ 24 \\ \hline \end{array}$	$\begin{array}{r} 33 \\ +\ 15 \\ \hline \end{array}$	+ 8 others
(2)	$\begin{array}{r} 206 \\ +\ 153 \\ \hline \end{array}$	$\begin{array}{r} 623 \\ +\ 312 \\ \hline \end{array}$	+ 8 others
(3)	$\begin{array}{r} 38 \\ +\ 46 \\ \hline \end{array}$	$\begin{array}{r} 17 \\ +\ 68 \\ \hline \end{array}$	+ 8 others
(4)	$\begin{array}{r} 397 \\ +\ 844 \\ \hline \end{array}$	$\begin{array}{r} 178 \\ +\ 669 \\ \hline \end{array}$	+ 8 others

tives would be a score of at least 80% correct. Children who scored eight, nine or ten of the items for a given objective would be described as masters of that objective. Thus a child who has mastered objective (3) will be able to perform the operation of addition using two-digit numbers plus carrying with at least 80% accuracy – an unambiguous description of what he or she is able to do. The boy or girl who gets seven or fewer items correct per objective is deemed to require further teaching or practice in the attainment of this objective. Thus only two 'states' are assessed: 'mastery' and 'non-mastery' of the objective. Given that these objectives are quickly mastered by most children a criterion of 90% accuracy might well be reasonable. (Problems of setting standards are more fully discussed in chapter 9.)

Opponents of criterion-referenced testing have pointed out some of its limitations. It is appropriate chiefly in the evaluation of learning where objectives can be clearly stated, where criterion performances can be established and where objectives are organized hierarchically. In our example, objective (1), too, has prerequisites although these are not specifically stated. They require that the child discriminate the signs which indicate the basic arithmetical operations, recognition of numerals and so. Some subjects, for example in basic mathematics or reading, have such a structure which can be presented in logical sequence and it is for this reason that most of the published criterion-referenced tests to date are in areas of elementary skill. In English literature, however, to cite one contrasting example, it is not at all apparent just what is the logical structure of the subject. A second objection concerns the arbitrary definition of 'mastery'. In our previous example a criterion score of 80% was specified to discriminate the two states but there may be other instances in which the teacher would set an even more stringent criterion. In other cases, where some learning of a later objective does not appear to depend upon complete mastery of one logically earlier in the sequence, somewhat lower demands might be set. In addition, whilst we can draw up logical sequences in the presentation of objectives, educational psychology has not yet reached a stage of theoretical or empirical precision which enables it to define just how much of a 'lower' objective need be mastered for attainment of one at a 'higher' level. Moreover, specifying a sequence in which all children should learn is to overlook the possibility that there are often many routes to attainment of the same objective, particularly where the material to be learned becomes increasingly abstract and where intellectual abilities and skills such as analysis and synthesis are required.

A third criticism of mastery learning is that it proposes a 'closed' or convergent model of teaching and learning: it implies a structured approach which all must follow and seems to remove the possibility of excitement and discovery. Those in favour of mastery learning argue that although criterion-referenced assessment may have its simplest application in learning basic skills, most subject matter in school can be thought of as organized hierarchically if only teachers were more systematic in their analysis of the tasks and demands they set children (Ausubel et al., 1978).

A further argument against the mastery model points to the absurdity which would result if it were blindly applied. If time spent in mastery of a criterion is of paramount importance then one could easily envisage some children taking years to reach a level of mastery attained by others within weeks! Quite probably this is already the case, but rigid adherence to the approach could lock slower learners into an inexorable and morale-sapping ritual, and bore the most able. Although mastery testing is indispensable in formal systems of individually prescribed learning (such as is practised in 'individually guided education' (IGE) developed for schools by psychologists and teachers at the University of Wisconsin)

Glaser (1968) has demonstrated that if the slower 5% of learners in schools are omitted from consideration, the ratio of time spent by slower to faster learners is of the order of six to one. If this is the case, teachers who favour mastery learning are faced with the tricky decision as to just how long they should require a learner to persist towards the attainment of a particularly obdurate objective. This would be easier to determine if we really were in a position to establish exactly what are the basic academic skills indispensable for a child's future survival. These are probably fewer than most teachers care to admit. Whatever they are, they seem likely to change with time. Many teachers already believe that the widespread availability of electronic calculators renders the learning of a good deal of basic arithmetic technologically – if not culturally – redundant! The suggestion by Gronlund (1971) that schools distinguish objectives which are minimum essentials from those which encourage maximum development and reserve the use of the mastery learning approach for the former begs the question. Recent discussion in Britain of the content of the 'core curriculum' has made some progress: the emphasis in the USA on the teaching of the elements of 'functional literacy and numeracy' has run into similar problems in identifying the functional 'elements'.

Perhaps the most fundamental objection to criterion-referenced testing and mastery learning concerns their psychological parentage. The use of educational objectives which are stated in terms of a pupil's observable behaviour can be traced to the principles of behaviourist psychology and represents a conscious extension of those precepts into educational practice. In behaviourism, learning is studied only at its observable level and all other terminology or interpretation in terms of hidden entities or mental processes is denied. Early behaviourism was influenced by a philosophical movement known as positivism which dismissed as meaningless all statements which were not empirically verifiable. Accordingly the cardinal educational principle derived from this set of beliefs was that the only meaningful goals of learning and teaching were those which are objectively measurable as observable outcomes. Other aims are dismissed as little more than pious hopes.

One notable exponent of a behaviourist standpoint on teaching was Skinner. According to his view, learners respond to stimuli from their environments and acquire behaviour as a consequence of the events which follow – that is by reinforcement. The technology of teaching is seen as the definition of goals, the search for appropriate reinforcers that will produce the desired behaviour and, finally, careful measurement of the reinforcer's effects. Not all users of behavioural objectives subscribe to the behaviourist traditions, however, and many are simply borrowing from it what seems to them to be a useful device to help precise specification of objectives in areas which are too often confused by the use of vague and lofty prescriptions. Nevertheless, blind application of the principles of behaviourism (and of its offshoot, the objectives approach) could easily end in an overemphasis by schools on training programmes to elicit from learners narrowly defined and 'correct' responses to specific stimuli. There are very many elements of understanding and of attitude which are legitimate goals of teaching but which simply do not submit to behaviourist analysis and objective assessment.

Some technical problems of criterion-referenced tests have not yet been overcome. No agreement has yet been reached as to the most appropriate method for establishing the reliability and validity: these difficulties are dealt with in some detail in chapters 7 and 8. Nevertheless criterion-referenced tests form a valuable addition to teachers' techniques of assessment. They provide information which complements that available from norm-referenced tests and enable the teacher to communicate far more precisely what children can actually *do* than is permitted by norm-referenced assessment. The two types of test are not mutually exclusive, however. A criterion-referenced test can easily be used to make norm-referenced statements about pupils: it may even describe in greater detail the actual structure of the differences which lie behind the discriminations made by norm-referenced tests. Because they include too few homogeneous items to establish mastery of an objective, norm-referenced tests are seldom used in a criterion-referenced way but a single test score on either test could be given either type of interpretation. We can say that 'Mary got 80% of the items correct in a test on the solution of two linear equations with two unknowns' (criterion-referenced) and, equally, that 'Mary did better than 85% of her class' in the same test (norm-referenced). Each has its uses, but the distinction between the two types of assessment becomes even more blurred when one realizes that the standards which form the criterion may well be levels of performance established by other children else-where!

The implication of this previous paragraph is that norm- and criterion-referenced tests do not represent discrete and mutually exclusive methods of assessment, but, that they reflect different emphases, interpretations and purposes of the teacher. Table 3.1 attempts to summarize these differences.

Table 3.1 – A comparison of norm-referenced (NR) and criterion-referenced (CR) assessment

Difference	Emphasis of NR assessment	Emphasis of CR assessment
(1) Purpose	To make comparisons between pupils and to relate these to the average performances by large numbers of similar children	To evaluate the achievements of pupils relative to an established criterion of performance
(2) Interpret-ation of score	If standardized, the score indicates the position of a child's score in a large normally distributed group of scores (see page 180). If unstandardized, the score shows the child's relative standing in the group to which he/she belongs (e.g. the class or year group)	Indicates the level of a child's mastery of a given objective. It does not refer to a distribution of scores by other pupils

Table 3.1 *continued*

Difference	Emphasis of NR assessment	Emphasis of CR assessment
(3) Diagnostic value	In the identification of relative performance to see *who needs* remedial work or special education	In the identification of actual strengths and weakness in performance to see *what kind* of remedial action is necessary.
(4) Variation in scores	Needs to be relatively high to discriminate effectively between pupils	Usually relatively low. Could be a useful test even if no differences between pupils are observed, e.g. when all achieve the criterion
(5) Reliability: 'How effectively does the test measure whatever it is it measures?' (see chapter 7)	Estimated using test–retest, parallel form or homogeneity methods	Estimated by the consistency with which the set of items for an objective classifies pupils as 'masters' or 'non-masters'
(6) Validity: 'What exactly *does* this test measure?' (see chapter 8)	Examined by reference to an external criterion (a present or future performance) and by studying its relationship to other tests, which claim to measure the 'same' attribute	Examined chiefly by comparing the actual content of each item with the statement of the objective
(7) Types of item in test	Usually a large number of different items designed to sample a *range* of skills and concepts	Each *objective* has a number of very similar items designed to test a narrowly defined skill or concept

Table 3.1 *continued*

Difference	Emphasis of NR assessment	Emphasis of CR assessment
(8) Selection of items to make up test	Item difficulty is an important criterion. Those answered correctly by about 50% of children who take it are chosen since these 'spread out' the final totals most effectively	Items tend to be easier and the spread of correct responses is relatively small
(9) Applicability to school 'subject'	Can describe relative standing of pupils in any subject for which information from group performance is available	Useful only in those subjects where precise objectives can be stated
(10) Role in education	In selection, grading, competition and career guidance. In comparing schools and the *relative* performance of children (These last named are probably of greater interest to researchers than to teachers.)	In evaluating the absolute success of instruction. In decisions as to the speed at which children are to be allowed to progress through a fixed sequence of instruction. In individualized instruction and the assessment of readiness
(11) Logical inference	'Child i exhibits an amount of x which is greater than or less than the mean amount of x in population y.'	'Child i exhibits an amount of x which is greater than or equal to c.' (c = Criterion score)

MODES OF ASSESSMENT

Rowntree (1977, 119) has collected the labels for eight modes of assessment prevalent in education. For convenience he has presented them as a set of polar opposites but they are best regarded as dimensions by which the emphasis of current practices may be described. They are:

formal	versus	informal
formative	versus	summative
continuous	versus	terminal (or final)
course work	versus	examination
process	versus	product
internal	versus	external
convergent	versus	divergent
idiographic	versus	nomothetic

(As Rowntree wryly comments: 'People in education contrive many more ways of finding out about students than they would dream of using on their family and friends.')

It is obvious that no one dimension represents mutually exclusive alternatives. Most schools employ a mixture of formal and informal methods, of continuous and terminal modes and many examination systems use both course work and final examination, with different weightings, in arriving at a classification, e.g. of a university degree. Few guidelines can be given as to the degree of emphasis which teachers could place on these types. What is important, however, is that teachers should be informed of the choices, available to them. Schools, departments within schools and teachers as individuals will decide on the programme best suited to their purposes. Only by knowing the relative strengths and weaknesses of the approaches can an informed choice be made.

We shall adopt Rowntree's useful classification and deal briefly with those of the above dimensions most frequently encountered in practice. The discussion departs from that provided by Rowntree (1977, 119–62) but interested readers may like to read his accounts for purposes of comparison.

Formative versus Summative Evaluation

This is a favourite distinction among American educators. The terms are used in a variety of ways but, so far as the writer can tell, choice of the word 'evaluation' rather than of 'assessment' is to indicate its application to a judgement of the effectiveness of an educational programme or curriculum rather than the perform- ances of children. Some assessment of one of the outcomes of major interest – pupil learning – would, of course, be part of the evaluation programme but many other facets would be considered (see Anderson et al., 1975). The basic distinction may be stated as follows. Formative evaluation focuses on the programme whilst it is in operation. In particular it provides information to help all those responsible for the development of materials used (books, worksheets, other resources for learning) and in the recording of all the unintended consequences (more often undesirable than desirable!) for the attitudes and motivation of pupils. Summative evaluation is concerned with evaluating the overall effectiveness of a curriculum or programme once it has been completed and especially whether the goals and objectives have been attained. Whereas formative evaluation is carried out principally by and for those responsible for the development of the programme or course of study, summative evaluation is more detached and is preferably carried out by someone not personally involved in its develop- ment. Quite obviously the results of summative evaluation may well have implications for future formative work.

Here again we see one of the cardinal principles of assessment: the method to be adopted depends on the purposes for which the work is carried out. Applying the formative–summative distinc- tion to the assessment of individuals we could say that formative aspects are present whenever the results of an assessment – how- ever formal or informal – are communicated to learners and these have feedback consequences for their efforts. Feedback can be corrective (showing how and where a learner 'went wrong' and how to improve) or confirmatory (a demonstration that what the learner has acquired in skills and concepts is suitable for the tasks which lie ahead). Assessment of a child's learning or performance is summative when information is not made available for feedback purposes, not necessarily because it is obtained for other parties but perhaps because it comes too late in a learner's career. Much of the day-to-day assessment of pupils is formative: helpful written and oral comments on children's work accomplish this function.

Continuous versus Terminal (or Final) Assessment

This is not so much a method as an indication of when and how often assessments are made. Continuous assessment was introduced partly because of complaints that it was unfair and unnecessarily stressful to learners to know that they were being examined on only a single occasion or over a short period of time where luck with the questions played a particularly significant part in their chances of success (Miller, 1976).

If assessors do take into account a child's performance over a longer period of time and in a variety of situations, it should be possible to obtain a more representative view of his or her capabilities than in the artificial context of the examination room. (Assessment as part of mastery learning is continuous in this sense.) Amongst other advantages claimed for continuous assessment are that it encourages steady application throughout the course, does not unduly penalize learners for one or two poor pieces of work and encourages more closely the development of a variety of problem solving skills which are inhibited by the need to develop examination 'tricks'.

In practice, continuous assessment has also been found to have its share of disadvantages. It has been reported (Rowntree, 1977) that only work which is to be assessed receives the attention of learners (at least in an examination you do not know what is going to come up). Also, it is often difficult to establish just what is and what is not the learner's own personal contribution (tutors known to the writer often find themselves spending considerable amounts of time investigating plagiarism) and anxious students have experienced only slightly less stress but over much longer periods of time than with terminal or final assessments. One thing seems clear. All assessment practice is potentially capable of raising levels of anxiety. This, according to one psychological theory, is not necessarily a bad thing but it depends upon the level of difficulty of the task being assessed for the learner (Child, 1977, 54). Where teachers are using an assessment to help pupils learn and not making decisions or norm-referenced judgements about them for other people's purposes, it can be minimized. In this case it seems important that the learner is helped to understand the purpose and be convinced that no other (ulterior) motive is in mind.

There seems little justification for a practice which may be more widespread in institutions of higher education than is sometimes thought, that is, making an assessment in order to determine a grade or mark which is then withheld from the student. If the grades are so unreliable that it would be dangerous for a student to know of them, then what is the point of applying them? If assessors lack confidence in their judgements to the point at which they cannot defend their assessments to students, then this problem must be faced not displaced onto the unfortunate learner.

Some institutions have decided to grade their students using a weighted combination of both continuous assessment and final examination grades but the weightings often appear to be largely arbitrary. Some have abolished examinations altogether: others have graded all pieces of work but have allowed students to submit only their best pieces of work for final assessment. Nevertheless it should be possible in schools to reduce the number of occasions on which it is necessary to supply anything resembling a terminal or final grade. One cannot for long remain a starry-eyed idealist about this, however. Although it may be highly desirable to emphasize the school's educative function and to de-emphasize its selecting and sorting functions, these apparently irreconcilable demands seem likely to constitute a tension on schools, teachers and pupils for very many years to come. Nevertheless, in reaching an overall grade for any pupil the teacher can profitably consider which of continuous or final assessment most adequately permits the development of skills and concepts which forms the educational objectives guiding the teaching. Teachers who have considered this point often conclude that both are required, but to varying degrees.

Course Work versus Examination

Although continuous assessment is more likely to be of course work it could incorporate the results of tests and even of examinations. Likewise, final assessment could consist of a summation of course work grades. Examination grades tend to enjoy greater respectability in the eyes of the public than course work grades: the latter can too easily be contaminated by favouritism and cheating and be achieved in a variety of conditions which render the principle of comparability inoperative. But whilst the external conditions of an examination (time limit, invigilation, unavailability of sources of reference and so on) remain the same for all examinees and the actual contents of the paper are the same for all, most examination papers allow choice from a larger set of questions or problems, such that the assumption that a common basis for comparison has been obtained can be illusory. As Rowntree has said, if a student is required to choose four topics out of ten, 210 different choices are available. (One examination paper known to the author requires the respondent to answer three from 24 questions. This allows for no fewer than 2024 possible combinations of questions chosen!) Moreover, examination questions are frequently set with only the haziest concept of difficulty in mind so the notion that 'all have sat the same paper' is true only in a limited sense where so much choice is available.

There are other difficulties inherent in the assumptions drawn from examination results. For example, the marks of examiners often differ quite widely in some subjects (see the section on the reliability of essay marks in chapter 7), the conditions under which the candidates have to answer bear little or no resemblance to any conditions under which people usually work in later life and are, therefore, of poor predictive validity (see chapter 8) and the results frequently testify to the luck or skill with which the candidate (or his teacher) has 'spotted the questions', or effectively revised.

Since all teachers will almost certainly have sat an examination paper at some time in their lives they will know from personal experience some of the deficiencies of assessing in this way. Little justification seems possible for premature examination (that is before the relatively later stages in a child's school career). If it is chosen as an appropriate method of obtaining information about children's performance then the teacher can consider how to ameliorate some of its worst features. Some institutions have experimented with so-called 'pre-set' examinations in which candidates receive the paper several days in advance but answer it 'under examination conditions'. The author has acted as external examiner to one such procedure. There some students have commented that the method places even greater demands upon them to write 'good answers' and removes from them the grounds for face-saving excuses when they fail to do so!

Quite clearly, arguments can be advanced for and against both methods of assessment. Teachers must decide where to place the emphasis in the light of evidence they acquire from use of both methods; in particular how far they encourage the attainment of objectives and motivate pupils.

Process versus Product Assessment

Teachers are most accustomed to the assessments of products, most frequently those by children using pencil or pen on paper or their equivalent. Quite obviously this kind of outcome is of great importance: the essay, the technical drawing, the painting, the 'page of sums' and so on. The demonstration of the pupils' ability to make something is an important educational objective, in art, craft, home economics, physics, chemistry, biology: right across the curriculum in fact. In those subjects where products are not the goal, assessment tends to be avoided: in contemporary religious education where the ability to discuss and to appreciate the point of view of others is encouraged; in sex education (where products would be viewed with mixed feelings!) and in all those situations where civilized conduct is implicitly and explicitly encouraged.

Process and product are intimately related – there would be no product without processes. Although it is easier to assess a product than the processes which went into it, we often assess both in the former. Our evidence of life in past civilizations is from their artefacts and written records; we infer process from products where direct observation of process is not possible. We reproduce Seurat's technique of painting by studying his pictures, we study a child's method of problem solving from the 'working' on his paper, we infer the difficulties faced in reading by a girl's stumbling attempts and errors and we assess the strength and movement of Egyptian peasants before Christ by an examination of the force required to turn the handle of an Archimedean screw. But these are retrospective assessments – they were not observed while they were being executed.

Although assessment of product is easier to carry out than assessment of process, studies of the concepts used by teachers in their appraisal of children show that they do indeed use many which refer to process. Amongst the most common are the processes of class participation and the children's approach to tasks (Wood and Napthali, 1975). The comments made about students in colleges of education often reveal that a final grade has been reached on teaching practice which includes assessment of relationships with children, with other staff and so on, as well as of the products produced by the children in their class – not to mention the ubiquitous 'TP file'. It is almost too obvious to point out that much of the assessment of a person's job performance is process-oriented, especially where this does not end in a tangible product. Nevertheless, the formal assessment of process has got off to a relatively slow start in British education where comparatively little value is attached to any process until it has been verbalized or otherwise made available as its product for sustained and critical appraisal – not without good reason, of course!

One of the reasons for the emphasis on product is the sheer difficulty of assessing process except in a very trivial sense (for example, studies of pupil–teacher interaction, Flanders, 1970). If we were interested in the processes by which children attempt to solve problems – as distinct from whether they are 'correct' or not – one way of doing this might appear to be through the method of introspection: that is by asking children to verbalize their behaviour whilst performing it, or immediately afterwards ('retrospection'). The problems here are both practical and logical. In the first place, numerous psychological studies have shown the human inability to perform two intellectual operations at one and the same time (two components of skill can be integrated but what appears to be 'doing two things at once' is often accomplished by a process which involves rapid switching of attention, as in landing an aircraft). We cannot logically require a child both to solve a problem and at the same time to observe him or herself solving it – *and* report on it! Practically, the method of introspection is seldom particularly informative with children especially where the intellectual demands are complex. Indeed, the results of introspective reports by even the world's greatest thinkers have often thrown little light on the process involved (see for example, Wertheimer's work with Einstein; Wertheimer, 1945). Readers who might envy the accomplishments of 'lightning calculators' and who would like to emulate them will receive very little guidance as to how to begin by a study of introspective reports during quick-fire arithmetical manipulation (see, for example, Hunter's account of Aitkin;

Hunter, 1962). In the first place, then, there is the sheer difficulty of 'getting at' the process in a good deal of human cognitive activity. Computers may stimulate human thought and provide valuable insights into effective problem solving strategies but these models do not provide help in the assessment of processes in children. In any case, models are formal structures and much of the process of everyday thought is intuitive. We proceed by a mixture of formal thinking, setting up hypotheses as to how we might proceed, using 'hunches' or by 'taking a chance'. Some solutions are even achieved by happy accident. The processes of intuition are, by definition, those of which the learner can offer no explicit account: he is unaware of the steps in the process by which a conclusion was reached.

In spite of these problems we pay lip service to the role of the teacher in understanding and adapting to the cognitive style of the learner (that is to the learner's preferred and consistent ways of thinking), in the development of the pupil's capacity for problem solving, to help pupils co-operate with others and to 'relate' to other people, amongst a host of other objectives which emphasize process. We may even succeed in some of these aims without knowing precisely how we have managed it. (We may begin to see some of the reasons why behaviourism concentrated its attention on the observable and denied all reference to processes hidden from view.)

The nub of the difficulty then is that where process assessment is possible it demands direct observation of the processes of interest whilst they are taking place (Green, 1970). Some assessments are explicitly directed at process (the 'oral' in a modern language is one obvious example). In some cases the product may provide a clue to process, but in others it is more than likely that a similar product can be achieved by markedly different processes. If one is simply interested in the children's ability to solve linear equations correctly (i.e. product) many teachers might consider it irrelevant whether they solved it by the method of substitution, by addition, by the equating or by the determinant method. But where the objective of the teaching *is* the development of process an attempt should be made to assess it.

No 'ground rules' for the assessment of process can be given. But if the teacher decides to attempt the task a number of possibilities suggest themselves. Although this chapter is concerned with the ways of carrying out assessments rather than with the instruments for doing so, the idea of process assessment is probably a little unfamiliar. In order to clarify some of the ideas one or two of the main types of instrument are briefly described here.

By the use of rating scales
These can be numerical, graphic or of the check list type. An example is shown in table 3.2.

By the use of an interaction schedule
This means a prior decision as to what is going to be observed, a list of categories and a matrix.

Example: for observing the relationships between children during a group activity.

(a) *Statements*. These include 'affective' (statements which encourage, discourage, blame, etc.), 'procedural' (statements about how to do the task, what should be done next, etc.), 'substantive' (resolving conclusions, evaluating the product, etc.).
(b) *Interchanges*. Those which involve a unit which consists of a question, a formal response and an evaluation of the response.

(This is a much simplified version of OSCAR (observation schedule and record) developed by Medley, Schluck and Ames (1969). It is used for illustrative purposes only.) Table 3.3 gives an idea of what such a schedule might look like. Tally marks can then be entered as the observations are made. A similar interaction schedule has been developed by Flanders for the study of teacher–pupil interaction (Flanders, 1970).

By the use of self-reporting devices, anecdotal records, etc.
Rating scales could be completed by pupils instead of by teachers. Teachers can prepare anecdotal records of incidents and record their comments. Over time both these techniques can provide a record of the longitudinal development of any pupil.

By simulation methods
Where performance in a task is to be assessed and provided the

Table 3.2 – Example of a rating scale

Examples A	To assess a pupil's participation in discussion (numerical)
Question	To what extent does a pupil participate in discussion?
Respond	Ring appropriate number

(1)	(2)	(3)	(4)	(5)
Unsatis-factory	Below average	Average	Above average	Out-standing

---

Examples B	To assess a pupil's level of concentration in laboratory work (graphical)
Question	How much concentration does a pupil display in class?
Respond	Mark an 'X' at the appropriate place on the continuum

(1)	(2)	(3)	(4)	(5)
Very easily distracted		Averagely attentive		Shows great con-centration

---

Examples C	To assess basic study habits by children during individual work (check list)
Question	Which of the following does the child display when working individually?
Respond	Circle the number in front of each statement which applies to the child

(1)	(2)	(3)	(4)	(5)
Has short attention span and weak powers of concen-tration	Seeks frequent help from teacher	Lacks confidence to get on by him- or herself		
			etc.	etc.

---

teacher can simulate that task in a realistic way, observation schedules can be applied to the performance of pupils during their carrying out the exercise. These seem more appropriate for the older pupils and fall into one of three categories:

(1) *In-basket exercises.* In these the pupil is presented with data, such as letters, reports, memoranda and so on and asked to reach decisions to a specified problem, e.g. the pupil is

Table 3.3 – Observation schedule for the assessment of process during group activity

| | | Children | | |
		1	2	3
(a) Statements	(1) Affective			
	(2) Procedural			
	(3) Substantive			
(b) Interchanges				

presented with documents relating to the conduct of a youth club member and is asked to decide on a course of action.

(2) *Situation tests.* Pupils play the roles in a lifelike context, e.g. an immigrant pupil new to a British school meets classmates and teacher.

(3) *Problem solving games.* Groups are given tasks to perform against a criterion, e.g. a time limit or to build a structure which supports weight across a 'stream'.

This section has served as no more than a brief introduction to the assessment of process. In choosing between process and product assessment, teachers will obviously be guided by which is the more appropriate for assessing the objective in mind. This decision having been reached, one may fairly safely conclude that product assessment is the only viable choice if the processes remain unobservable (despite the ingenuity of the teacher), if methods for describing and measuring products are already available and where the product itself provides evidence of the processes of interest.

This chapter concludes with a brief commentary on some of the remaining modes of assessment identified by Rowntree.

Internal versus External Assessment

To a very large extent teachers are unable to decide this question but are more likely to have a practice thrust upon them. Current practices in British educational institutions are very variable.

GCSE examinations incorporate substantial internally assessed components with external papers in reaching the final grade. University examinations are set and marked internally but with external moderation of a sample of the work. Unlike universities and schools in many other countries, British schools are not yet considered sufficiently respectable for all external assessment to be redundant. External examinations are absent in many countries often regarded as competitors in the academic stakes (for example, Japan).

In favour of internal assessment is the argument that the teacher knows the pupil 'better' than an outsider (this could work both ways). Without some sort of external 'check', however, charges of favouritism and antagonism are difficult to refute. The big argument in favour of external assessment is that it forces a comparison of local and national standards and provides a check on the complacency which may result if teachers remain in ignorance of levels of achievement by similar children elsewhere. The danger of external assessment comes when teachers passively allow the objectives of others to become their own. On the other hand, floundering teachers may be helped by this.

Thus external assessment can take two forms. In the strong sense it applies to the assessment of children's achievements in tests externally set and externally examined. In the weak sense it points to the possibility of teachers accepting the tests set or published externally (and the objectives which they imply) but marking them internally in accordance with the test's specification. Where the goals of teaching form a core of widely accepted objectives, an external test is likely to have wide application across regions and schools within regions (a diagnostic reading test, for example). Where teachers have adopted structured sequences of instruction or have developed their own objectives which effect local needs or a new curriculum, teacher-made instruments are more likely to form the appropriate way of carrying out internal assessment.

CHOOSING AMONGST THE ALTERNATIVES

The purpose of this chapter has been to inform teachers of some of the options in assessment open to them. Faced with the bewildering array of modes (let alone instruments!) available, how is the choice to be made? No rules, obviously, but a few guidelines may be advanced. Remember we are talking about the main modes described in the chapter. The strengths and weaknesses of the available instruments are discussed elsewhere. Obviously a given instrument (such as a test, rating scale or check list) whether objective or subjective, could be used in more than one mode. For example a standardized test could be used in either continuous or final assessment. By contrast some tests are more closely associated with one mode of assessment than with what appears to be its opposite in Rowntree's list (1977, 119). An obvious example is a test to assess mastery of a given objective which is likely to find its principal use in criterion-referenced assessment although it may also be used to discriminate among individuals – this, however, would be more probably for secondary purposes only.

The assumption is made that by this time the teacher will have his or her ideas of the relative merits (and the unintended side-effects) of the types discussed through personal experience and reading chapters 2 and 3. In making decisions it is recommended that teachers apply the following principles:

(1) *Identify the constraints.* For example, school custom may well require that a termly or yearly rank order be drawn up for children in the class or year group. Here a norm-referenced statement is required. Is this purpose best served by setting the same test to all pupils or can this aim be achieved by a summative report based on the cumulative records of the results of criterion-referenced assessment? If the latter is true, then no *extra* testing is required over and above that which informs the day-to-day decisions of teachers as to those children who are ready to move further in the instructional sequence. If there is an 'exam timetable' then there's probably little or no room for manoeuvre! Other constraints obviously include whether or not you have to 'prepare' children for an external examination.

(2) Be clear on the objectives and 'spirit' of your teaching and choose a method of assessment which encourages (or, at least, is not antagonistic to) the exercise of the skills and concepts you have been trying to teach. This is probably the most important choice point once you have established what

you are free or not free to do. Many examples could be given. If your aim is to encourage children to *learn* how to organize their own ideas and to express them effectively, then essays as part of continuous assessment are indicated. If the aim is to encourage the development of problem solving skills then process assessment is required (for example, in 'Nuffield Science'). If major attention is paid to building up children's background of knowledge, this would best be accomplished by formal objective tests rather than by *ad hoc* informal testing. The 'golden rule' is: see what method is congruent with your educational aims – the aims come first.

(3)   Be clear on the kinds of information you wish to acquire from the assessment and the kinds of inference you wish to draw. For example, if you wish to study the results of different methods of presenting the same objective with a view to improving upon your teaching you will need to adopt formative methods. If a teacher wants to study the progress of one or two 'special' children in his or her class, an assessment which is informal and continuous (looking for change) seems best suited to this end. By contrast, if your aim is to advise a pupil on his or her suitability for a particular choice of subject or career, cumulative records may be backed up by an aptitude test which is norm-referenced. If you wish to predict a pupil's chances of high performance in a future criterion you might try a norm-referenced and external test known to have high validity for this purpose. The general advice is: make sure you get what you want from the assessment – if you do not know what you want, you deserve what you get!

(4)   From your knowledge of the characteristics and personalities of pupils in your class consider whether certain types of assessment might not be suitable for them. A pupil known to have a history of failure can probably be more appropriately assessed using a criterion-referenced test where each criterion is suitably poised for his/her level of competence. Norm-referenced testing is only likely to reinforce the sense of failure so it should be avoided where possible. With children who become highly anxious in formal assessments, try informal and continuous assessment in preference to final testing.

The converse of this principle also applies. When pupils or classes have been poorly motivated under continuous assessment try a termly or final exam. Require the pupil who is complacent (but without justification) to take a norm-referenced test with age norms. (Teachers, who might object that this principle implies a method of assessment *per child* should consider the assumptions inherent in the practice where all children take the same test.)

(5) Examine available published methods of assessment to see if one is available that fulfils your objectives. Assessment takes time – the teacher's and the pupils'. Teachers' time is spent in devising the assessment (possibly in constructing the instrument) and in 'marking'. If a test already exists that meets your objectives then external assessment (in its weaker sense, p. 60) may be appropriate. If a need exists to diagnose children's learning difficulties in basic subjects a test in print will probably meet this need. But if no test exists (e.g. to examine exactly why so many children cannot 'do' logarithms) then develop your own criterion-referenced tests and study the mistakes, not the correct answers.

(6) Decide who is going to use the results of the assessment. Teachers will know the meaning of the various types of assessment. Parents, employers, children may not understand. Unless teachers wish to emulate doctors in the assumption that it is 'not good for patients (pupils) to know what is wrong with them' choose a method of assessment which enables the results to be communicated simply but accurately in a form which helps in the education of the child. Informal assessment is often the most useful type of assessment in the day-to-day interaction of pupils with teachers. Standardized test scores may be most appropriate where the child's standing in a large peer group needs to be described.

4

Constructing Tests

WHY TEACHER-MADE TESTS?

The strengths of teacher-made tests are as follows:

(1) They provide a closer fit between test and course content, except perhaps in basic subjects where courses are common to most schools for children of corresponding age.
(2) Tests which match the educational objectives of teachers can provide more day-to-day, formative evaluation of pupils and their progress. Tests which correspond with units of a course provide a check of the effectiveness of teaching and learning.
(3) Teacher-made tests can provide a more extensive sampling of specific areas of learning. Commercially produced tests normally sample a wide range of knowledge, skills and concepts.
(4) Teacher-made tests can consist of a small number of relevant items and provide immediate feedback in the form of knowledge of results to both pupil and teacher.
(5) Teacher-made tests provide information regarding a pupil's attainment relative to specific objectives which then provide a basis for report to parents concerning his/her educational progress.

CONSTRUCTING TEACHER-MADE TESTS

It is not expected that teachers will have a great deal of time available in which to build tests but it is certainly not recommended that they 'knock something out' two or three days before tests are to be used! Of course, published tests can and do suffer from a variety of deficiencies in spite of the concentration of time, skill and attention paid to them by professional test constructors. Indeed, many of the side-effects of a test, or the ambiguities or special difficulties presented by an item, may not come to light until after several years of usage. Examples can be given where items have proved more difficult to particularly able pupils than to pupils of average ability because the former have perceived problems hidden from even the authors of the items! Nevertheless, and without pursuing a counsel of perfection, a systematic approach to the construction of a test or instrument – which still allows considerable scope for the creativity and ingenuity of teachers – can be recommended. An attempt has been made to provide such a framework in the pages which follow. As with all learning, the skills of testing would be acquired gradually, but it repays time and effort if teachers accumulate their own files of good items with experience and application. There are very many books on the subject, progressively concerned with suggestions for the improvement of the technical efficiency of the assessment. Books have been written on single aspects of testing (e.g. the construction of multiple choice instruments; the statistics of item analysis; methods of ensuring a higher degree of examiner's consistency when making essay or other open-ended tests). The recommendations offered here do not assume that teachers have little else to do than to construct tests! They propose a minimum set of activities which, if followed, provide a working basis for the construction of instruments more likely to meet educational criteria than tests constructed hastily the night before they are required by a head of department or head teacher, or as yet another annoying appendage to the teacher's main task. In addition, as teachers become more practised, these skills are capable of transfer to the many *ad hoc* occasions on which informal assessment is made in the classroom.

What and How to Test: Sorting Out your Objectives

The simple answer to the question: 'What to assess?' is of course, 'the objectives of the course of teaching and learning'. We identify a teacher's objectives when we pose the question: 'What are you trying to achieve and what kinds of changes do you hope to make to your pupils' capabilities?' But we do not always receive very precise answers, as we have already discussed in chapter 2. For this reason, definition of objectives in behavioural terms is often held to be a fundamental stage in both teaching and testing. Now the language of behavioural objectives is somewhat limited in its expressive potential but it is often useful in the statement of the ends we hope to achieve where these are the actual 'new' or extensions to pupils' accomplishments in the cognitive domain.

One influential source of ideas for educational objectives is the *Taxonomy of Educational Objectives (for the cognitive domain)* by Bloom et al. (1956). Although many who have used it find it unnecessarily restricting and think that the advance specification of objectives inhibits spontaneity in learning (as, indeed, anything can if followed slavishly), others have found it a useful means of correcting an overemphasis on a narrow range of outcomes, in particular the ubiquitous demand for recall and memory for knowledge that makes up so much of traditional examination.

The classification is into six major categories. Metfessel et al. (1969) have proposed a number of verbs which specify the kinds of activities native to each level of the classification. These verbs are representative, but since too much time can easily be spent in trying to show their unique suitability for the heading under which each has been placed, they are quoted here only as one possible guide to the amplification of the category (see table 4.1).

There is no room here to provide a complete breakdown of the classification, but each major category is itself divided into sections. Thus, for knowledge (from Bloom et al., 1956):

1.00	Knowledge
	. . . involves the recall of specifics and universals, the recall of methods and processes, or the recall of a pattern, structure or setting
1.10	Knowledge of specifics
1.11	Knowledge of terminology
1.12	Knowledge of specific facts
1.20	Knowledge of ways and means of dealing with specifics
1.21	Knowledge of conventions
1.22	Knowledge of trends and sequences
1.23	Knowledge of classifications and categories
1.24	Knowledge of criteria
1.25	Knowledge of methodology
1.30	Knowledge of the universals and abstractions in a field

Table 4.1 – Taxonomy of educational objectives

Levels in taxonomy	Verbs to define the relevant activity
1.00 Knowledge	to recall, reorganize, explain, define, identify
2.00 Comprehension	as *translation* to change, give in own words, rephrase, illustrate, translate
	as *interpretation* to illustrate, represent, reorder
	as *extrapolation* to conclude, deduce, estimate, generalize, infer, predict
3.00 Application	to apply, calculate, classify, develop, organize, transfer
4.00 Analysis	to distinguish, detect, classify, categorize
5.00 Synthesis	to unite, tell, relate, produce, derive, organize, formulate
6.00 Evaluation	to argue, judge, compare, contrast, appraise

1.31   Knowledge of principles and generalizations
1.32   Knowledge of theories and structure

It is not suggested that teachers will find it particularly rewarding to classify minutely all their objectives in teaching for knowledge using the above scheme. But an awareness of the qualitative differences in the objectives at the six main levels enables teachers to analyse the very different types of outcome they are seeking to achieve. And if teachers do not know what they are trying to achieve (and many, privately, express this doubt) it is difficult to see how they can plan learning experiences intelligently. A clear concept of the objectives is an indispensable focus for determining the content and form of the teaching and learning experiences as well as an indication of what can, and what cannot, be assessed.

Many writers have urged the desirability of writing objectives only by using verbs which match the various levels in Bloom's taxonomy. But others have argued that it is often very difficult to write a 'pure' objective (that is one which belongs exclusively to only one level in the classification) and have suggested that so long as ambiguity is excluded and the objective is phrased in terms of desired learning outcomes this is sufficient for most teachers' practical purposes. Moreover, a great deal of time and effort has already been expended to determine whether or not the levels in the taxonomy correspond with separable psychological processes. It is clear, however, that it would be a mistake to confuse a formal analysis of educational outcomes with a psychological theory of human ability.

As a rule-of-thumb it is helpful for teachers to be as analytic as possible in the identification of what it is they want children to be able to do (as process or as product) as a result of teaching: this will then constitute the teaching objectives. The question: '*Can they do these things?*' then makes up the assessment objective. The question of the context in which the learning is demonstrated remains to be decided of course, and it is here that knowledge of Bloom's taxonomy proves useful. If the teacher wishes to assess knowledge or comprehension (levels 1 and 2) the context of the assessment can correspond very closely with that in which the *original* learning was presented. If, however, the teacher wishes to assess the extent to which pupils can transfer what they have learned to a *new* situation, then an item which tests application (level 3) should be prepared. Since the total context in which something is originally learned provides valuable clues to recall (psychologists have called this tendency 'episodic memory') teaching for levels 1 and 2 is likely to prove 'easier' than for level 3 – at least in the short term.

Examples of rule-of-thumb objectives (see preceding paragraph) are given by the following.

Can my pupils:
(1)   Add two-, three- and four-digit numbers with decimals?
(2)   Label the chambers and blood vessels into and out of the heart?
(3)   Draw and label a diagram to show total internal reflection in a 60° prism?
(4)   Summarize the chief features in the character of Lady Macbeth?
(5)   Recall Boyle's law?
(6)   Recall the features of 'chernozems' and 'podsols'?

(7)   Construct and use a simple clinometer?
(8)   Give the perfect tense of the following French irregular verbs: *aller, être?*
(9)   Remember the main incidents in the campaigns of Boadicea?
and so on.

Readers may object that this advice is scarcely innovative and point out that even a year's work would soon accumulate a vast number of objectives. This latter point is undoubtedly true. Nevertheless, we can make a distinction between 'core' and other objectives, the former being those which the teacher holds to be indispensable or of central importance when learning a particular topic or subject. We are not arguing that teachers everywhere will agree as to the constituents of that core although there will be a good deal of common ground in basic subjects, but rather that the teacher implicitly in the way he or she teaches will emphasize those that 'matter' in a variety of ways. The exercise might work the other way: the process of seeing these objectives on paper can well lead one to reallocate a rank order of importance by 'downgrading' some, 'upgrading' others and discarding those found by formative evaluation to be unrealistic. One point cannot be over-emphasized: verbs which are open to a wide variety of meanings are avoided where possible. Although the verb 'to know' plays an important part in teachers' discussions about their aims, it is not sufficiently precise to serve as a specific objective. A simple illustration will do here. Suppose a teacher believes that children ought to learn about the EEC and decides that at least children should know where Strasbourg is. 'Knowing where Strasbourg is' could be manifest in a variety of highly dissimilar ways: by *recalling* that Strasbourg is in France: by *naming* a dot on a map as Strasbourg; by *locating* and *naming* a dot on a map; by stating its position in latitude and longitude, miles from London, and so on. One can easily see that very different teaching would be required to achieve these objectives and different kinds of 'knowledge' would be involved. Indeed, some of these would not be classified as 'knowledge' by Bloom's taxonomy.

As might be expected, reliance on behavioural objectives is open to serious criticism. Some of these were described in chapter 2, in the third objection. A good summary of the pros and cons of this approach has been provided by Payne (1974, 41–2) which readers should consult. The chief dangers of slavish adherence to the objectives approach seem to be:

(1)   the trivialization of the goals of education and the possible danger of under-emphasizing the most important;
(2)   the process can become mechanical; and
(3)   the pre-specification of objectives can conceivably prevent the teacher from capitalizing on the unexpected opportunities which occur in classrooms.

Preparing the Specification Table (sometimes called the 'Test Blueprint')

Having determined the objectives of teaching (and, presumably, taught for their attainment) or having identified the outcomes judged to be educationally worthwhile which were attained but not planned in advance, the next task is to prepare a table which shows the way in which the test or instrument is to reflect that content. This is an important aspect of a test's content validity (see chapter 8). By and large it is unfair to pupils to incorporate material not covered by the teaching or other learning activities into a test: such a test would be constitutionally incapable of use in the formative evaluation of teaching effectiveness. The table can be constructed *before* teaching has begun as part of course preparation but left incomplete to enable the unexpected but worthwhile to be incorporated.

Most published specification tables have employed a version of Bloom's taxonomy by which to classify the abilities or performance involved in the objectives (vertical dimension) and their conceptions of the structure of the 'subjects' to classify the contents (horizontal dimension). There is clearly no *one* way in which to classify the material: a suitable method is to study the syllabus with an eye to the process–product distinction and to make some differentiation between levels of outcome ranging from recall of essentials ('knowledge' in the taxonomy) to problem solving, if appropriate. A useful example has been provided by Child (1977, 324) taken from the Nuffield Chemistry Project. In keeping with the process-oriented objectives of the project, the content was classified as 'activities' required in study of: (a) composition and change in materials; (b) practical techniques; (c) patterns in the

Table 4.2 – Specification table: Nuffield Chemistry Project

		Activity/content					
		(a)	(b)	(c)	(d)	(e)	Total (%)
Knowledge	1						21
Comprehension	2						42
Application	3						18
Analysis/evaluation	4						19
Total (%)		24	9	16	32	19	100

behaviour of materials; (d) essential measurement; and (e) concepts. This represented the broad headings under which the various parts of the syllabus could be grouped. Four levels of Bloom's taxonomy were used and the final form of the grid was as shown in table 4.2.

From the totals (which appear in the margins) we can see that greater importance has been attached to comprehension than to the other abilities involved and that measurement (d) was rated almost four times as important as the practical techniques involved (b). Obviously, no rules for determining the weights can be given (indeed they are omitted from this version of the table): they may be arbitrary but will almost certainly express the explicit or implicit value attached to the cells by the teacher. For example, as measurement is the most important activity (d) one might expect a distribution of marks to be awarded for the knowledge level (1) as follows:

Knowledge of composition of changes in materials	5
Knowledge of practical techniques	2
Knowledge of behaviour of materials	4
Knowledge of essential measurement	6
Knowledge of concepts	4
Total	21

If the test designers decided to set one multiple choice question for each point, then the number of items is determined by the emphasis to be placed on the different aspects of knowledge. If weights are applied *initially*, that is before teaching begins, they will certainly be tentative. When teaching begins one may find an inordinate amount of time being spent on the teaching of one aspect of a syllabus, when the table is drawn up an overemphasis of a narrow aspect of the syllabus may be identified: in both cases the specification table is a potential corrective. Construction of the specification table implicit in teacher-made tests often reveals an imbalance: too much emphasis on the recall of isolated factual material or the reproduction of computational skills learned by rote is often seen as a fundamental defect. If a final examination is prepared in this way pupils could be given the specification table to guide them in their revision. If the distribution of weights is justifiable on educational grounds then there seems no fundamental objection to pupils distributing their revision time and efforts accordingly. But if the test is designed to sample (and therefore estimate) the pupils knowledge of the *entire* course this would clearly be a mistake. Generalizations to a child's competence in the domain of learning being tested cannot be obtained if the children are encouraged to learn only a small part of that domain.

Possibly the chief difference between a specification table for norm-referenced and criterion-referenced tests is that the former will express a much broader range of objectives than the latter: in certain cases, a specification table for a criterion-referenced test will consist of a single cell (i.e. one level of ability × one content). Other examples of specification tables may be inspected in Gronlund (1971) and Mehrens and Lehmann (1978).

Deciding upon the Type of Test Item

Having made a decision as to the objectives to be assessed, and the items which embody the levels of ability and contexts in which they are to be examined, the next decision concerns the type of test to be constructed. Broadly speaking teacher-made tests fall into two categories: the objective test or the essay type. Objective types are those in which criteria for the correctness of an answer are set up in advance of the pupil's responses and in which the scores are affected – if at all – in only very minor ways by the subjective

Table 4.3 – Types of teacher-made test

Objective tests	Other name

(1) Recall or completion type
   (a) single word, symbol, formula, etc.
   (b) multiple words or phrases
	Supply type

(2) Alternative response type
   (a) true/false; yes/no
   (b) multiple choice
	Selection type

(3) Matching type	Selection type
(4) Context dependent or unit type	Either supply or selection

Essay tests	
(1) Restricted response (paragraph length)	Supply type
(2) Extended or discussion response	Supply type
(3) Oral	Supply type

judgements or opinions of the markets. One useful classification of teacher-made tests is modified from Lien (1976) and is shown in table 4.3.

Each of these tests has a typical type of *item* associated with it and many variants.

A number of permutations of types of items could be made to make up a total test although it is probably better, if different types are to be used, to keep items of a similar type to the same part of a test. (It is very confusing for children to have to switch types rapidly since each type has a different kind of instruction to respondents.)

In the sections which follow a few examples of each type will first be given; these will be followed by a discussion of their advantages and limitations and a few tips on how to distinguish 'good' from 'poor' items will be offered.

TYPE A1: SIMPLE RECALL/COMPLETION TYPE

Examples:

Question Type

    (1)   What is the name of the capital city of France?
    (2)   Who is the present British prime minister?
    (3)   What is the formula for the 'refractive index'?

Completion Type

    (5)   The chemical formula for sulphuric acid is . . .
    (6)   Solve $5x + 4 = 24$; $x = \ldots$
    (7)   Draw the Ordnance Survey map sign for a church with a tower.

Advantages
These items are limited to those cases in which a single correct answer can be given. They are useful in mathematics and the sciences not only to test knowledge of specific facts but also where computation is required. Although teachers are likely to use these predominantly as tests of knowledge of bits of information, their format is not limited to these occasions. Reference to Bloom, Hastings and Madaus (1971) reveals several examples where this type has been used to test comprehension and application. For example, the item:

    (8)   A car accelerating from 48 to 80 km/h in four seconds has an average acceleration of . . . km/h per second

requires knowledge of the relevant formula, the ability to substitute the values into the formula and to work out the value for *a*, the acceleration. In this case the item would not be very useful in the diagnosis of errors. If three separate stages in answering the item are required the teacher will not know which one or combination of these has 'broken down' if an incorrect answer is selected.

    In general type A1 is a fairly easy item to construct in order to test for the knowledge of technical terms, the symbols used in a discipline and definitions. The chief limitations of such items are

that, if relied on exclusively to assess how much has been learned, they can encourage the child to depend on the rote learning of highly specific and unrelated facts. A second disadvantage is that they are restricted chiefly to the 'lower' levels in Bloom's taxonomy and place a premium on the child's ability to recall. Mehrens and Lehmann (1978) are of the opinion that the testing of synthesis and interpretation are extremely difficult subjects for this type of item, for example. Thirdly, the ease and speed with which these items seem to be constructed can often lull the teacher into believing that 'any fool can write them'. One common mistake is to fail to notice that an apparently objective item can be answered in a number of ways, thus setting the respondent an ambiguous problem and the marker a subjective decision (which defeats the object of the exercise!).
For example:

(9) Where are the athletics in the 1992 Olympic Games to be held?
(10) A circle has a diameter of five inches; what is its area?
(11) Columbus discovered America in . . .

are all indefinite: item (9) because 'Spain' and 'Barcelona' are both applicable, item (10) because the degree of accuracy required is not specified, and item (11) because the sentence can be completed in a number of perfectly correct ways ('a boat which sailed from Europe' and 'the fifteenth century' are just two of many responses which present the marker with a subjective decision on whether or not the answers are to be allowed). These items could be improved as follows:

(9) In what city are the athletics in the Olympic Games of 1992 to be held?
(10) A circle has a diameter of five inches. Its area, correct to two decimal places, is . . . square inches.
(11) In what year did Columbus discover America?

Hints on writing recall/completion items
In general, then, the rules for writing (and not writing!) items of type A1 are:

(a) Require short, definite answers in response to complete sentences.
(b) Specify the degree of accuracy required in computational items.
(c) If the item is of the completion type make sure the blanks occur at or near the end of the sentence to ensure that the readers have not forgotten the requirements by the end of the sentence. (This is particularly important when testing young children whose retention span is small and who find it difficult to comprehend 'backwards'.)
(d) Try and *avoid* items that can be answered by general ability rather than by the knowledge being tested.
(e) Specify the terms in which the answer is to be given (for example in item (9) above, 'in what city' is much better than 'where').
(f) Do not write a completion type which is long and includes many blanks. Items with a large number of gaps are often ambiguous and set the child the task of guessing what was in the item-writer's mind.

An extreme example:

(12)   If . . . solution is . . . using . . . electrodes . . . is deposited at . . .

And while on the subject of blanks, keep them all the same length and do not vary them with the number of letters in the missing word.
(g) Avoid giving external clues to the answer, e.g. of a grammatical kind, which may lead the children to the correct answer independently of their knowledge.

TYPE A2a: ALTERNATIVE RESPONSE TYPES

True/False Type

In these, children are presented with a proposition that is either true or false and are asked to underline which answer they consider correct.
    Examples:

(1)   True   False   In the play, Hamlet is killed by his wife

(2)   True   False   In a truly normal distribution, the median, mode and mean coincide

Sometimes, especially in the assessment of attitudes, opinions and beliefs, a yes/no format is adopted:

(3)   Yes   No   I prefer reading a good book to attending a good party

(4)   Yes   No   Capital punishment should be restored for all murders

A further variant is known as the cluster type. In it there is a statement (or 'stem') followed by more than one item requiring a response:

(5)   The arithmetic mean is

    True   False   (a)   the value about which the sum of the deviations is zero

    True   False   (b)   another word for median

    True   False   (c)   less affected by extreme scores than is the median

The disadvantages of true/false items are probably more apparent than their advantages. The probability of obtaining a correct answer by guessing is high, the items are restricted in use to those propositions which are unequivocally true or false, tests containing only few items are very poor at discriminating among children and the tendency to respond 'true' when in doubt (known as 'acquiescence') confounds the interpretation of the score.

The advantages of true/false items are that they can be scored very quickly indeed, they permit coverage of a large area of content in a relatively short time and, contrary to the misconception of some teachers, can be extended to test comprehension and understanding if constructed with ingenuity. For example:

(6)   True   False   Given that an electric kettle is rated '2kW, 240 V' and when filled with cold water takes five minutes to

boil, the average weekly cost of boiling the kettle six times each day is 21 pence if 1 kW costs three pence.

Hints on writing true/false items
(a)   Avoid any source of ambiguity or imprecision. Examples of words or phrases which signal this difficulty are 'most important', 'never', 'largely', 'always', 'essential', 'only'. If children are 'test-wise' they will have learned that certain words of this type (known as 'specific determiners') are more likely to signal that the proposition is false than that it is true. Conversely, any proposition which contains words like 'may', 'might', 'can', 'sometimes' is more likely to be true than false.
(b)   Avoid the use of negative statements. Try answering this one:

True   False   It is not true that Baldwin was Prime Minister in 1920

(c)   Avoid using words which are open to more than a single interpretation: use quantitative rather than qualitative terms where possible. For example:

True   False   Many people voted Liberal in the 1979 General Election

presents a problem because 'many' is open to different interpretations.
(d)   Only use this type of item for propositions which are unequivocally true or false.
(e)   Balance the number of true and false statements in the test but keep the length of statements roughly equal. (Extra long statements, such as those containing subordinate clauses or qualification often indicate that the item-writer has taken special care to construct a true statement.)
(f)   Avoid lifting statements verbatim from text books: the children may have memorized passages.

TYPE A2b: MULTIPLE CHOICE TYPE

Teachers will be very familiar with this type of item, but it is difficult to construct effectively. The basic structure is in two parts: a 'stem', which states the problem and a set of possible answers or 'options' one of which (the 'key') is correct and the others of which are incorrect (the 'distracters'). There are many variations on this format. Stems can be direct questions or incomplete statements: only one, or several options can be correct; with stems which are difficult to prepare the candidate may be required to select the 'best' answer. The concern of this section is to describe those which the teacher can construct with little difficult rather than to demonstrate the extent of the ingenuity exhibited by professional item-writers. Whole books and lengthy chapters have been written on this topic and the interested reader is referred to the thorough descriptions provided by Gerberich (1956) and by Wesman (1971, chapter 4). The chief varieties are now given.

Single Correct Answer Type

(1) Who invented the sewing machine?
  (a) Singer   (d) Fulton
  (b) Howe   (e) White
  (c) Whitney

(2) If 36% of the variance in test X can be predicted from test Y, what is the value of the correlation coefficient?
  (a) 0.36   (d) 0.70
  (b) 0.50   (e) 0.80
  (c) 0.60

'Best Answer' Type

Whereas the previous examples have a single correct answer, teachers may wish to extend the multiple choice format to examine the children's knowledge in an area where several versions of 'fact' have been proposed. This type of item bristles with problems: the item-writer has the responsibility of providing the evidence that experts agree on the 'best' answer or to inform the respondent of the source or authority for the best answer. The respondent must, of course, be directed to select the 'best' response from among the options.

    (3)   What was the basic purpose in setting up the National Health Service?
        (a)   To supply cheap medical care to the community
        (b)   To keep an election promise made by politicians
        (c)   To remove the privileges of those who could pay for private care
        (d)   To make medical care available to all regardless of income
        (e)   To improve the health of underprivileged sections of the community

Incomplete Stem Type

    (4)   The correlation coefficient between test X and test Y is 0.71. The amount of variance in Y which is predictable from X is
        (a) 3%   (c) 50%
        (b) 7%   (d) 71%

Multiple Response Type

If several correct answers to a question exist it is sometimes a stringent test of the child's knowledge to include two or more correct answers among the options. (The teacher would obviously have to prepare an instruction that the child is allowed to pick one or more than one of the options.)

    (5)   What factor or factors are chiefly responsible for the clotting of the blood?
        (a)   Contact of blood with injured tissue
        (b)   Oxidation of haemoglobin
        (c)   Contact of blood with a foreign surface
        (d)   Presence of unaltered prothrombin

Where questions are set which have several equally acceptable answers as in the above example, writers have sometimes prepared a negative version of the multiple response type. The respondent is instructed to mark the option which does *not* correctly answer the question.

(6) Which of these statements is *not* true of a virus?
  (a) It can live only in plant and animal cells
  (b) It can reproduce itself
  (c) It is composed of large living cells
  (d) It can cause disease

(the above two examples are taken from Wesman, 1971).

Incomplete Alternatives Type

This type can be used where a unique but simple answer exists to a problem and where the teacher wishes to make the respondent a little more active than in other types. It is particularly useful for arithmetical problems.

(7) If you calculate the square root of 27, what number should appear as the second decimal place?
  (a) four   (d) eight
  (b) five   (e) nine
  (c) seven

Substitution Type

This type has been extensively used to assess children's ability to detect errors of style or syntax in well-written prose. A short extract from a written passage is presented but with alterations to include errors (e.g. of punctuation, grammar, spelling). These are underlined and identified with a number. For each number the child is required to select the phrase (either the original or an alternative) which provides the best expression. Unfortunately they often have a somewhat contrived appearance.

(8) 'Star Trek' is fantastic story about the future. The aim of the crew of the star ship 'Enterprise' is to boldly go[1] where no man has been before. The crew consists[2] of a motley array of men and women of many national ities, but each one seems to spend most of their[3] time sitting[4] at a computer terminal.

Item
(1)	(a)	to boldly travel	(3)	(a)	their
	(b)	boldly to go		(b)	his
	(c)	to boldly go		(c)	his or her
(2)	(a)	consist	(4)	(a)	sat
	(b)	consists		(b)	in front of
	(c)	comprises		(c)	sitting

As can be seen from this example it can be difficult to choose plausible alternatives and items of this type are probably most easily constructed by the pedantic!

There are many more types but this has dealt with those most frequently encountered. Each type presents its own source of difficulty but certain 'rules for writing' are generalizable.

Tips on preparation of multiple choice items

(a) Ensure that the *instructions* to the children are clear. For example, a set of single correct answer items could be introduced as follows:

'Each of the questions below is followed by several answers marked (a), (b), (c), (d) and (e). From these, you are to choose the *one* answer which is correct. Mark your answer by underlining the letter alongside the one you choose.' (This would be followed by an example showing how it is to be done. If separate answer sheets are to be provided the children could be asked to respond by placing the letter of the chosen answer in a space provided.)

(b) Stems which present a direct question are easiest to write.

(c) Keep the stem short and the options of roughly the same length as one another in a single item. If this is not done and one option is longer or shorter than the others the child may suspect that it is the correct answer. In general, avoid making the correct option systematically different from the distracters.

(d) Make all options equally plausible. This is sometimes quite difficult. As an example of alternatives which are *not* equally plausible consider the completion item:

(9) The logarithm of 27.56 is
(a)	1.4702	(c)	1.3712
(b)	1.4507	(d)	1.4402

This item was set presumably to test the child's ability to read the body of the logarithm table and to interpolate using the table of differences. Options (a), (b) and (c) are, therefore, quite implausible since none occurs in the required line of the table.

(e) Make sure that all options are mutually exclusive unless you have deliberately written an item of the multiple response type. Payne (1974, 113) has provided a good example of an item which 'fails' on this tip:

(10) If a test has a reliability of 0.78 what percentage of an observed score is attributable to errors of measurement?

(a) over 5%	(c) over 20%
(b) over 10%	(d) over 30%

The precise answer is 22% and the closest option (c), but (a) and (b) are also correct.

(f) Do not overwork the option 'none of the above'. It suggests that you have run out of plausible alternatives but the biggest objection is that a child may get the answer correct (when 'none of the above' *is* the correct answer) for the wrong reasons. For example:

(11) What is the area of a circle whose radius is 5.2 inches? Give your answer to two decimal places (take pi = 3.14).
- (a) 83.09 square inches
- (b) 84.95 square inches
- (c) 84.98 square inches
- (d) 85.91 square inches
- (e) none of the above

Any child who got an answer not found among (a) to (d) inclusive would choose (e), the correct answer. But this would not necessarily mean that he or she had calculated the answer correctly as 84.91 square inches. 'None of the above' can be used if the correct answer *is* one of the other options provided.

(g) In the incomplete stem type make sure that the alternatives are grammatically consistent with the stem and parallel with each other. The oldest mistake with this type of item is to give a grammatical clue to the correct item, most commonly the use of the article 'an', which applies to only one alternative.

(h) Eliminate the use of the same wording in stem and option. If there is a common term in stem and one option this provides a clue to the correct answer.

(i) Place the correct option at random throughout the tests. In other words, do not place more of the correct options in any one position than in any other. This can be accomplished by shuffling cards.

(j) Use four or five options. The problem here is one of compromise between what is practicable and what ensures greatest reliability. Theoretically, the larger the number of *plausible* alternatives the lower the probability of obtaining the correct answer by chance. But really plausible alternatives are quite often difficult to prepare and take up time and space. By convention, then four or five options are usually adopted.

These tips by no means exhaust all the advice that could be given on the writing of items, but if followed they should help the teacher avoid some of the most common errors in the preparation of this type of item. The purpose in setting high standards of item preparation is not, of course, to improve the technical properties of the test for the sake of it. It is to reduce as far as possible the sources and magnitude of the error variance in the test as a whole. Chapter 7 explains the importance of the concept of error variance and shows how it may be calculated.

One of the most useful ways of spotting deficient items is by consultation with the children who have taken the tests. They are often capable of picking up many of the often unforeseeable problems in items. Gradually the teacher can build a bank of items classified by content and by ability required or tested in their solution. Good items can be retained, poor items discarded or rewritten.

HOW TO DEAL WITH GUESSING

One of the most hackneyed but fundamental criticisms of the types of item we have been considering is that children can gain marks by guessing even when they are ignorant of the answers to the tests or quite unprepared to take them. Guessing cannot entirely be eliminated even from essay type tests but the chances of gaining marks by guesswork are much higher in multiple choice items. Suppose there are just two options to a question, as in the true/false items. By chance alone one might expect a child to get half marks (that is even if he or she 'knows nothing' of the content being sampled). Similarly in a test composed of items each having four options, a chance mark of 25% would be expected.

Faced with this problem a number of solutions have been proposed:

(a)   the use of instructions designed to discourage or equalize the effects of guessing;
(b)   the use of 'correction formulae' which are designed to penalize guessing;
(c)   the use of weights to modify the scores in the light of the degree of confidence expressed by respondents when choosing options.

Methods (a) and (b) are those most commonly encountered. But there are problems with both methods. Some writers have favoured the use of instructions which tell children only to respond to those items where they are certain of their answers. This seems to run counter to our common experience that the knowledge we possess is held with very varying degrees of 'certainty' which is itself, in any case, open to a number of interpretations. Given that the personalities of children are very different this instruction could serve to reward the disobedient! Some writers have agreed that the best way to proceed is to instruct the children not to guess and to tell them that they will be penalized if they do so. Another view is that children should be told to attempt all items but without threat that a penalty for guessing will be exacted; the formula for the correction for guessing is, then, applied as part of the scoring procedure. Probably the most commonly used formula is:

$$S = R - \frac{W}{n-1} \qquad [4.1]$$

where

S = corrected score
R = number correct
W = number incorrect (not counting omitted items)
n = number of options per item

The rationale for this formula is simple (too simple!). If there are n choices per item the chance of a correct guess is $1/n$, and of an incorrect guess $n-1/n$. Thus for every $n-1$ incorrect guesses we expect one guess to turn out correct. Thorndike (1971, 59–61) gives a full account of the difficulties in dealing with guessing. The obvious problem with the 'correction formula' is that its assumption is wrong: 'guessing' is not a chance phenomenon any more than 'knowledge' is an all or none affair. Although this problem has been extensively studied, no final answer has been reached. It has been reported that the 'correction formula' reduces reliability (see chapter 7) but increases validity (see chapter 8). Other statisticians have suggested that instructions not to guess have made a slight increase in the test's power to predict a criterion. It is known that, if everyone guesses (as would, perhaps, be the case if the test were grossly unfair to all respondents) the size of errors of measurement (see chapter 7) shoots up. On the other hand, if all pupils have the time to answer all items and, indeed, do so, there is a perfect correlation between corrected and uncorrected scores, i.e. the rank order of scores will not change (Tinkelman, 1971).

The suggestion that teachers require each child to indicate (on say a four–five point scale) the degree of confidence with which an option has been chosen, followed by the practice of weighting the option accordingly (that is, of giving greater credit when a correct answer has been chosen and rated five for 'absolutely confident' than when it is chosen but only with rank two – 'not at all confident') seems not to have been widely practised. This method is deficient in that it offers no particular hope of a common basis for comparison between the respondent who is a 'natural gambler' and one who is shy, timid and self-deprecatory.

Sound advice on dealing with this problem has been provided by Cronbach (1961). This is to provide the respondents with encouragement to answer as best they can with a cautionary note that blind guessing can lower as well as raise scores. However, guessing is likely to operate extensively only where something is to be gained by 'chancing one's arm'. If the multiple choice test is

used in criterion-referenced assessment and pupils understand that
it is part of the process by which they are to decide whether or not
to continue to the next most advanced topic, one might expect
them to be as interested as is the teacher in a reasonable assessment of their readiness and to admit their ignorance if remedial
help is available. Perhaps guessing is less prevalent in a relaxed
atmosphere of assessment free from competitiveness.

TYPE A3: MATCHING TYPE

This is a further variety of multiple choice item but one which
conserves space. The child taking the test is presented with two
lists. The instructions require the child to make the correct link
between an entry in list A with one in list B and indicate this link in
the blank space.
   For example:

(12)   Painters and painting
       Famous painters are listed in list A and paintings in
       list B. Place the letter corresponding to the painting in
       the space next to the artist who painted it.

List A	List B
(1) Paul Cézanne	(a) Bal Champêtre
(2) Auguste Renoir	(b) Young woman pow-dering herself
(3) George Seurat	(c) Rocks – Forest of Fountainbleau
(4) Antoine Watteau	(d) The Fiddler
	(e) La Première Sortie
	(f) The Supper at Em-maus

Mehrens and Lehmann (1978) have described this type of item as
most suitable for the 'who', 'what', 'when', 'where', type of learning and for any others which involve simple relationships. Many
examples will come to mind. They require relatively little reading
time and providing the matching requirements within an item deal

with a single area of knowledge (painting and painters in the above example) they can sample quite a large content. The type is less well suited to the assessment of the abilities higher than 'knowledge' in Bloom's taxonomy and is quite difficult to construct (the reader should try to spot the deficiencies in our example).

There are many variants of this type: in fact Gerberich (1956) lists no fewer than 38 versions! They can be used to test comprehension or knowledge of cause–effect relationship. Child (1977, 325–6) provides one such example drawn from the Nuffield Chemistry Project:

(13)   Directions: the group of questions below consists of five lettered headings followed by a list of numbered phrases. For each numbered phrase select the one heading which is most closely related to it. Each heading may be used once, more than once, or not at all.

Classify the following changes into one of the categories (a)–(e):
(a) radioactive decay   (d) cracking
(b) catalysis   (e) oxidation
(c) hydrolysis

(1) the conversion of heat alone of an organic liquid consisting of one compound only, into a mixture of components which are gaseous at room temperature
(2) the production of thermal energy from the fossil fuels
(3) changes in the nuclei of atoms

Experience with these items has shown that, despite their advantages in efficiency in use of time and space, they are particularly open to irrelevant cues and the task of producing plausible alternatives is often very difficult. If you do decide to use them the following points should be observed:

(a)   Write responses which are related (our examples were all paintings or physical/chemical processes) but mutually exclusive.
(b)   Keep the number of stimuli small (say four or five but let the

number of responses be larger, by about two or three). Long lists are more difficult to construct homogeneously and will involve the child in a much larger number of comparisons between stimuli and response. If the number of stimuli equals the number of responses a child may get a correct answer simply by the process of elimination. The practice (adopted in the Nuffield example) of requiring the child to respond 'once, more than once, or not at all' may help to minimize guessing.

(c)   Write the directions for matching and responding clearly. (The Nuffield Chemistry item as presented here tells the respondent to classify and select, but not where/how to do so.)

(d)   Present the responses in some sort of logical order (in the painters' list the artists are presented in alphabetical order of surname). This has been shown to help the respondent scan the lists quickly.

TYPE A4: CONTEXT DEPENDENT TYPE

So far we have concentrated on the production of items in which every one is independent of every other, in the sense that each contains all the information the child is offered. Occasions arise, however, especially where the teacher is assessing comprehension rather than knowledge, in which it is convenient to provide respondents with a stimulus about which a number of questions is posed. These fall into two main types: the *pictorial type* or the *reading type*. Space will permit only a single example but the reader is referred to many examples present in standard texts.

Pictorial Type

These are most frequently used to present stimulus material in the form of graphs, tabulated data, maps or scientific and mechanical diagrams.

Example (9–10 year olds):

(14)   The graph below shows the number of bicycles sold by one shop in one week last year. Study the graph then answer the questions which follow.

(1)   On which day were fewest bicyles sold?
    (a) Monday   (c) Thursday
    (b) Tuesday   (d) Friday

(2)   How *many more* bicycles were sold on the 'best' day than on the 'next best' day?
    (a) four   (c) three
    (b) two   (d) five

(3)   How many bicycles were sold altogether on the *two* 'poorest' days?
    (a) one   (c) two
    (b) four   (d) three

If you decide to use the pictorial form the following points should be borne in mind:

(a)   Choose pictures/graphs because they are appropriate to what you wish to measure, not just because they are novel or interesting.
(b)   Use pictorial material which is clear and uncluttered with detail unless you *wish* to test for perceptual analysis.
(c)   Adhere to the principles of multiple choice construction as have already been described.
(d)   Make the instructions to children very clear. You are assessing the ability of children to deal with the information in the picture not their comprehension of the instructions.

Reading Type

Typically, this type consists of a piece of writing (usually of good quality though one can often detect material written especially for the purpose) followed by multiple choice questions requiring comprehension and application of the material. The special difficulties with this type of test include the time taken to select passages and to construct interesting questions (especially plausible options, where interpretation is being assessed); the low reliability relative to the time taken to enable children to respond, and their inappropriateness for a wide range of ability in view of the demands placed upon reading skill.

If teachers do intend to try this type of item:

(a) Choose material which is worth interpreting.
(b) Rewrite or edit it to incorporate the interpretations desired. Include several distinct ideas that lend themselves to questions clearly differing in content.
(c) Make sure the resulting material is within the reading ability of the children for whom it is intended.
(d) Base the items on the material in the passage: do not write items which depend on background or general knowledge.

THE ANALYSIS OF OBJECTIVE TEST ITEMS

We shall defer for a while consideration of the type of test beloved by British teachers – the essay type – to study the methods by which items may be examined. No matter how carefully the items have been constructed some will turn out to be 'better' than others – but 'better', of course, needs to be defined. 'Item analysis' refers to all the techniques available for the examination of the responses of groups of children to each item. This section will concentrate on those methods within the competence of classroom teachers.

A very large number of techniques of item analysis is available at varying levels of sophistication. Since rather stringent criteria of item preparation have been advocated which will take time to master, it is recommended that teachers do carry out item analysis in order to retain, for repeated use where appropriate, those which have the most satisfactory properties. For purposes of simplification, we shall restrict the discussion at this point to the analysis of items which are to form part of tests designed to discriminate among pupils; that is, of norm-referenced tests. We shall assume that individual teachers will be too busy to conduct extensive 'try-outs' of items although this will be possible if teachers join working parties or collaborate in the development of new curricula as in the Nuffield projects. In practice, the actual assessment is likely to constitute the try-outs of the items. But other informal opportunities may be devised, perhaps with small groups of pupils as part of their normal lessons or in another school where the items are appropriate to the teaching objectives.

The aims of the try-out are as follows:

(a)   To identify items with such weak construction that they should be discarded on the grounds of their ambiguity, misleading instructions, undue complexity or lack of plausibility in the distracters, if used.

(b)   To determine the degree of difficulty of each item. Items which are 'too difficult' or 'too easy' are of little or no use in norm-referenced assessment.

(c)   To examine the plausibility of the distracters.

(d)   To determine the effectiveness of the item in discriminating pupils who are 'high' or 'low' in the ability or achievement being tested.

(e)   To gain information on the number of items to make up the test and to determine the time limit for the final test.

(f)   To examine the relationships among the items chosen in order to eliminate redundancy of information if the test is to be used for norm-referenced assessment (i.e. to see the extent to which items are measuring the same or different attributes of the group of respondents).

Aim (f) demands rather complex statistical treatment and will be dealt with in chapter 6. The 'bare bones' of the processes by which aims (a) to (d) may be realized are now considered. We divide the processes into steps.

Step 1: Conditions for the Try-out

Ideally the items should be tried out on a sample of children comparable with the group for which they are intended. It would be quite easy to do this if, say, an entire age group in a single school had followed a course of study. In practice, however, no more than two classes (say 60 pupils) may have followed a similar course of study; in this case the group may be smaller than desirable. If a group of teachers were to pilot items on, say, a year group in a comprehensive or middle school, a short cut might be adopted. In this case the items could be divided at random into subsets containing equal numbers of items. Each subset would constitute a 'mini-test'. The year group would then be divided at random into test groups and a 'mini-test' allocated at random to each test group. In this way attainment of a large number of objectives can be studied and the behaviour of a large number of items examined without the need for any child to take all items. This economical method is known as multiple '*matrix sampling*' but the random requirement and at least 20 children per subgroup must be adhered to if the results are not to be misleading. Teachers may obtain information about the performances of pupils and the characteristics of items using a number of basic types of sampling. These are, respectively: (a) using the population; (b) using a pupil sample; (c) using an item sample; (d) using matrix sampling; and (e) using multiple matrix sampling. These are illustrated in figure 4.1.

Strictly speaking type (a) is not a form of sampling since all items are administered to all pupils. In (b) all items are taken by a random sample of pupils whereas in (c) a random sample of items is administered to all pupils. In type (d) only a sample of items is taken by a sample of pupils whereas in type (e) subsets of items are administered to subsets of pupils. Type (e) is the most economical in gaining estimates of performances of the largest number of pupils.

Assuming the teacher has constructed the items with care, only few ambiguities should go undetected at the try-out stage. One way to gain relevant information of the try-out and the assessment on one and the same occasion is to invite pupils – especially those in secondary schools – to mark an item 'unfair' if they detect a source of difficulty inherent in the structure of the item. The teacher can then guarantee to discount performance on that particular item if a number of pupils mark it, provided a reason can be given by the children concerned.

Step 2: Finding Item Difficulties

Arrange the answer papers in rank order from the highest total to

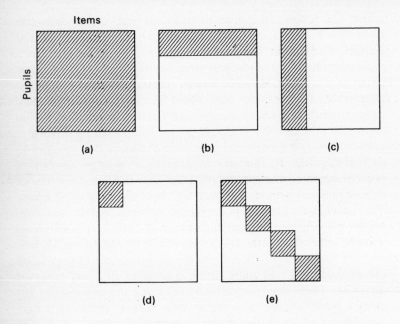

Figure 4.1   Types of sampling: (a) population type; (b) pupil sample type; (c) item sample type; (d) matrix sample type; (e) multiple matrix sample type.

the lowest. This will be done for the entire group of children who took the test but if matrix sampling has been adopted it will be carried out for each separate 'mini-test'. Then record the number choosing the correct answer if the item is in multiple choice format or supplying it if the item is open ended, and calculate the difficulty index.

This and subsequent steps are illustrated using a small sample of data acquired from a mathematics test taken by all pupils on entry to a large comprehensive school. In order to simplify the arithmetic involved, the papers of 120 children were extracted at random for item analysis. The test consisted of 64 items but the chief points can be made with reference to only a few of these.

To calculate the difficulty index
The following numbers of correct responses to the first five items were obtained:

	1	2	3	4	5
Correct response	68	69	59	56	46

$$\text{Difficulty index} = \frac{R}{T}$$

where
R = number of correct responses
T = total number of children

Hence the corresponding difficulty indexes[1] are

	1	2	3	4	5
Index	0.57	0.58	0.49	0.47	0.40

Some people refer to this as the *facility index*. We can obtain a simple alternative 'difficulty index' which actually does indicate how difficult each item is using

$$\text{Difficulty index} = 1 - \frac{R}{T}$$

Thus the corresponding values for this index would be

	1	2	3	4	5
Index	0.43	0.42	0.51	0.53	0.60

Item number 28 in the test proved particularly difficult. Only 13 got it right. Corresponding indices for this item therefore are 0.11 and 0.89 respectively. It does not matter which index you use, but be sure you get hold of its *meaning*!

---

[1] Although this is called the 'difficulty index' it actually indicates how *easy* the item was, because the higher the index the *more* children get it right.

The use one makes of these values depends on the purpose for which the items were used. If the teacher wants to compile a test of items which maximally discriminates among the children in terms of total test scores then items with value for the index of between 0.40 and 0.60 are best for this purpose (actually at 0.50, but for practical classroom purposes the above range is suitable). If one uses each item primarily as a test of an objective, as in criterion-referenced tests, then no particular value can be specified. But assuming item 28 (and any others with very low values for the difficulty index) is not technically deficient (badly worded, ambiguous) it clearly indicates a state of non-mastery by almost all respondents. What view do we take of items with facility values greater than 0.90? Apart from the fact that it is a very easy item and not likely to help discriminate between levels of achievement, its incorporation into a test may be justified on the grounds that it helps anxious pupils to settle into the test-taking routine. By and large, however, and as a compromise, most tests useful in assessing achievement will consist of items whose difficulty values lie within the range of 0.30 and 0.70.

Step 3: Checking Plausibility and Discrimination Values

For each item in the multiple choice or matching type, examine the behaviour of the correct answer and its distracters. This is done by dividing the total sample into levels of achievement on total scores. If the teacher has only about 30 or 40 pupils available, two levels ('upper' and 'lower') each with half the number of pupils will be suitable.

In an example of 120 pupils division into fifths seems a reasonable decision. Item 32 in the mathematics test will be used to illustrate the procedure.

(32)   A litre of paint will cover approximately 50 square feet. How many litres of paint will you need to buy to paint the walls of a room 12 ft long, 10 ft wide and 8 ft high?

(a) 2   (d) 10
(b) 6   (e) 20
(c) 8

Table 4.4 – Distribution of responses to item 32

Option / Range of pupils on *total* scores	(a)	(b)	(c)	(d)	(e)	Omitted	Pupils not read item	Total
Top fifth		1	21	2	—	—	—	24
Next highest fifth		1	18	3	2	—	—	24
Middle fifth		2	14	6	1	1	—	24
Next lowest fifth		5	10	7	—	2	—	24
Bottom fifth	1	9	6	2	1	2	3	24
Total	1	18	69	20	4	5	3	120

Table 4.4 shows the distribution of responses to item 32. Of the total group of 120, 69 pupils got the answer right (keyed (c)). Thus the item has a difficulty index of 0.58, and is well within the range specified in step 2 as desirable. Distracters (b) and (d) seem to have proved fairly attractive but the response rate to distracter (a) shows that pupils regarded it as an implausible one probably because it is so disparate from the others. Distracter (e), also, showed a large discrepancy, probably for the same reason but in the opposite direction. The way in which the correct answer (c) worked (the number correct decreases with decreasing overall ability) is satisfactory and only few children omitted the item altogether. The overall conclusion from the analysis is that item 32 is some use but needs to be improved by the provision of more plausible alternatives than options (a) and (e).

To reiterate: the number of divisions into which the range of total scores can be grouped depends on the size of the group. Less than 20 children per division is probably not adequate. Division into top and bottom halves is often quite appropriate. If the teacher were to find items having an inverse relationship to overall score (i.e. being answered correctly more often by pupils 'low' than by those 'high' in ability) this item should be treated with caution and scrutinized for a possible explanation.

Step 4: Calculating the Discrimination Index

For each item, compute the discrimination index. This is a simple technique to examine how well the items discriminate between 'high' and 'low' scores overall. Where large numbers of children are available most authorities recommend a comparison between top and bottom 27% of scores (Henrysson, 1971). Using the data of table 4.4 we find that of the top 32 pupils (approximately 27% of 120) 26 got the item correct and of the bottom 32, eight were correct. So 26 out of 32 (0.8125) and eight out of 32 (0.25) in top and bottom groups of scores were successful

$$\text{Discrimination index} = p_1 - p_2$$
$$= 0.8125 - 0.25$$
$$= 0.56$$

where
p_1 = proportion in top 27% responding correctly
p_2 = proportion in bottom 27% responding correctly

Obviously the higher the value for the discrimination index the more effectively performance on the item reflects performance overall. If the discrimination index is near zero the item, whatever else it may be doing (like encouraging the poorest pupils), is redundant in terms of differentiating levels of ability or achievement in the test as a whole.

Step 5: Deciding on the Length and Time Limit of the Test

This is not strictly an aspect of item analysis but the results of item analysis play a part in these decisions. In tests which are criterion-referenced, knowledge of the difficulty of an item is not very helpful. As a rule-of-thumb for criterion-referenced tests, each objective tested required about eight to ten similar items. In norm-referenced testing the inclusion of a few very easy items at the beginning is recommended: all pupils who are required to take a test should be given a reasonable opportunity to get at least some right because the use of tests to destroy any semblance of self-esteem is strongly deprecated. Similarly, the practice of including a few really difficult items is also recommended. This is to challenge the most able pupils and to offer some basis for discrimination at the top end of the ability range. The majority of the items (say

80%) should, however, be of average difficulty (those in the range 0.30–0.70 as already indicated).

Deciding on the length of the test is a matter of the teacher's judgement but some pretty obvious considerations apply: the purpose of the test, the age and ability of the pupils and the level of reliability required are probably the most important.

If the test is used to assess a term's work or year's work it will need to be longer than for a short unit of work or a small number of objectives. If the purpose of the test is principally diagnostic, more items per objective will be necessary.

Quite obviously, young children read and write more slowly than older children. Similarly, brighter children think, read and write more quickly than less able children. With objective tests, having four or five options in multiple choice form, 45 item tests can be taken in about one hour. Children aged over 11 years should certainly be capable of an hour of testing. For pupils in the early years of junior schooling 30 minutes is probably sufficiently long. You can obtain your own estimates by supplying each child with three coloured pencils, giving the test and asking them to mark in one colour the point reached after 20 minutes, in another the point at 30 minutes and in the third at 45 minutes, to get some idea of what is a reasonable expectation of the speed of responding by motivated children.

Reliability is a big concept and is fully examined in chapter 7. There you will see that, all other things being equal, the longer the test the more reliable it seems to be. No one can state what a reliability *ought* to be. Reliability is usually expressed as a co-efficient and most published tests in the cognitive domain have values of around 0.95 (a value of 1.0 would indicate that *no* measurement error is present). Teacher-made tests can approach this value but as the amount of error increases as the coefficient falls, a target reliability of 0.85 seems not an unreasonable one to aim for in teacher-made tests.

Teachers will be guided by experience in these important aspects of testing. If the test is seen to provide valuable information teachers will feel justified in spending time on it. If testing is haphazard and does not form part of a coherent programme of assessment more than a few minutes on tests may justifiably be begrudged. So far as a time limit for a test is concerned, if teachers are in doubt it seems preferable to be generous and to allow as many to complete as is organizationally feasible.

ALTERNATIVE METHODS OF ITEM ANALYSIS

What have been suggested so far are extremely simple but quite valuable methods of item analysis. For a variety of reasons, measurement theorists have been dissatisfied with these methods, however, and have developed more rigorous statistical techniques. If teachers opt for the simpler techniques they will, by now, have decided which items to retain, which to modify and which should be discarded. Items which fall into the last category because of the difficulty of finding plausible options but which nevertheless appear to be appropriate for a given objective can sometimes be salvaged for presentation in a true/false format. Gradually files of items of known difficulty can be built which, in the long run, greatly economize on time and effort in the preparation of future tests. Notice, however, a rather stringent limitation in what has been done so far: item difficulties are sample dependent. It is certain that the values will vary from sample to sample. Our item number 32 in this chapter would obtain a proportion of near zero if administered to an average group of seven year olds and near 1.0 if taken by A level students of mathematics (one or two might make careless errors). This, of course, is an extreme example since if items are written to satisfy the criteria of the teaching objective they would not be applicable to the learning by pupils ranging from seven to 18 years of age. Nevertheless, the point still holds with reference to different ability groups within an age band. If the items are for use with a representative 'all-ability group' (as would be the case with the mathematics test taken by all entrants to a comprehensive school or by all on transfer from junior to middle school) and the teacher can be sure he or she is using them on a similar group each year, item difficulty values would be expected to remain relatively stable provided similar teaching programmes have been followed.

CONSTRUCTING THE ESSAY TYPE

This is probably the most extensively used type of item in Britain outside mathematics and the physical sciences. Although it is not much loved by measurement theorists, who have demonstrated its deficiencies over many years, it remains a standard device for the assessment of achievement over a wide range of the curriculum. Many who hold the objective test in the deepest suspicion have continued to set essays, and generations of learners at all levels have been invited to 'write brief notes', 'to explain', 'to discuss', 'to describe', 'to compare and contrast', and so on, on a wide variety of topics.

As a working definition the essay may be thought of as a test item which requires the respondent to compose a response in sentence form, and in which the productions cannot be regarded as correct or incorrect but, rather, vary in a number of respects in quality or merit which experts in the subject can recognize and evaluate.

At a superficial level essay tests are the easiest possible to prepare: it takes only a few minutes to permutate the standard introductory phrases and a variety of topics. Yet this ease is deceptive. Not only is it difficult to decide what essays actually do assess, but, more importantly, it is difficult to know just what inferences about ability can be drawn from them. Allied to this is the subjective nature of essay marking and the frequently low agreement between markers acting independently. All this has been known for decades, so unless the persistence of essays is attributable to the sheer inertia in assessment practice there must be reasons for their longevity.

Amongst the advantages claimed for essay tests is that they uniquely assess the cluster of intellectual components required to marshal facts and present an argument; secondly, they are a versatile means whereby tests may be quickly compiled by most teachers whereas objective tests, by contrast, are popularly thought to demand mastery of a skilled technology; thirdly, the almost unquestioned assumption that the production of language and the verbalization of thought is the most scholarly of all activities, lends support to their continued use; and finally, unlike objective tests which have an undesirable effect on teaching and learning, essays are thought to encourage learners to develop study habits which will stand them in good stead in higher education.

Types B1 and B2

Very many types of essay items come under our working definition but an arbitrary classification as *restricted* (B1) or *extended* (B2) type will be sufficient for classroom purposes. In the *extended* type no limits are placed upon the respondent in regard to the type of organization to be adopted, the material adjudged to be relevant or the points to be discussed; a maximum length can, however, be specified. Typical examples might be:

(1) Compare and contrast objective with essay type tests.
(2) Describe the factors responsible for the distribution of population in India.
(3) Which inventions of the twentieth century do you consider have been most important in the well-being of people in Britain?

In each of these, children have to decide which aspects of their knowledge are relevant to the answer and which are most important; to retrieve this knowledge, organize it and present an argument or opinions in a logical manner as well as using syntax and spelling of a sufficiently high standard not to put the marker off! Many intellectual skills are involved: understanding, recall, application, synthesis, judgement, writing skills and so on, and no two productions will embody these in similar proportions.

In the restricted type, a deliberate constraint is imposed on the answer required. Example (1) in the extended version could be rewritten thus:

(4) Discuss the advantages and disadvantages of objective and essay type tests with respect to: (a) reliability; (b) validity; and (c) usefulness in evaluating teaching objectives.

In its restricted form, the specific areas of the required answer are indicated by the use of organizational headings, whilst sufficient scope for respondents to organize and express their ideas within them is retained. One advantage of the restricted form is that it increases reliability in marking and helps the less able learner: one major disadvantage is that it reduces the opportunity to assess the ability of the respondent to recall and synthesize and to impose an overall organization which is logical and progressive.

Careful construction of essay tests enables the teacher to retain some of their advantages but at the same time to elicit certain comparatively clearly defined mental processes. As examples (in no particular order and with no particular age range in mind):

(a)   Understanding cause and effect

Give three reasons why more cars are sold in Britain than in Iceland.

(b)   Summarizing

Summarize in 100 words or less the story of Beowulf.

(c)   Decision for or against

Should the death penalty be restored for terrorist murders? Defend your answer.

(d)   Application of rules or principles

Where would you weigh more, on the moon or on Mars? Explain your answer.

(e)   Analysis

Why is there so much violence on football terraces?

(f)   Formulating questions

Two children stole a packet of biscuits from a supermarket. What questions should the teacher ask before deciding whether to punish them?

(g)   Criticism of the adequacy or relevance of a statement

Criticize or defend the statement: 'The central conflict in *Far from the Madding Crowd* is between Boldwood and Troy'.

(h)   Giving examples or illustrating principles

Name three examples of the use of the lever in your home.

(i)   Making comparisons

Compare trawling and drifting as methods of catching fish.

(j)   Explanation

Macbeth says 'Life's but a walking shadow, a poor player,
That struts and frets his hour upon the stage'.
Explain the meaning of this statement.

Items of this kind can provide quite a stringent test of a variety
of teaching objectives. Care needs to be given to the key words
which indicate specifically the process required. There are, however, many pitfalls in setting and marking essay type tests. Before
looking at these the claims and counter-claims for their usefulness
are summarized in table 4.5.

Some General Considerations in Presenting Essay Test Items

(1)   Be fair to your pupils. Children cannot write many essays in
a fixed period of time. Whereas one or two badly constructed
objective test items may not have very serious consequences,
a badly thought-out essay title can be damaging.
(2)   Write the question in such a way that it indicates the level of
response you are looking for. Titles that are wide open are
inappropriate especially for children in primary and middle
schools. Try to ensure that the title makes clear what you are
looking for in the answer, or provide a structure (headings)
to aid organization.
(3)   With children in primary and middle schools it is preferable
to use a number of questions which require short answers
rather than a few which involve long answers.
(4)   Avoid questions of the 'who' or 'what' variety: these can
usually be dealt with more effectively by the objective item.
(5)   Remember that some of the advantages claimed for the essay
test are less applicable for the level of maturity expected in
children of primary and middle school age ranges than for
older pupils. Adapt the length of the response to what may
reasonably be expected of pupils of the age range being
assessed. There are considerable limitations in the younger

Table 4.5 – Arguments for and against the use of essay tests

Pro-essay	Anti-essay
(1) Ease of construction. Item for item, it takes much less time to prepare an extended or restricted response test than a corresponding objective test	(1) In the time available for testing, only a small part of the content of a course can be assessed by essays
(2) It has a great potential for assessing the writer's ability to organize, integrate and synthesize his/her knowledge	(2) It has very low reliability (i.e. agreement amongst markers). The mark given depends too much on who reads it
(3) It encourages a range of approaches to learning, in particular 'good study habits'	(3) It presents the respondent with ambiguous options on how to respond. It involves the child in guessing what the teacher is 'looking for'
(4) It fosters the development of substantive (i.e. 'in own words') rather than rote learning	(4) An inordinate amount of time is needed to read and mark essays. The task cannot be made automatic and requires the availability of another expert if the degree of agreement is to be measured
(5) It provides great scope for exercise of the candidate's creativity	(5) Marking is too contaminated by extraneous features of a child's response: handwriting, spelling, etc.
	(6) Except in short and restricted form, the essay is not a suitable item for younger children still mastering the mechanics of writing a connected piece of prose

child's ability to conceptualize and organize information in free response and whilst children learn to write by writing, do not expect too much.

(6) If the essay item is being used in norm-referenced testing do not provide optional questions. No comparisons of achievement are possible if children in a class tackle heterogeneous items of differing levels of difficulty.

(7) Do allow time for pupils to write their answers. There is little justification for measuring handwriting speed under the guise of an essay test.

Marking Essay Tests

Generally speaking, teachers in primary and in the first years of middle schools are likely to use essay tests in assessment which are of the restricted, short answer (up to 100 words) type. Only in secondary schools will long answers be expected and even here (except in the 'essay question' in English language) examinations such as the new GCSE seem likely to require them comparatively infrequently. For these reasons we shall concentrate on marking the short answer type but the principles are capable of extension to longer answers of the extended variety.

We shall assume that the questions set match the teaching objectives and are prepared with the preceding points in mind. Given that all reasonable care has been taken in these important aspects two approaches to marking may be considered: these are the analytical and impressionistic (sometimes called 'global') methods.

The analytical method

This consists of the production of a check list of points considered essential to a good answer to the question. Deciding in advance which points to look for and the number of marks to be allocated to each point permits easier and fairer comparability between papers, helps consistency between markers and provides a ready-made set of points by which to help the child understand the reason for the mark given (and how he or she could have improved the answer). This last point is particularly important where the assessment is seen as part of a continuing process of formative or criterion-referenced assessment. No guidelines can be given as to an appropriate differential marking scheme since the importance

Table 4.6 – An example of a scoring key based on Diederich's scale for grading English composition in Jewett and Bish (1965).

1 = inferior; 2 = below average; 3 = average; 4 = above average; 5 = superior

(a) Quality and development of ideas	1 2 3 4 5		
Organization and relevance	1 2 3 4 5	_____ subtotal	× 5
(b) Style, individuality	1 2 3 4 5		
Wording and phrasing	1 2 3 4 5	_____ subtotal	× 3
(c) Grammar, sentence construction	1 2 3 4 5		
Punctuation	1 2 3 4 5		
Spelling	1 2 3 4 5		
Legibility	1 2 3 4 5	_____ subtotal	× 1 Total (%) =

of the points will depend upon the objective of the teaching. Although teachers may object that preparation of a scoring key takes more time than they can afford, it is often a way of coming to recognize the difficulties faced by pupils in answering the questions and, if the testing is competitive, it provides a basis for a demonstration that fair comparisons have been made. It should not be too onerous for use with the short answer restricted type, however. Teachers can in fact adopt a sort of 'halfway house' between analytical and impressionistic marking. The scoring key need not refer to actual points of content (as would be the case in fully analytical assessment) but to certain headings, rather than making an overall global judgement as in impressionistic marking. One such example is given in table 4.6.

The impressionistic method

This applies where teachers wish, for whatever reason, to award a grade or mark for the essay as a whole. This method is usually defended on the grounds that teachers' reading time is limited and that the purpose of the assessment is not norm-referenced. The number of points on the scale is often quite arbitrary: some may have only two points, the five-point scale is very common and, where marks are given, a maximum of ten is frequently adopted.

Many teachers will claim that a grading is of no interest to them or to their children. But, even here, verbal comments of a summary kind are often given – or even just a tick! (We are not defending these practices: one teacher said 'at least a tick shows the child you've looked at it'.) Where the marking or acknowledgement of the essay is only of this kind, the purpose in setting the essay is presumably to provide a stimulus for the child to write something. It may be that the teacher employs an implicitly analytical scheme by which to identify the strengths and weaknesses of a pupil's answer but that its purpose is purely diagnostic or to inform the direction and content of future teaching and learning activities.

If impressionistic marking is to be used in norm-referenced assessment a minimal requirement is to establish some sort of standard of comparison. Let us suppose that the marking is to a five-point scale of quality, such as

    5 = superior
    4 = above average
    3 = average
    2 = below average
    1 = inferior

(the actual choice of label is unimportant for our purposes). A rather tedious method of standard setting is to prepare model answers to represent each grade. (It is not a bad thing to make teachers answer their own questions!) A less onerous method is to select from the actual answers papers to represent each grade. In public examinations experienced markers are asked independently to select answers which exemplify the grade and other examiners meet to be trained in application of the system. Rapid reading is then undertaken to place each paper in the relevant pile. In order to determine a measure of inter-judge consistency or concordance (see chapter 7 on essay reliability) a second reading should be undertaken by a further independent reader. Any discrepancy of more than one point is then resolved in consultation with a senior examiner. Admittedly little of this is likely to take place in schools, but a teacher with, say 30 answers could assign papers to piles on first reading and then carry out a self-imposed check to determine the level of 'self-consistency' (chapter 7). It is fairer to children to provide them with the average grades given more than one marker (or of the teacher's two grades if they differ) and for teachers to grade only one question at a time for all papers (i.e. read all answers to question one first, then two, and so on) otherwise you switch from standard to standard and cannot hold them properly in mind).

Type B3: The Oral Test

Oral examinations are seldom held but informal assessment of oral output is one of the major sources of teachers' inferences about children. As has been argued in chapter 3 assessment of one person by another is an inevitable part of social processes, and teachers receive numerous and accumulating impressions of children from their informal observations of children's oral production. Formal use of oral tests is found most frequently in universities, in secondary school examinations of a foreign language, in assessments by educational psychologists and, of course, in oral reading tests in primary schools. This last named is excluded from this discussion because whilst other varieties of the oral test are a kind of 'unwritten essay', reading from print cannot be thus regarded. Yet, potentially, the oral is of great use with children who for various reasons are unable to take written tests; if conducted with skill it can reassure the anxious child and can exhibit a flexibility for eliciting a variety of responses in interaction with pupils which are not permitted by static written tests.

In this section the concern is simply to draw the attention of teachers to the advantages and limitations in the use of oral information. Probably the chief limitations are: it is time-consuming, transient (unless recorded), limited in its sampling width, especially vulnerable to halo effect (chapter 3) and low in reliability. Chief amongst it advantages are its flexibility in enabling the teacher to assess a level of knowledge and understanding especially where the pupil has writing difficulties, the way it permits a free response by pupils, and how it can institute a very stringent test of a child's ability to reason in a specified context (most of Piaget's information on children's thinking came from the use of oral tests).

To some extent study of the presentation of oral tests is the study of the art of questioning. Very often the child gives an incorrect response not from lack of knowledge but because wording is not clear or because of misinterpretation of what was asked for, or what was only partially heard. To spell out the implications of these difficulties for the assessment of a child's oral response to questions would require a book in itself. All teachers will have been aware of the dangers in the impulsive assessment of a child's oral work, although use of questioning over a period of time will inevitably lead to their developing generalized assessments of this ('takes little or no part in oral work'; 'quick and eager to answer'; 'always ready with an intelligent answer' are typical of the type of description made). If teachers wish to incorporate an assessment of oral work, it is advisable that this be done systematically if any comparisons are to be made between children. *Ad hoc* assessment is far too easily influenced by halo effect resulting from speech style, dialect or accent to form the basis of the study of children's capabilities. Whilst it is always dangerous to infer lack of knowledge from the absence of response to a question in whatever medium it has been posed, different factors inhibit the exploration of a child's knowledge through oral questioning (especially in the presence of other children) from those involved in testing in the written medium.

Some of the principles of good oral assessment are similar to those proposed for the setting of objective items. High on the list is the need to set questions which are neither too long nor involve subordinate clauses, especially with younger children whose span of apprehension and attention is limited. Similarly, teachers should make clear that a question is to be posed, either by an introductory phrase (such as 'I'm going to ask you some questions; listen carefully') or by the use of familiar interrogatives. It is also advisable to state the terms in which the answer is required ('Where is Paris?' is much less satisfactory than 'In what country is Paris situated?') and the context which makes the question meaningful if this is not obvious from the question itself.

Inevitably, slipshod questioning will occur. The important point is that it should not be allowed to occur if the teacher wishes to draw inferences about ability from the answers received. Quite recently the writer observed a lesson in a school in the centre of a large industrial city where all the children were second-generation immigrants. A discussion on safety in the home was taking place with infant pupils aged five to six years. By and large, the children were inattentive when suddenly the question: 'What must we remember to take out at night, Mohammed?' was posed. Mohammed was not the only participant to find the point of the teacher's question somewhat elusive!

Item Analysis of Essay Tests

Most of the methods of item analysis described in earlier sections of this chapter are inappropriate for essay type tests. The essay 'item', by its nature, assesses a very large number of intellectual skills. It is obviously possible, if analytical marking is adopted, to break down the knowledge components and theoretically possible to evaluate the extent to which alternative organizational headings elicit or fail to elicit the required factual knowledge. Where a correct answer is supplied as one of four or five options as in an objective test and the item is refined as a result of item analysis, failure to respond correctly can be attributed with a high degree of confidence to a property of the respondent. But failure to supply the information required by the marking scheme used in analytical assessment of an essay can never be thus attributed: it is always possible that it is the item which is at fault. The fact that one cannot determine in advance the responses to essay items is one of their most attractive features: interesting answers are often produced to items which are not worthy of them!

Unfortunately, even in higher education, students respond to essay titles by writing all they can think of about the key concepts *in* the question but at the same time overlooking – possibly deliberately – the relational terms or key verbs in the title which specify the demands made upon them by the teacher who set the question. (One would not normally expect qualitatively different responses from a group of teachers in training to essays which begin 'discuss', 'evaluate', 'examine', despite the clear differences in meaning between these three terms, for example.)

The analysis of essay items, therefore, is best undertaken as follows:

(1) Record your impressions of the answers to given essay questions, in particular the features of the responses which match the demands of the analytical marking scheme (these will be 'good' items) and where the responses 'do not answer the

question' or omit the fundamental components of a model answer (these might well be 'poor' items).

(2) Note the frequency with which different items/titles are chosen if optional. Where items are consistently ignored, try to determine whether this is because they do not match the course content or whether they contain features which are perceived by the respondents as conferring particular complexity. This will be done in consultation with the students themselves.

(3) Try out substantially the same item but with alternative organizational headings. See which is associated with the most satisfactory answers. Compare responses to an item when presented in its extended form with those to its restricted form. (The restricted form of items, is, however, almost always to be recommended for use with children up to, say, fifth form level, except, of course, in English language.)

(4) Examine your own literary style to eliminate ambiguities and excess verbiage from titles. This, of course, is mainly an aspect of preparation, but study of the responses to items often indicates the presence of ambiguities unidentified at the preparation stage.

The chapter up to this point has been concerned with the following aspects of teacher-made test construction and use:

(1) Identifying the potential strengths of teacher-made tests.
(2) Matching items to the objectives of teaching.
(3) Preparing the specification table, or test blueprint.
(4) Deciding upon the type of test item.
(5) The preparation of various types of objective test item: a comparison of their advantages and disadvantages, with examples.
(6) Methods of item analysis and improvement.
(7) Preparing and marking essay type tests. Advantages and disadvantages of essay tests.
(8) Analysing the results of essay type tests.

ASSEMBLING THE TEST

During the course of this discussion we have seen that different
types of item tend to be suited to the assessment of different types
of intellectual objective. There is no one-to-one correspondence
here: the multiple choice test is potentially versatile and can be
used to assess objectives at all levels of Bloom's taxonomy, for
example. But the essay type of test does call for the integration of
a number of intellectual skills in a way that no other type of item
can. We have seen, however, that this advantage can be achieved
only at the expense of lowered objectivity and reliability. One
question that arises, therefore, is how does one assemble an
instrument for the assessment of a fairly lengthy course of study
which has sought to enable learners to acquire a variety of knowledge, skills and concepts across a relatively large content area? We
have seen how a specification table aids the construction of a test
to assess comparatively 'compact' sets of teaching objectives but,
as such, it leaves open the question of the type of item best suited
to the assessment of each objective. There will, of course, be many
constraints on the final form of a test and it is all too easy to throw
together a variety of items which, though good in themselves, do
not constitute an appropriate mixture overall by which to assess
children's abilities in subject areas.

To specify what the overall test instrument *should* look like
would be to run the risk of violating one of the cardinal principles
of assessment: teacher control of the objectives, emphasis and
evaluation of the teaching. A few writers have, however, tried to
set up guidelines to help the assembly and arrangement of tests.
Gronlund (1971) has suggested that the test will be arranged in
such a way that items progress from lower level intellectual abilities (recall of knowledge) to the most complex that can reasonably
be expected from knowledge of the teaching that has taken place
and level of ability of the group for which the test is intended. Thus
tests might begin with simple recall as measured by the completion
or true/false type of item, progress through short answer or multiple choice items to the essay type of item. Keeping items of
similar type together will make it easier for the examinee to
understand and comply with the instructions without switching
from one type to another and, of course, make the test easier to
mark. It also helps if the actual items within types are as homo-

geneous as possible in respect of the teaching objectives. (In multiple choice items those that deal with, say, knowledge of terminology should be kept together and those that deal with knowledge of principles should be separated from those which deal with comprehension, and so on.) This will aid the teacher considerably in his or her analysis of results and in the identification of those objectives which have been most successfully mastered, least successfully, and so on. If items have been the subject of a try-out and difficulty values are known it seems desirable for them to be arranged in order of difficulty.

Many other technical recommendations on the layout of tests could, of course, be made. Thorndike (1971) provides a useful, comprehensive and comparatively brief source of information of value to teachers in these aspects. The chapter will conclude, however, with brief reference to the psychological rather than the technical aspects of test taking and administration.

PSYCHOLOGICAL ASPECTS OF 'BEING ASSESSED'

All test results are contaminated by factors other than those ostensibly assessed. Modern assessment methods try to increase motivation by the use of interesting tasks and decrease anxiety by relaxed conditions for assessment, by negotiating results with pupils where suitable and encouraging self assessment where possible. One assumption which is commonly made is that the child being tested is doing the best he or she can do at that time. The importance of motivation to a child's test score has been repeatedly demonstrated by controlled studies (for example, by Flanagan, 1955, and McClelland, 1966) and by common sense. It is true that children differ in the extent to which they 'lay blame' on external or internal factors for their own performances. Children who attribute their successes and failures to the amount of their effort are sometimes described as 'internals'; children who see success because the task is 'easy' and failure when it is 'difficult' are correspondingly described as 'externals' (Bar-Tal, 1978). But all learners are aware that sometimes they 'try hard', at other times they do not. Lack of effort in test taking has various origins: in some cases it may reflect lack of interest in the test because it is not expected that the results can be put to positive advantage.

Equally, lack of effort may be a consequence of a defensive attitude on the part of the child in the face of anticipated failure (Goldman, 1971). No matter how able, a child who has no motivation to perform is not going to obtain a high score on the test. Thus we distinguish the motivation to acquire the knowledge and skills which are being assessed by the test from the motivation to exhibit that knowledge in the test itself.

We have already implied that motivation to take the test is greater where the child sees the pay-off in taking it (the pay-off can take many forms, of course). But motivation is also more likely where the child sees the point of what he or she is being asked to do. Donaldson (1978) has quite convincingly demonstrated that very young children can think about problems which make sense to them but are defeated by problems involving similar logic where the task presented is arbitrary or is set in an abstract context. The implications for pupils who are 'culturally disadvantaged' or who are naive in test-taking skills are clear. We take it for granted that children will understand the point of the 'testing game' we are asking them to play but it seems very unlikely that young children especially will understand the unspoken customs (particularly where the tester is an outsider chiefly interested in obtaining data for his research project!).

To sum up, we can go some way towards minimizing the error due to motivational differences amongst pupils if we ensure that they understand the point of assessment and the benefits which may result from accurate assessment. Secondly we can see to it that children who are not 'testwise' are instructed in the principles and procedures of test taking. This is particularly important in norm-referenced assessment: in criterion-referenced assessment the test is continuous with the learning. Thirdly, testing may be more acceptable, particularly to older learners, where their part in helping them to learn is explained and where the entire procedure and content of the tests is fair. In carrying out standardized testing it is important to adhere to the manual's instructions, but the motivational levels of pupils in normal classroom testing are influenced to a far greater extent by a classroom climate and teacher–pupil relationships which are psychologically supportive of the individual.

Closely allied to the motivational aspects of testing is the topic of anxiety. There are two chief views of this ubiquitous phenomenon. Some psychologists believe that anxiety is a pre-disposition or state of the individual looking, as it were, for an object or outcome to which to attach itself. Others have seen anxiety as a learned response to a threatening stimulus. The actual role of anxiety in human performance seems to vary with the individual and with the degree of complexity of the task he or she is asked to attempt (Gaudry and Spielberger, 1974) but the experience of anxiety in taking a test or when the pupil knows an assessment is taking place is probably universal. Psychologists have concluded that whilst a certain amount of anxiety enhances the general alertness of many pupils, test anxiety tends to depress test performance. Others, of course, are 'intellectually frozen' by it! (Karmel and Karmel, 1978). Some writers have claimed social class differences in the extent and productive use of anxiety, however, but there is no universally effective practice of ensuring optimal anxiety in test taking. It would be futile to try to remove it altogether. Everyone experiences anxiety in taking tests especially if the results are to have long-term implications for the type of secondary school to be attended, if vocational opportunity is at stake or where the label 'fail' is to be applied. Regular formative classroom assessment of learning is generally free from the worst excesses of those practices and teachers will normally seek to inform pupils of the purposes of testing and the uses to be made of the results in as relaxed a manner as possible. The teacher who is aware of the limitations of the inferences which can be drawn from any assessment will probably emphasize its formative aspects and reduce to a minimum the occasions on which judgements which appear to be final are made.

It is not unknown for teachers themselves to feel threatened by tests and this anxiety can easily be communicated to the pupils. This is likely to be more prevalent in external assessment or in programmes which attempt to evaluate teacher effectiveness. Knowledge of the effects of anxiety on individual pupils is just one of the factors to be taken into account in trying to reach a just appraisal of a child's work.

5

Criterion-referenced Assessment

Criterion-referenced assessment (CR) is often exonerated from many of the criticisms of testing outlined in chapter 2. Several writers have suggested that its increasing use in education will provide for clearer 'targets' for learning than traditional norm-referenced tests (NR), enhance the motivation of pupils to achieve, and play a major part in the raising of educational standards. If this optimism is borne out in practice chapters like chapter 4 will no longer be read and techniques like those in chapter 5 will, like the State, wither away (writer's irony!).

The Education Reform Act (1988) intends that the performance of pupils, schools, groups of schools and the entire national system be regularly monitored for their attainments. One group set up to examine ways of realizing these intentions (the Task Group on Assessment and Testing, TGAT) has devised a scheme of assessment which looks likely to place great stress on, amongst other things, the formative use of CR assessment and the use of well-defined 'attainment targets' across the primary and secondary range. The underlying assumption is that levels of achievement are too low and that new examinations and schemes of assessment have an important part to play in encouraging more effective methods of teaching and learning. A major requirement for new assessment techniques is that they emphasize objectives and acknowledge 'positive achievement': through their capacity to enhance motivation and encourage participation, no pupils need be condemned to 'fail'.

Recent years have seen three major trends in the development of assessment techniques in Britain. These have been identified by Weston and Evans as follows: 'widening the scope (of what is assessed), making learning targets explicit and trying to involve pupils in the assessment process' (1988, 28). The first of these refers to attempts to assess a far greater variety of pupils' competences than can possibly be assessed by written and formal examinations, which will demand the use of modes of assessment developed for the purpose. The second, that new assessment methods (including those emerging in the new GCSE) indicate as precisely as possible what pupils are expected to learn and explicit criteria by which different grades of achievement are to be awarded. The final trend can be observed in, for example, moves towards self assessment and negotiated statements of achievement as part of profiles and records of achievement (see chapter 10) which require more participation by pupils than do traditional tests and examinations. Criterion-referencing is at the heart of all these changes.

It is not our concern to examine the political and practical problems in the implementation of such profound changes, nor to speculate on the likelihood with which high hopes for raised standards through assessment innovations will be realized. Instead, it is to provide guidelines for the construction, use and interpretation of the kinds of CR assessment which are within the capabilities of teachers to devise. Although there are differences between writers in the exact role for CR tests, most conceive of their integration into planned sequences of learning and teaching as being something similar to the diagram shown in figure 5.1. Read horizontally it indicates the sequence for learners, vertically the processes of planning and using the test or assessment instrument. In this model – applicable for systematic learning of the 'targets' or objectives – test construction is seen as integral to the process of learning. Pupils and teachers have explicit targets in view and are assumed to be motivated towards their attainment. It is planned, systematic and, to some, far too mechanical and time-consuming. Whilst teaching along these lines looks likely to increase in pursuit of the targets within the national curriculum it is important to realize that valuable educational aims of an expressive or creative kind cannot be attained in this way.

Changes in methods of assessment are said by some to be 'driving the curriculum' (GCSE, for example, is forcing changes, yet to be evaluated, in the methods of learning and teaching, and in the kinds of thinking pupils are encouraged to adopt). Thus criteria not only provide a focus for the teaching and learning but also permit diagnosis of learner-difficulty and, as important, more detailed description of a learner's achievements. The entire approach has sometimes been called the 'intended outcomes' model of learning and assessment.

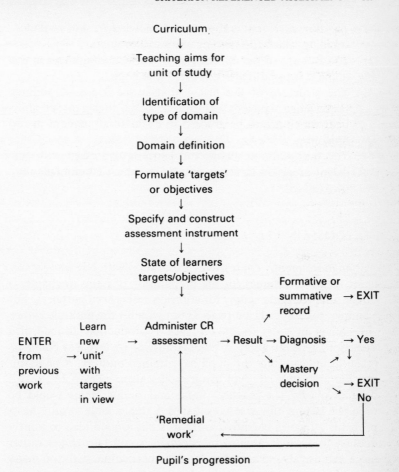

Figure 5.1   Planning and using the CR test.

Fortunately, very many of the interactions within classrooms yield educationally worthwhile outcomes which are unforeseen by pre-specified learning criteria. We are not arguing that only learning and assessment which is criterion-referenced is worthwhile, for in areas of the curriculum which encourage inventiveness, discovery and expression they are impossible to specify in advance of the activity. Learning towards criterion-referenced assessment then, need not 'close down' other valuable kinds of curriculum experience as some opponents have feared.

Constructing criterion-referenced tests requires careful attention to a number of aspects to be dealt with in more detail below:

(1)   The domain – that is the area of knowledge, skill or under-
       standing which the teacher wishes to evaluate.
(2)   The content of the unit of study by which attainment in the
       domain is to be realized – or so it is hoped.
(3)   The structure of the test – that is the kinds of abilities
       (knowledge, concept acquisition, skills, higher order abili-
       ties) which are to be studied to evaluate attainment in the
       domain.
(4)   The targets for teaching and learning expressed with suf-
       ficient precision to act as criteria by which attainments may
       be assessed.

THE DOMAIN

Although frequently contrasted (favourably) with NR assessment,
many of the techniques for the preparation of items in chapter 3
can be adapted quite simply for criterion-referenced purposes. For
example, take item 11 on page 83 but without the multiple choice
alternatives in order to make it into a 'production' instead of a
'selection' type of item. A correct answer to this test could be
taken to indicate that the pupil has attained mastery. 'Can calculate the area of a circle of given radius, using pi = 3.14, to two
decimal places'. In practice, more and similar items would be
required before this was considered a dependable result. Most
probably (since in cognitive areas it is not a good idea to limit a
domain to a single ability) the domain would be defined rather
more extensively, so as not to load the curriculum with too many
objectives to be manageable. In this case the domain would
probably be thought of as 'Ability to calculate the area of the
following common plane figures' – a more inclusive domain. Some
authorities would recommend that the conditions under which
attainment in this domain would be assessed should be stated more
precisely (with or without calculators; with or without the formulae being made available, for example).

   One can, of course, think of domains in quite large chunks if it
helps learning and assessment to do so since many domains are
organized hierarchically with others. One of the working parties of
the Secondary Examinations Council (Geography) recommended
that GCSE examinations sample five global domains: specific

geographical knowledge; geographical understanding; map and graphic skills; applications of geography to economic, environmental, political and social issues; geographical enquiry. A similar differentiation of domains may be helpful in domain specification within units of study as well as at national examining level (see the later discussion on test specification).

Our discussion has introduced the idea of thinking of the outcomes of teaching and learning to be assessed (in so far as they consist of the acquisition of knowledge, skill and understanding) as organized into 'domains'. Indeed, Black and Dockrell have gone so far as to say that 'criterion referenced tests without domain definitions are difficult to construct' (1984, 50). Whereas in NR assessment the instruments are designed to sample a range of achievements and to differentiate among pupils, CR tests attempt to assess the learner's mastery of relatively discrete areas of competence and performance – the 'domains' – but without being able (except in exceptional cases) to sample all the items which make up that domain.

Types of Domain

Black and Dockrell (1984) whose study is an excellent account of the vicissitudes of CR test construction have found that teachers encounter considerable difficulty when attempting to define the domain in which mastery is to be assessed. To help in this task they suggested that domains could be defined *explicitly* (before the construction of the test) or *implicitly* (through the items which make up the test). Before showing how this can be done, we must identify a simple classification of domains since it is of great importance that teachers have as clear an idea as possible what it is they are trying to assess – the more so if diagnostic information is required. Recall that it would be futile to suggest that all school subjects or topics within subjects lend themselves to domain specification or can become the subject of CR testing. We would recommend that the 'core' objectives for teaching be the focus for CR testing. Indeed, the 'attainment targets' which may form the bases of the national curriculum constitute such a list, at least for many teachers since pressure to teach them is bound to be strong if not irresistible.

Black and Dockrell (1984) have identified three types of domain: 'single act', 'closed' and 'open'. Some of the intended outcomes for learning constitute single act domains where the description of the domain is very similar to the target objective. When learning to drive a car, for example, several discrete acts must be coordinated so it is doubtful if it is a true example of a single act domain. However, 'the ability to run 100 metres in 12.0 seconds', 'to cut lengths of ½ inch dowel into lengths of up to one metre to within a tolerance of plus or minus one millimetre' and 'to type 80 words per minute' are examples. It is true that reference to conditions under which these performances are to be observed would be needed for a complete specification of the objective but, in practice, some degree of vagueness will be tolerated since overspecification yields far too many objectives to be of much use to teachers. The usefulness of single act domain definitions in assessment lies in the fact that the performance target *is* the criterion, it does not stand as an index of any hidden or inferred characteristic of the pupil, unlike those affective domains where any number of observations may be taken to indicate that a criterion has been demonstrated ('showing interest' or 'demonstrating understanding', for example).

Where the area of knowledge to be assessed consists of a specifiable number of related items or elements we have an example of a closed domain. Consider the following: Roman numerals in use today; symbols for the 105 chemical elements; conventional signs and symbols as used on the 1:50,000 Ordnance Survey map; international road signs; basic safety rules in the school laboratory; the binomial expansion applied to the tossing of up to and including five coins; methods of borrowing money from a bank or building society. All these are closed domains. Defining the domain, then, amounts to a statement of those outcomes which are to be assessed. In closed domains the tests only sample from the potential outcomes; for example a test might assess only knowledge of the 50 most commonly encountered chemical symbols.

Most objectives for learning relate to much larger domains than these. Suppose the teacher adopts the target proposed by the Kingman Committee (1988) for 11 and 14 year old pupils: 'the ability to spell correctly'. The domain to which this target refers is as large as the number of words in the English language! Even Kingman's suggested target for seven year olds: 'the ability to spell *common* words correctly', is undefined. To be assessable, such targets – if they are to serve as criteria – must be re-phrased in terms of those words which are going to be considered as 'common'. Such domains are termed 'open' since in this particular case there is virtually no limit to the ways in which 'correct spelling' can be demonstrated. If the domain is to be tested then it must be defined.

The book by Black and Dockrell (1984) constitutes a more detailed guide to CR test construction for diagnostic purposes than is possible within the confines of a single chapter. It does not seek to disguise the difficulties that can occur. They suggest, correctly, that the majority of educational targets refer to open domains. Any target of the form: 'The pupil will demonstrate understanding of X' will inevitably belong to an open domain since a very large number of instances of the relevant understanding or ways of expressing it could, potentially at least, be tested. Again, defining the domain is stating which representative outcomes will be assessed by the instrument.

DEFINING THE DOMAIN

Some writers have taken a very demanding position on domain definition. Hambleton (1980), for example, has written that there are two requirements for specification: (a) that all the items that *could be* written from the content domain to be tested must be written or known, and (b) that item selection must be by a random process from all the items that make up the domain. We shall see that in open domains the number of items that could be written could be extremely large and teachers would find the task prohibitive.

Recall that one of the purposes of CR assessment is to describe, compare and report performance relative to a criterion which 'belongs to' the domain being tested. Whereas most texts recommend domain definition before the assessment task or instrument its drawn up ('explicit definition'), Black and Dockrell found that it was more straightforward in many instances to define the domain 'through the creation of the instrument itself' (1984, 44). They call this latter method 'implicit definition'.

Explicit definition of single act and closed domains is usually simple because the intended outcomes of the learning resemble the domain very closely indeed. One consequence is that teachers of a given subject are usually able to agree as to what constitutes achievement in that domain. For example, if the (closed) domain is knowledge of the symbols for the chemical elements the performance sampled by a suitable testing instrument would be either recognition or recall of a sample of these elements – probably those which figure most prominently in school chemistry. Similarly, if the (single act) domain is 'running 100 metres in 12.0 seconds' then the sprint has only to be timed to assess the pupils' performance against that criterion. Most skills or algorithms (rules which ensure a 'correct' answer); measuring, weighing and so on; cutting materials to a given size; present few problems for domain definition: all that is required is a precise indication of the conditions under which the performance will be assessed and, if necessary, the margin of error which will be tolerated (in measuring, weighing, cutting) and the criterion of satisfactory achievement or mastery (80% is typically set) in other tasks.

In many instances, where single act and closed domains are being assessed, the performance can be observed and the criterion applied during normal classroom activities. There is a great deal to recommend assessment whilst children are working normally not only because of its immediacy for formative evaluation but also because a child's performance in context is often a much more valid indication of competence than in decontextualized activities artificially set up for test purposes. For these reasons we are likely to see greater use of standard tasks in which pupils can be assessed whilst carrying out worthwhile activities, especially when assessing children in the primary school. We return to this topic later in the chapter.

Problems of definition in open domains can be illustrated by two examples. Concept attainment (some prefer to distinguish 'acquisition' from 'application') is a major intended outcome in all areas of the curriculum. Consequently, objectives of the form 'Pupils will demonstrate that they have acquired the concept X by . . .' are frequently formulated (these are usually followed by a description of the processes by which this demonstration is to be made). Domain definition prior to test construction requires that the meaning of concept acquisition be spelt out in assessment terms (test items) and it is most unlikely that teachers working independently of one another would define the domain the same way.

As a second example – and to show how the problems may be resolved in practice – consider an important intended outcome of modern language teaching: 'The pupil should demonstrate communicative competence.' Recognizing the extremely open nature of this domain teachers decided to limit their first attempts at definition to competence when shopping for basic requirements. Defining the domain tentatively as 'competence to shop effectively', further clarification was sought by a method familiar to all those who have been encouraged to try 'criteria setting'. First, a situation was constructed in which pupils could simulate shopping, with a teacher as shopkeeper. Pupils were then observed (after some preparation) either singly or in pairs performing this task and the observing panel of teachers asked to grade the performances 'using marks out of five'. When this had been done teachers described as fully as possible the features of the behaviour given each of the scores, one to five. A list of statements descriptive of each score was then compiled and discussed in an attempt to identify those features which most clearly and consistently define each point on the scale. What it is to 'shop effectively' emerged as a consequence of the procedure and the criteria for each point on the scale are ready for trial as the first version of the assessment instrument. The instrument has defined the domain ('implicit definition').

Now that the reports of the Assessment of Performance Unit (APU) are widely available teachers can consult these to examine examples of well-constructed CR tests. To give an example, the test of 'structured conversation' (figure 5.2) has been reproduced by permission. It describes the setting, the task of the assessor and the criteria for each score awarded. There is no indication of mastery level.

An alternative method of definition for an open domain consists of asking teachers to *imagine* a level of performance which merits each of the points on a five-point scale. This short-cuts the process but seems to yield more statements that are less directly tied to the observable features than the first and, from the limited experience of the writer, to demand more discussion before agreement is reached. It can also be objected to on the grounds that devising criteria by a comparison of 'best' and 'worst' performances merely reinforces existing thinking about differences between pupils – a norm-referenced concept! However, whilst there may be many different but equally acceptable ways of communicating in shops,

Illustration 4.2 *Structured conversation*

You are on a beach in France with your family. You want to find out from a French girl where you can buy an ice-cream. The assessor will play the part of the French girl. The things you have to say are underlined.

1. <u>Say hello.</u>
2. <u>Ask her if there is a café nearby.</u>

    She says there is, and she is going there too.
3. <u>Ask her where it is.</u>

    She says it's at the end of the beach. You walk along together.
4. <u>Ask her if she speaks English.</u>

    She prefers to speak French.
5. <u>Say you will speak French then.</u>

    She asks if you are on holiday
6. <u>Say yes, for two weeks.</u>
    She asks when you arrived.
7. <u>Say on Monday.</u>

    She asks if you are camping.
8. <u>Say no, you are in a hotel.</u>

    You reach the café.
9. <u>Say you would like an ice-cream.</u>

    The French girl says something to you.
10. <u>Say you don't understand.</u>

    She is asking if you want a vanilla ice-cream.
11. <u>Say you prefer chocolate ice-cream.</u>

    The French girl gives you your ice-cream and your change.
12. <u>Say thank you very much.</u>
    She is going to leave the beach.
13. <u>Say good-bye.</u>

    She asks if you come to the beach every day.
14. <u>Say yes, you are coming tomorrow at 10 o'clock.</u>

Table 4.2   *Scale of performance. Structured conversation*

5	Can convey the message in all cases, using expressions which a native speaker might use in the context.
4	Can convey the message in all or most cases, almost always using appropriate expressions.
3	Can convey the message in at least half the cases, sometimes using appropriate expressions, at other times producing incomplete utterances.

2	Can convey the message in some cases, mostly in incomplete utterances. OR Can convey the message in few cases using appropriate expressions.
1	Can convey the message in a very few cases, and generally in incomplete utterances.
0	Nothing recognisable as relevant to the task set.
–	Not attempted.

Figure 5.2   A well-structured CR test.

Source: Assessment of Performance Unit: *French Foreign Language Performance in Schools, Report on 1985 Survey of French*. London: HMSO. Reproduced with the permission of the Controller of Her Majesty's Stationery Office.

some are clearly more effective and efficient than others and this example seems to be the kind of element where 'evaluative' as distinct from 'purely descriptive' criteria must be applied.

In principle, a group of experts can adopt this kind of procedure to draw up an agreed domain definition for almost any open domain. The example above illustrates a general feature of many of the assessment tasks which have been suggested by TGAT (DES, 1987b): setting up a task and suitable conditions under which a range of desired responses for assessment may be elicited.

We can sum up this section by saying that in *explicit definition* the test instrument is driven by the domain definition, whereas in *implicit definition* the definition is driven by the test instrument. The method of implicit definition can be used to obviate abstract discussion where domains are open or fuzzy (that is, difficult to clarify) or where considerable disagreement exists between teachers working together. However, the importance of domain specification in the construction of CR tests cannot be overstated: only when we know the nature of the domain can we establish the validity of any test or assessment task for testing attainment in that domain.

SPECIFYING THE TEST AND CONSTRUCTING THE INSTRUMENT

Two major stages are involved: specifying the content and structure of the test and realizing the specification in the first version of the instrument.

The existing literature on this topic is extensive (for example, Hambleton, 1980; Berk, 1980; Royd and Haladyna, 1982; Clough et al., 1984; Lloyd-Jones and Bray, 1986) and some of it is very technical. Unfortunately, it cannot all be integrated into a teacher-friendly set of principles generalizable to all tests in all types of domain. The guidelines below are intended to draw attention to basic considerations: they have proved of value in enabling teachers to assess pupil learning of core objectives and units of study. There are of course other ways of going about it and no 'best test' can be said to exist.

Specifying a test or assessment instrument involves the following considerations:

(1)   The structure of the test; that is, the relative balance between various kinds of ability – knowledge of specific facts and propositions, concept acquisition, skills, and higher order abilities (such as understanding, evaluating, synthesizing). A test could be written to measure ability at only one of these levels.

(2)   The content of the test; that is, the details of the stimulus to be presented to the testee (text, map, diagram, picture, numerical data) and of the type of item and responses the children are to make.

In order to summarize, we recommend a standard description of the test:

(a)   The domain name or definition.
(b)   The age group for whom the test is designed and any prerequisites or limitations (only for those whose first language is English, for example).
(c)   The presentation mode – usually whether oral or written.
(d)   The task mode – the content and whether intended for groups or individual testing.

(e) The response mode – usually oral, written and whether selective or productive.
(f) The criterion score or criteria of mastery, if relevant.

In specifying structure, the most important consideration to be borne in mind is whether the test represents the relative emphases on the kinds of ability to be acquired through the unit of study or essential to the target tested (for example, if the learning has emphasized the acquisition of skill with little concentration on knowledge acquisition, is this emphasis reflected in the structure of the test?). Regarding content (especially if the test is to be diagnostic) the stimulus material, type of items and kind of responding should correspond with the intended outcomes of the unit of teaching.

The general question: Is this test testing what I intend to test? helps to keep the question of content validity in mind. Two other kinds of validity are desirable but the extent to which they can be realized without putting the test into practice is debatable. *Discriminant validity* refers to the ability of the items making up the test to discriminate masters of a criterion from non-masters. This is of particular importance when learning is taking place in a sequence where success in one unit is a pre-requisite for proceeding to the next. *Decision validity* is the utility of the test in helping inform the decisions which are to be based on the result. It is specially important in summative evaluation.

Deciding on Content and Structure of the Instrument

We will take single act and closed domains in science by way of examples. Suppose first year secondary pupils study a unit entitled 'Introduction to Science' and one of the objects is that the 'pupil should be able to read the scale of a laboratory thermometer and make appropriate measurements to a tolerance of plus or minus 0.2 degrees Celsius'. Given the close similarity between domain definition and the objective, the assessment task was to provide a context in which the accuracy of measuring temperature could be observed. Following discussion the teacher set up four thermometers as follows:

A   suspended in air using a clamp and stand
B   suspended in a beaker of crushed ice

C   in a vacuum flask containing hot water (top of flask plugged
with cotton wool)
D   in a vacuum flask containing warm water.

(Regular checking was required by teacher just prior to the
individual task.) The task was adjudged to be a simple one and a
criterion of 4/4 was set. Summary specification was:

(a)   Domain definition: ability to read scale of laboratory thermometer
(b)   Age group: 11–12 years, first year science topic
(c)   Presentation mode: oral
(d)   Task mode: 'hands on' (the actual instrument is used)
(e)   Response mode: written or oral
(f)   4/4 correct.

A re-test was held to be desirable (to be taken during normal
lessons) approximately two weeks later. Comparison of scores on
the two tests enabled the dependability of the scores to be studied
using the method of tables 7.4 and 7.5 (see chapter 7). In a class of
28 children taking the tests the coefficient of consistency was
calculated at 0.54, indicating only a moderate agreement between
the two tests of the criterion. It reflected the effect of the practice
gained on the first test and of intervening learning. Inspection of
the scores would provide diagnostic information only in the sense
of enabling errors and those who need more teaching to be
identified. This criterion was regarded as a basic target for first
year science learning, so results were recorded in the summative
statement of first year attainment, dated and initialled by the
teacher. Similar tests were constructed for the measurement of
length; mass, using a top balance; time; and volume of liquids
using a measuring cylinder.
   The first year science teachers also attempted to assess closed
domain attainments. One example was: 'knowledge of common
laboratory hazards'. The relevant target was as follows: The pupil
should be able to recognize 20 common laboratory hazards, for
example:

(1)   Pupil writing near bunsen burner
(2)   Heated test tube pointed toward pupil . . . through to:

(20)   Apparatus too near edge of work bench.

In order to test this, a drawing of a laboratory showing a class at work was prepared within a rectangle measuring 7½ × 6 inches. Hazards were depicted, one to each 1½ square inches. Pupils were given oral instructions to 'use a red felt pen to draw a ring around each of the hazards you can see in the picture'. Scoring was accomplished by placing a transparent grid over each child's picture and the total number correct obtained. Scoring was stringent, 18/20 being the criterion. Summary specification of the test was, therefore:

(a) Knowledge of common laboratory hazards
(b) 11–12 years; first year science pupils
(c) Oral: individual test
(d) Pictorial
(e) Written ('circling')
(f) 18/20 correct

(Notice that the emphasis of the test is on 'knowledge as displayed through recognition'.)

Specifying content and structure of an instrument designed to test attainment in open domains is more controversial and considerable scope exists for creative writers of assessment tasks. As already stated, one GCSE Working Party has recommended that the entire subject area of geography should be thought of as structured into five domains. Such a large domain definition is probably necessary in assessment for external accreditation but teachers are more likely to want their CR assessment and diagnosis to be more finely tuned to units of study which make up the course. It has been found useful, therefore, to assess core objectives or target domains by a standard specification of up to five kinds of ability as appropriate. These are:

(a) Knowledge of specific facts and propositions (using productive or selective or open-ended items)
(b) Acquisition of concepts } the distinction is often clearer
(c) Application of concepts } in theory than in practice
(d) Acquisition and use of skills
(e) Higher order abilities.

It is not easy to recommend how the above should be balanced, only that they should reflect the relative attention paid to each type of ability in the unit of study or the relative importance of the abilities in the study of future units.

ASSESSMENT CRITERIA

Knowledge of Facts and Propositions

So far as assessing knowledge is concerned, items of types A1–A4 described in chapter 4 seem suited. Concept acquisition is more difficult to assess since it can be tested in many ways. Teachers and others are known to disagree on just what it means to say a concept has been 'acquired' and how a child can reasonably be expected to demonstrate that acquisition. From a psychological standpoint, Klausmeier and Ripple (1971) have shown that many types of response could be taken as indicating 'acquisition' and it would be a very lengthy process indeed to prepare a test to 'tap' all of them.

Acquisition and Application of Concepts

We can show two ways in which children's acquisition of concepts can be assessed. The first is similar to that recommended by Black and Dockrell (1984) based on Markle and Tiemann (1973) (see figure 5.3). Essentially it assesses children's ability to distinguish instances from non-instances. Proceed as follows:

(1)   Name the attributes which define the concept (call it X) to be tested.
(2)   Prepare instances of X.
(3)   Prepare non-instances of X.
(4)   Present list of instances and non-instances and ask children to differentiate examples (by 'Yes/No' or 'Probably/Probably not').

Teachers planning to test concept acquisition reached agreement that the defining attributes of the class 'mammals' were 'warm-blooded', 'vertebrate', 'female mammary glands', 'thoracic diaphragm' and 'four-chambered heart'. The unit of study, however, had emphasized only the first three, so these were considered

Animal	Yes	No	Reason for choice
A. This cold-blooded creature lives in the sea; it has a very long tail and lays eggs in gravel. These hatch after about 4 months.	☐	☐	
B. Lives most of its life in trees. When young is suckled by mother till about 9 months of age. Can walk erect.	☐	☐	
C. It lives in and out of water and lays its eggs under leaves. It is cold-blooded and hibernates in winter.	☐	☐	
D. Lives on land and is a source of food for humans. Mothers deliver up to two young four months after fertilization. These rival one another for her milk.	☐	☐	
E. Lives in water. Warm-blooded and swims quickly because of a powerful tail. Only one young which is suckled by its mother for up to 6 months.	☐	☐	

Figure 5.3 A short test of concept acquisition.

sufficient to define the class among the relevant age group. Knowledge as to *which* animals are mammals can be tested by recall or recognition types of item (A1 to A4). Acquisition of the concept 'mammal' was tested by providing a short description of five animals lettered A to E. For each description the child was asked to decide whether or not it was a mammal (Yes/No) and to supply his or her reason for that decision.

The test shown in figure 5.3 can be criticized on a number of grounds: too few items to permit a reliable 'mastery' decision, an unequal number of positive and negative instances and vagueness in the descriptions are three of the more obvious weaknesses. Generally speaking we may expect the reliability of a test to increase with its length and this principle gains in importance with the target being assessed. Limitations on testing time have to be taken into account but experience suggests that a test of 10 items (permitting equal numbers of positive and negative instances) is needed for acceptable reliability. Study of the reasons given for the decision provides diagnostic information on the extent to which children have 'understood' the essential features of the concept 'mammal'. For example, that blood temperature, backbone (inferred from presence of a tail), suckling (which entails mammary glands) are relevant attributes but habitat, incubation period, number of young, hibernation are irrelevant in defining the concept.

Many concepts can be assessed in this sort of way but it is not clear whether preformance on the test is correctly described as 'concept acquisition' or 'concept application'. It is difficult to see how a concept can be 'applied' before it has been 'acquired' but the reverse seems conceivable especially if the concept has been stored by rote memorization. Some theorists have dealt with this difficulty by thinking of rotely learned material as 'merely verbal learning' by contrast with meaningful learning: thus they deny that a concept has in any significant way been attained until the child can use it: verbal recitation is not sufficient. Test constructors can sidestep this problem, however, by stating (in the form of an objective in the test specification) several ways in which concept attainment is to be demonstrated whilst recognizing that many other ways could be derived. That is to say, the pupil will demonstrate that he/she has attained the concept of mammal by:

(a)   Stating the attributes (orally or in writing) which define the concept 'mammal' (a *product* or *supply* item).
(b)   Distinguishing instances from non-instances of the concept by classifying correctly five animal descriptions (a *selection* item).

The criterion for (a) would be the inclusion of 'female mammary glands', 'vertebrate' and 'warm-blooded' or acceptable synonyms as descriptive of animals. Thus the criterion would be 4/4 for content, ignoring stylistic, grammatical or syntactic features.

The criterion for the second test would be 5/5 correctly classified.

The approach, admittedly, presents a rather limited view of what constitutes observable evidence of concept acquisition. A far more detailed analysis is recommended by Klausmeier and Ripple (1971). They distinguish objectives which require pupils to *select* or *identify* responses from those in which they have to *produce* or *supply* responses. Their scheme identifies ten types of objective for initial concept learning and three for the application of concepts to other concepts, principles and problem solving (Gagné, 1970).

In the example given in figure 5.4 the target concept is 'quadrilateral' but it can be taken as an exemplar of most class concepts (that is those defined by combinations of attributes).

Once teachers have got the 'hang' of thinking of responses as 'selecting' and 'producing', objectives for concept learning can easily be written following this scheme, 'mammal' lends itself to this kind of definition. If the teacher wishes to test only initial concept acquisition, item 10 to 13 would be irrelevant. Some kinds of concept would not require all items. The concept of 'justice', for example, would not need items of type 1, 2, 6 and 7. Alternatively, teachers could abbreviate the tests by producing two parallel versions, one which involves only 'selection' items, the other 'production' items. Few, if any, British authors recommend such detailed specification of objectives for concept acquisition. Nevertheless, it provides several model objectives for concept attainment.

Can Normal School Activities be used?

The previous example is an extremely systematic way of assessing concept attainment but it finds little favour with those who argue that the assessment task itself should be intrinsically interesting. Such critics object, quite fairly, to the decontextualized nature of tests and their oppressive or restricting consequences for the children's individuality and creativity. The challenge, from this perspective, is to set up interesting group or individual tasks during which the responses which it is desired to assess may be elicited. This has considerable merit but, because the response is influenced by many factors besides the child's ability which is being tested, the results contain more uncertainty or 'noise' than objective test items. Returning for a moment to the mammal concept test, children (individually or in groups) could be asked to prepare

Intended outcomes	*Sample item*

1a. Selects an instance of the attribute, given its name (closed figure)

1a. Which drawing is a *closed figure?*

A.   D.

B.   E.

C.

1b. Produces an instance of the attribute, given its name (closed figure).

1b. Draw a closed figure.

2a. Selects the name of the attribute given an instance of the attribute (closed figure).

2b. Produces the name of the attribute, given an instance of the attribute (closed figure).

2b. What term accurately describes all three figures?

3a. Selects an instance of the concept, given the concept name (quadrilateral).

3a. Which figure is a quadrilateral?

A.   D.

B.   E.

C.

3b. Produces an instance of the concept, given the concept name (quadrilateral).

3b. Draw a quadrilateral.

4a. Selects a noninstance of the concept, given the concept name (quadrilateral).

Intended outcomes

Sample item

4b.   Produces a noninstance of the concept, given the concept name (quadrilateral).

4b.   Draw a plane figure that is *not* a quadrilateral.

5a.   Selects the name of the concept, given an instance of it (quadrilateral).

5a.   ▱   This figure is a

A.   parallelogram

5b.   Produces the name of the concept, given an instance of it (quadrilateral).

B.   square
C.   rhombus
D.   quadrilateral
E.   rectangle

6a.   Selects the name of the relevant attribute (4 sides) of the concept, given the name of the concept.

6b.   Produces the name of the relevant attribute (4 sides) of the concept, given the name of the concept.

6b.   List the characteristics which are true to all quadrilaterals.

7a.   Selects the name of the irrelevant attribute (4 right angles) of the concept, given its name.

7a.   Not all quadrilaterals have
A.   4 right angles
B.   4 sides
C.   closed sides
D.   straight sides
E.   4 angles

7b.   Produces the name of the irrelevant attribute (4 right angles) of the concept, given its name.

8a.   Produces the name (quadrilateral) of the concept, given its definition.

8b.   All plane closed figures with 4 sides may be called . . .

8b.   Produces the name (quadrilateral) of the concept, given its definition.

9a.   All quadrilaterals are
A.   plane closed 4-sided figures
B.   plane closed 3-sided figures
C.   plane open 4-sided figures
D.   plane closed 4-sided figures with opposite sides equal
E.   plane closed 4-sided figures with no sides equal.

9a.   Selects the definition (plane closed 4-sided figures) of the concept, given its name.

Intended outcomes   *Sample item*

9b.   Produces the definition (plane
closed 4-sided figures) of the concept,
given its name.

10a.   Selects the name of a concept
(polygon) superordinate to the one
given.

10b.   Produces the name of a concept   10b.   Triangles and
(polygon) superordinate to the one   quadrilaterals may both be
given.   called . . .

The following items test the pupil's understanding of the relationship of the concept to other concepts and principles, and its use in elementary problem solving.

11a.   Selects the name of a concept   11a.   Which is true?
(trapezoid) subordinate to the one given.   A.   All hexagons are also
                                                    quadrilaterals.
                                               B.   All trapezoids are also
                                                    quadrilaterals.
                                               C.   All circles are also
                                                    quadrilaterals.
                                               D.   All triangles are also
                                                    quadrilaterals.
                                               E.   All pentagons are also
                                                    quadrilaterals.

11.b   Produces the name of a concept
(trapezoid) subordinate to the one given.

12a.   Selects the principle that relates
two concepts, given the concept names.

12b.   Produces the principle that relates   12b.   What is the perimeter of a
two concepts, given the concept names.   quadrilateral?

13a.   Selects the correct answer by ap-   13a.   Which is the correct way to
plying a principle to a given problem.   find the perimeter of the quadri-
                                               lateral below?

                                               A.   a × b
                                               B.   a × b × c × d
                                               C.   a + b + c + d
                                               D.   a + b
                                               E.   2a + 2b

Intended outcomes   *Sample item*

13b.   Produces the correct answer by
applying a principle to a given problem.

Figure 5.4   A test of objectives for concept attainment.

Source: H. J. Klausmeier and R. E. Ripple (1971): *Learning and human abilities*,
3rd edn. New York: Harper and Row. Reproduced with permission of
the publisher.

wall charts 'to show why some animals are called mammals and
others not' to teach the concept to other children, to 'design'
animals using hypothetical but simple genetic engineering techniques to meet certain adaptive requirements and so on. These
tasks seem more interesting but certainly more demanding than
tests. The problem is how to 'abstract' the criterion of concept
acquisition where a cluster of unrelated abilities is entailed in an
outcome to the task.

Almost everything children do in schools can be taken as the
opportunity to make informal but systematic assessment – and it is
quite simple to set up tasks in which attainments in more than one
area of the curriculum may be assessed. A good example is
provided by TGAT (DES, 1987b) in which 'integrated tasks' are
presented to groups of children who are encouraged to conduct
simple experiments in order to permit teachers to observe target
abilities for assessment (Example 21). Pupils collaborate in small
groups to determine the most effective shape of a boat given
certain standard materials with which to carry out the investigation. Process and product assessment is undertaken; this particular task being designed to evaluate 'effectiveness of group discussion', 'oral presentation' (report back to class), 'clarity and
appropriateness of written records', 'mathematical and scientific
operations involved'.

This is an interesting example of the wider scope of educational
assessment than formal traditional tests and the task appears
interesting, motivating to pupils and intrinsically worthwhile.
However, the processes and products depend to a considerable
extent on the composition of the group so it is not clear how much
of the assessment is applicable to individuals (and therefore of little
use in diagnosis). As a check on the collective ability to demon-

strate scientific skills and concepts in action and providing feedback to the teacher, assessing group tasks has considerable
potential. Disaggregation of the group assessment to the level of
the individual presents a problem since the level of understanding
or concept attainment by a given individual may not be congruent
with the collective understanding of the group. Certain characteristics which many educators regard as desirable objects of assessment emerge only in groups ('leadership', 'co-operation', 'relationships with others', for example) and, if one is assessing for 'leadership potential', group problem solving may be the favoured setting
in which to make the judgement. However, many writers have
seen problems in describing such qualities as 'personal' and their
use in summative and personal assessment requires far more
thought than they have received to date.

Criteria for Higher Order Skill Assessment

A considerable body of CR assessment consists not so much in
setting tasks which are carefully prescribed but in the application
of descriptors to performances in situations where the child must
impose structure on an open-ended demand. Essays (including
shorter pieces of extended writing) belong to this category. Black
and Dockrell (1984) have written at some length on the diagnostic
potential of essays which they see as the best procedure for 'higher
order skills' assessment. (Just how many abilities are involved in
essay writing was considered on page 101). Quite clearly, essays
often provide a rich source of errors which suggest a need for
diagnosis but our concern is with the task of referencing them to
usable and interpretive criteria. Broadly speaking two approaches
may be recognized. One is to use analytical marking (see
page 106) and to describe the essay relative to each separate
component (quality of ideas; organization; style, grammar, legibility, punctuation, spelling). This is exceedingly time-consuming
and provides far more material than could be recorded given the
number of extended pieces of writing in arts subjects.

A second approach is to provide descriptions, one for each
grade to be awarded. These descriptors would constitute the frame
of reference to be used by teachers when reading and assessing the
essay, and also the criteria for the award for all essays within a
given subject area, 'across the curriculum', or specific to the given

topic. As an example of the second type consider the following descriptions on a 4-point grading scale for student essays in a university school of education. (Note the evidence of NR thinking in some of the statements and the ambiguity and imprecision in others.)

D: *Unsatisfactory*

Insufficient evidence of understanding of main issues and concepts. Serious weakness in coverage of content and sources, internal consistency and organisation of argument and/or style of presentation (i.e. punctuation, spelling, grammar, referencing, etc.). Use of sources inadequate, uncritical, irrelevant, and/or casually paraphrased or plagiarised.

C: *Satisfactory*

Main issues and concepts understood and described sensibly and coherently, although without much analysis of underlying principles and themes. Coverage, internal consistency, organisation and style of presentation are satisfactory. Some interpretation, evaluation and comparison of sources are attempted.

B: *Good*

Clear understanding of main issues and concepts is demonstrated. Underlying principles and themes are identified. Coverage, internal consistency, organisation and style of presentation are good. Material from sources is carefully critically selected, interpreted, compared and evaluated.

A: *Very Good*

Clear understanding of main issues and concepts is coupled with attention to underlying principles and themes. There is some evidence of original or imaginative insights and approaches. Coverage, internal consistency, organisation and style of presentation are very good to excellent. Selection, interpretation, comparison, evaluation, and integration of material from sources demonstrate ability to analyse and synthesize.

As well as providing some sort of frame of reference for assessors during their reading of the essays, these grades communicate broad differences between pieces of work. However, even the 'best' essays often contain some of the features characteristic of low grades and the 'poorest' some of the criteria of the highest. The choice of descriptors is intended to indicate only some of the factors which markers normally look for when deciding to place essays in one of the categories, but they fail to acknowledge any of the other ways in which a very good essay could be distinguished. In other words, the domain of essay performance has been defined implicitly by the marking scheme but, even so, considerable room is left for individual interpretation of the terminology employed. ('Plagiarism' is defined, however.) This accounts for a certain lack of agreement between markers although experience in the department suggests that discrepancies of more than one grade are not common. A somewhat more precise scheme for grading essays and other pieces of extended writing against criteria – geared to a particular topic – is given by Black and Dockrell (1984, 143). The principle of stating the criteria for given grades is the basis for assessment and reporting in 'grade-related tests'. The practice is likely to increase in the GCSE exam.

Many teachers and examiners object to the subjective nature of using essays to assess higher order skills and prefer to construct objective tests of analysis, synthesis and evaluation – the 'upper reaches' of Bloom's taxonomy of objectives (see page 66).

Analysis is assessed by tasks which require the pupil to break down a communication or text into its constituent elements. According to Bloom et al. (1971) analysis objectives are very difficult to learn and teach. The discussion by Bloom and his colleagues is by far the best analysis of the assessment of ability to analyse. They have identified six types of analysis, each of which requires its own kind of assessment task. Unfortunately the items they suggest are in multiple choice format and considerable difficulty has obviously been experienced in writing plausible alternatives. However, they recommend that the material to be analysed should be unfamiliar and remain on view throughout the assessment. Meaningful senses of the verb 'to analyse' include: using given criteria to classify the elements of a communication; drawing inferences from clues in a passage to detect the structure of the writing (Bloom et al., 1971, 177–91) or to see the gist of a passage whilst disregarding irrelevant and distracting material.

Synthesis involves the construction of a 'whole' out of elements by arranging them in a pattern 'not clearly there before' (Bloom et al., 1971, 193). Essays seem to be the best way of assessing these abilities. For example, requiring pupils to present an argument from information drawn from several sources. These types of synthesis may be separately assessed: producing an argument, producing a plan for dealing with a problem and, most demandingly of all, developing a theory of explanation to account for a given phenomenon, set of data or observations.

Evaluation is described by Bloom as 'among the most complex cognitive behaviors'. Generally, it entails the making of judgements about materials, ideas, explanations, methods and so on, using given criteria or with criteria generated by the pupil. It obviously involves a great deal more than opinion-stating since a justification using explicit criteria is required. Types of material to act as assessment tasks for evaluation include documents, written and art work, arguments (oral as well as written), theories, and sets of data and information relating to an artefact (a 'Which? report' is an example of an evaluation).

Quite clearly, a complex of skills, knowledge, analysis and synthesis is involved when making an evaluation and it is a matter of expert judgement to set criteria by which an evaluation may be assessed. Bloom et al. have provided several examples ̇of how different 'evaluation behaviors' may be assessed across the traditional school curriculum, examples which give an excellent idea to the interested reader of the high level of skill necessary to construct objectives and prepare test items in this domain.

Since analysis, synthesis and evaluation are higher order abilities, one is not likely to find much need for specified criteria until the later years of secondary schooling. However, to minimize the effects of previous knowledge when assessing abilities to analyse, synthesize and evaluate, the task should involve new or unfamiliar stimuli and the items should sample one or more of the behaviours suggested by Bloom et al. as involving the relevant ability. In the absence of clear criteria the best method that can be suggested is either to compare the pupils' effort with those made by experts in the relevant field *or* to use grades (no more than five to avoid the spurious impression that very fine distinctions can be made) similar to those found useful in judging essay tests.

EVALUATING A CR TEST

The discussion will be restricted to what teachers can reasonably be expected to do and not attempt to provide a 'complete guide' to the many technical analyses recommended by, for example, Hambleton (1980) or even Black and Dockrell (1984).

Does the Test Assess what it Purports to Assess?

Several aspects are of importance: the validity of the items, that is, how far each item can be thought to measure the domain as specified in the definition and, therefore, the targets for learning. We can look at four strategies for assessing tests.

(a)   Hambleton (1980) argues that the most effective way to answer this question is to involve judgements by experts (teachers) who are involved in the teaching. They would be asked to judge the item on its 'match' with the content of the domain using a 5-point scale from 1 ('poor') through 3 ('good') to 5 ('excellent'). This review of each test item would take place periodically: unsatisfactory items (those with a mean rating of less than 3 ('good') would be revised or eliminated from future versions of the test).

(b)   A second possibility is to judge each item for its 'instructional sensitivity'. If the item is a valid measure of the domain then teaching directly towards attainment of the target it embodies should increase the score on that item. Black and Dockrell (1984) compare three procedures for doing this. If the test can be taken as a 'pre-test' (i.e. before the unit is studied) and as a 'post-test' (i.e. after studying the unit) a useful index is provided by:

$$I = \left(\frac{\text{Post-test per cent}}{\text{correct}} \right) \div \left(\frac{\text{Pre-test percent}}{\text{correct}} \right)$$

where I = Instructional sensitivity of the item.

Alternatively, and if pre-tests are impracticable, the following index may be used:

$$I = \left(\begin{array}{l} \text{No. of non-masters} \\ \text{on post-test but} \\ \text{masters after} \\ \text{remedial teaching} \end{array} \right) - \left(\begin{array}{l} \text{No. of non-} \\ \text{masters in} \\ \text{post-test} \end{array} \right) \times 100$$

Items which are most sensitive to instruction (those with the highest values of I) are regarded as valid for testing attainment.

(c)   A third way is similar to the first. Since all tests contain error variance and often measure unintended outcomes the scores are contaminated by the effects of abilities which are not part of the domain being referenced. Asking 'what else (i.e. other than the domain) could this item/test be assessing' helps to suggest contaminating effects. No test is, of course, a 'pure' measure of anything but some contain fewer additives than others. Black and Dockrell (1984) present a classic example. In an attempt to make testing 'fun' teachers in their study set a simple crossword puzzle to assess knowledge of 'safety in the kitchen'. Not only were clues ambiguous but assessment was clearly contaminated by 'crossword-taking skills' unrelated to the domain.

(d)   Other sources of error in the presentation and administration of the test can threaten validity. Tests must continually be appraised for clarity of instruction, motivation of pupils to perform and take an interest in the task, and suitability of stimulus and vocabulary to the level of pupils' abilities.

These four strategies cannot establish content and construct validity but they can provide evidence in support (or denial) of claims that it does measure what it claims to measure.

Is the Mastery Decision Valid?

This can be evaluated for the test as a whole by comparing the test performance of two groups (as large as possible) one of which has received the teaching and one which has not. The decision validity of the test and criterion for mastery is evaluated by comparing the two groups in relation to the criterion score. Thus the percentage of taught pupils who reach and exceed the criterion is compared with that of the untaught pupils who do so. If the test contains items unrelated to the content of the domain and can be answered as easily by non-masters as masters this will lead to misclassification.

Need the Test be Composed of Homogeneous Items?

This question is raised because of a clear difference of opinion among experts. Some experts regard homogeneity as highly desirable, while others have argued that homogeneity is less important, especially in a diagnostic context where what is being evaluated is the pupils' mastery of a unit of study. In single act domains items are homogeneous since the same performance is observed but at different times and, probably, under slightly different conditions (running 100 metres in wet and in dry conditions, for example). In closed domains (like mastery of the 1:50,000 Ordnance Survey signs) each test item will sample those signs and domain definition will ensure their homogeneity. To this extent, test items are measuring the same thing (by definition) and homogeneity could be demonstrated by, for example, correlating scores on pairs of items (high positive correlation being taken to support the hypothesis of homogeneity). This method is not entirely suitable especially if all, or nearly all, the pupils in a sample reach (or fail to reach) the criterion. In these cases, if scoring is dichotomous, there will be little or no variance in the items: this of itself ensures zero correlation between them. For this reason it is probably worthwhile to calculate facility values for each item (page 95) to alert the teacher to this interpretation for the inter-item correlations (if facility values are near 1.0 or zero). Black and Dockrell have shown how facility values themselves can be used to study test homogeneity. To do this, find the facility value for the test as a whole and for each item separately. Consider the test as homogeneous only to the extent to which the range of facility values for the items (i.e. difference between highest and lowest value) falls within plus or minus 0.15 (or 15%) of the value for the entire test. Any individual item which falls *outside* that range is considered to be measuring 'something different' from the others.

However, the position is less clear for open domain items, especially if the teacher is rash enough to try to assess the higher order skills. Here, as we have argued, understanding, synthesis and evaluation can be demonstrated in a number of ways and (hence) test items. Given that there might be sound pedagogical reason for *not* conceiving of the domain as homogeneous (this of itself would be anathema to some CR experts, of course) we would not expect the test to be homogeneous in the sense that each and every item measures the same thing. Some critics would say that – if these are the desiderata – then no meaningful domain has been specified! Nevertheless it seems likely that many domain definitions for units of study will not be assessed by items which one might expect to correlate highly (that is, they *deliberately* measure different abilities). The implication of this seems to be a need for more careful description of 'mastery states' (or degrees of mastery) or more detailed descriptions of the 'can do' variety to indicate the 'patchy' nature of pupils' achievement rather than a complete reconstruction of the test in the pursuit of 'homogeneity'. The best text on item analysis in CR testing is probably that by Berk (1980, chapter 3).

How Long should the Test be?

It is clear from the chapter on reliability that, all other things being equal, the longer the test the greater the dependability of the score it yields. Nevertheless, lengthening the test is subject to the law of diminishing returns so the teacher's problem is to find a reasonable balance between reliability and length, given the constraints on the latter. A few intuitive rules-of-thumb may be given: never assess mastery on a single item, a minimum of five parallel items is necessary; reserve a larger number of items for the core objectives – preferably ten; if you have time and interest compare length with dependability of the score by calculating split-half correlations for tests of different lengths. As soon as the test yields a split-half correlation (after correction, see chapter 7) of, say, 0.80 stop adding further items. (Do this only for tests where variance exists among pupils' scores, i.e. not where all or most children either reach or fail to reach the criterion.)

This chapter has not sought to minimize the complexities in constructing CR tests. Nevertheless, specifying the criteria by which pupils' competence is differentiated and awarded grades or marks is indispensable if the limitations of traditional global tests and reports are to be overcome.

The Statistical Description and Interpretation of Test Scores

In an idealistic educational system, free from competition and comparison, most assessment would probably be of the criterion-referenced type. The purpose of the criterion-referenced mode of assessment, it will be remembered, is twofold:

(a) the objective description of the strengths and weaknesses of a child's performance in relation to a specified standard (this is sometimes known as 'telling what the child can actually do'); and

(b) (where what is being learned can be thought of as organized hierarchically or sequentially) the level of mastery attained of a given objective.

Comparatively few problems arise in the description and interpretation of criterion-referenced scores. If an objective has been described as in the case of the addition of numbers or the solution of linear equations in chapter 3, and a level of mastery set at 90% (nine out of ten items testing each objective correctly answered) then that is what mastery means, by definition. But few, if any, schools have given up the more traditional forms of assessment, and other interpretations of the scores obtained are required. Questions typically posed about the interpretation of scores include: 'What is the average score?'; 'How did the children taught mathematics in set A compare with those in set B?'; 'How much overlap is there between the scores in the two groups?'; 'You say Mary is outstanding in biology, but how much better is she than the average for her class?'; 'I see John has a standardized score on the English test of 132. What does that really mean?'

In order to answer questions such as these or to give a really informative answer to the parents' anxious query 'How is she getting on?' some understanding of the statistical methods basic to educational measurement is required. There are already very many excellent books available and one is inclined, pessimistically, to believe that if readers cannot achieve a basic competence from the mass of material now available one further chapter is likely to be of no significance. Yet it is hoped that readers will appreciate that good reasons exist for attempting to master the elementary ideas contained in this chapter and be encouraged by the fact that the arithmetic required is well within the competence of many of the pupils who are being assessed! Moreover, many of the cheap electronic calculators now available will perform some of the basic operations to be described here and greatly reduce the drudgery of number crunching.

LEVELS OF MEASUREMENT

It is undoubtedly the case that naive beliefs held by teachers about measurement have helped to inhibit a high level of professional expertise in assessment methods and to maintain current primitive standards of interpretation of test scores even in some schools which pride themselves on their 'academic excellence'. (Such schools are, of course, usually referring to the achievements of pupils rather than of themselves.) Quite obviously, measurement of children's ability and achievement differs in several fundamental respects from measurement of their physical attributes, say their height or weight. In the first place, when we measure height we do so by employing a series of real numbers having order, an origin (nought) and a fixed distance between adjacent numerals. Because we have a zero point which actually indicates the absence of height we are able to carry out certain algebraic operations on the numerals: for example, we can say that John who is five feet ten inches tall is twice as tall as his young brother who is two feet eleven inches; and that Mary, who is five feet two inches tall is that much taller than Susan (five feet nought inches) as is Susan than Helen (four feet ten inches). But the first type of statement cannot be made about mathematics scores. Even if Nigel *scored* nought on a test it would make no sense to say that he had *no* mathematics ability or that he knew *no* mathematics. (Teachers may often be heard to say this kind of thing but since one could easily put into the test items which all children could answer, the scale of ability in mathematics has no true zero point.) Scales which have a zero point, then, are often called *ratio scales* of measurement but we do not have any such scales for educational data.

For practical purposes, educators often assume that their scales of measurement have some of the properties of ratio scales, but not the zero point. To revert to our hypothetical mathematics test: John scored 50 marks, Peter 40, but Norman only 20 marks out of a total of 75. This is usually interpreted to mean that the difference between Peter's score and Norman's score is twice as great as that between John's score and Peter's score. This interpretation is based on the assumption that intervals along the scale are fixed: for this reason the scale is called the *interval type*. Quite a lot of assessment data is of this type.

Quite often, in education, the numerical data which are obtained by assessment do not imply fixed intervals along a scale. We could use our mathematics test to put children in rank order. Although the original scores were on an interval scale the distances between abilities in adjacent ranks are not. Indeed, in a class list, for example, the top two may be close together in raw scores and get many more marks than the third, but the mere statement of the ranks ('first', 'second', 'third') would disguise this fact. Because this type of measurement scale has order but lacks properties of distance and of a zero point it is known as an *ordinal* scale of measurement.

Some writers have argued that there is an even simpler scale of measurement than this. It is known as the *nominal* scale and really consists only of the assignment of numbers in order to differentiate whole categories of objects or events. Thus one might, for purposes of data analysis, use 'one' to represent the girls, 'nought' to stand for the boys in a class. In this case 'one' does not mean 'more than nought': we have neither the concept of order, nor of distance and no zero point. If we adopt Stevens's (1946) definition of measurement as assigning numerals according to rules, this would presumably qualify as measurement but we have no further use for nominal measurement in this chapter.

What is the relevance of this distinction between levels of measurement for teachers? In the first place it is an important aspect of the meaning (interpretation) of data. For example, the statement 'John scored 50 in a mathematics test' cannot be fully interpreted because the scale is an interval one and has no zero point. Secondly, different types of score allow different kinds of arithmetical and statistical operations to be carried out on them. We can never interpret scores to mean that one child has half, twice or three times as much ability in the subject as another child, for the same reason (no zero point). Thus, if scores are of the ordinal or interval type they cannot be interpreted as if they were on ratio scales and they require different kinds of processing if they are to be made meaningful.

In the examples which follow we shall assume the data obtained in education to be interval type unless otherwise stated. Actually it is not all that easy to decide which type of score we have. Take grades, for example. We can say that grade B is higher (more of the attribute used to grade the child) than grade C which in turn is higher than grade D, without being contentious (i.e. we can claim ordinal properties for the scale). But can we claim that the interval between adjacent grades remains the same? Almost certainly not. Yet grades are often treated as if they were on an interval scale and extensively used in averaging and so on, especially in the USA.

SUMMARIZING THE DATA

Because interval and ordinal scores have no zero point, we often need to interpret them in terms of the distribution of scores to which they belong. Tabulating the distribution in one way or another is a first step in summarizing the data. Table 6.1 represents the scores obtained in a geography test taken by 32 children aged 12–13 years. They appear in alphabetical order just as they were recorded in the teacher's mark book.

The purpose of statistical treatment is to describe scores like these and to bring out their meaning by relating any one score to certain important characteristics of the scores of the entire group. One simple way to begin is by putting the scores in rank order. It is then easy to tell at a glance who has achieved the highest score and who the lowest score, how far apart these are (the 'range'), how often a particular score occurs (the 'frequency') and so on. Ranking is usually done from highest to lowest score using a table such as table 6.2. A slight reduction in the space taken up can be

Table 6.1 – Scores of 32 pupils on geography test (maximum mark = 50)

Pupil	Score	Pupil	Score	Pupil	Score	Pupil	Score
Paul A	25	Charles F	40	Nigel L	29	Anne S	35
William B	36	Richard E	26	Geoffrey L	43	John S	34
Jean B	33	Robert F	21	Sandra M	36	Susan S	31
Mary C	24	Dean G	22	Elizabeth M	38	Sarah T	30
Peter C	32	Margaret H	38	James N	28	Clive T	42
Sylvia D	41	William H	23	Dennis O	39	Anthony W	34
Ken D	33	Norman K	35	Joan P	37	Marlene W	27
Jim D	37	Peter K	27	John R	37	Jane W	39

achieved as in the third and fourth columns of the table where each score and its frequency (the number of times it occurs in the group) is tabulated.

Notice that several ranks are 'tied'. Two children scored 39, for example: where this happens it is usual to assign the average of the ranks to each score. Thus, three children scored 37 and as there are eight scores higher than 37 these are assigned the average of ranks 9, 10 and 11. Quite a lot of ties have occurred, but this often happens with real data.

Several simple things can be done with these data to bring out their meaning.

Finding the Inclusive Range of the Scores

The highest score obtained in the geography test was 43 and the lowest 21. In statistics we think of each score not as a point on a scale but as occupying the mid-point of an interval on it. For example, 43 covers the interval from 42.5 to 43.5, 21 from 20.5 to 21.5, and so on. The reason for this will become clear later. *The inclusive range* is therefore found as follows:

$$(\text{highest score} - \text{lowest score}) + 1 \qquad [6.1]$$

In our example the inclusive range using formula [6.1] is:

$$(43 - 21) + 1 = 23$$

Table 6.2 – Geography scores in table 6.1 in rank order with frequencies.

Score order	Rank	Raw score	frequency (f)
43	1	43	1
42	2	42	1
41	3	41	1
40	4	40	1
39 39 }	5.5	39	2
		38	2
38 38 }	7.5	37	3
		36	2
37 37 37 }	10	35	2
		34	2
		33	2
36 36 }	12.5	32	1
		31	1
35 35 }	14.5	30	1
		29	1
34 34 }	16.5	28	1
		27	2
33 33 }	18.5	26	1
		25	1
32	20	24	1
31	21	23	1
30	22	22	1
29	23	21	1
28	24		——
27 27 }	25.5		n = 32
26	27		
25	28		
24	29		
23	30		
22	31		
21	32		

Some writers report the *range* of scores. The range of scores in table 6.2 is simply 22 (i.e. highest − lowest). (Notice that for some types of scores, the interval would not be equal to the score ± 0.5. For example, if we asked people to report their age *last birthday* all

INTERPRETATION OF SCORES 155

people who report themselves as, say 35 years old would lie within
the interval '35 years old today to 36 years old tomorrow'. Here
the interval would be 35.00 to 35.99 years. If, however, we asked
them their age to the *nearest birthday* the interval would be 34.5 to
35.5 with a mid-point of 35.)

Constructing a Frequency Polygon

This is a simple form of graph. A figure is drawn in which the mid-
point of each score interval has been placed along the horizontal
('*x*') axis and the frequency up the vertical ('*y*') axis. For our
example, to simplify, the scores have been grouped into *class
intervals* of two. Class intervals, frequencies and frequency polygon are shown in table 6.3 and figure 6.1.

The same data could just as easily be depicted using the *histogram,* familiar to most pupils in primary schools but not shown
here. Where large numbers of scores are obtained covering a much
larger range, class intervals may have to be as large as, say five.

Using Quantiles

This is a very useful method of describing scores and of giving
meaning to the score of any pupil. *Quantiles* is the name of a group
of examples of which the *percentile* is the most familiar and the
only type to be calculated here. A quantile is the point on the scale
which divides the scores in a distribution into a number of equal
groups. For example, if the entire range of scores is divided into
four quarters then this can be accomplished by three points on the
scale called *quartiles* (Q_1, Q_2 and Q_3). When the entire group is
divided into 100 sets of scores this is done using 99 points known as
percentiles (P_1, P_2, . . ., P_{99}). Similarly, *deciles* (D_1, D_2, . . ., D_9)
divide the scores into ten groups. Data in table 6.3 are used below
to show how percentiles are determined.

Determining percentiles
Scores must be arranged from highest to lowest, frequencies
plotted and the cumulative frequency determined as in table 6.4.
The cumulative frequency is simply the number of scores at or
below the score. For example, the number of scores in or below
interval 24–25 is five. We shall illustrate by finding the 75th
percentile (P_{75}).

Table 6.3 – Class intervals and frequencies of 32 scores used to construct the frequency polygon of figure 6.1

Score	20–21	22–23	24–25	26–27	28–29	30–31
Frequency	1	2	2	3	2	2

Score	32–33	34–35	36–37	38–39	40–41	42–43
Frequency	3	4	5	4	2	2

Figure 6.1   Frequency polygon of 32 scores in table 6.1.

The summary of steps to calculate P_{75} is as follows:

(1)   Find $0.75n = 24$

(2)   Find lower limit of score class containing 24th score:

$$L = 35.5 \text{ (i.e. } 36.0 - 0.5)$$

(3)   Subtract the cumulative frequency up to L from 24:

$$24 - 19 = 5$$

(4)   Divide results of (3) by the value for f in the interval containing the 24th score and multiply by the width (2):

Table 6.4 – How to determine percentiles in the frequency distribution.

Score	Frequency	Cumulative frequency
42–43	2	32
40–41	2	30
38–39	4	28
36–37	5	24
34–35	4	19
32–33	3	15
30–31	2	12
28–29	2	10
26–27	3	8
24–25	2	5
22–23	2	3
20–21	1	1
	$n = 32$	

$$5/5 = 1, 1 \times 2 = 2$$

(5)   Add result of (4) to L:

$$P_{75} = 35.5 + 2.0$$
$$= 37.5$$

This result could have been obtained by inspection since 25% of scores (eight out of 32) are either in or greater than the interval whose mid-point is 38.5. The method is generalizable to the determination of all percentiles, however, and to the calculation of other quantiles simply by placing the required coefficient of n in step (1).

The advantages of quantiles are that they provide a useful summary of data which is easily obtained and understood by children and parents alike. Simply reporting the inclusive range of scores and providing certain percentile values enables the reader to build up a picture of the data quickly and easily with a little practice. Moreover, as we shall see later, these values can easily be related to other measures which summarize distributions, pro-

Table 6.5 – Construction of an ogive for data of table 6.4.

Score	Cumulative frequency	Rounded cumulative percentage
42–43	32	100
40–41	30	94
38–39	28	88
36–37	24	75
34–35	19	59
32–33	15	47
30–31	12	38
28–29	10	31
26–27	8	25
24–25	5	16
22–23	3	9
20–21	1	3

vided certain assumptions are made about the shape of the distribution of scores.

Constructing a Smooth Curve or Ogive

The word 'ogive' (pronounced 'ojive') is an architectural term which describes the shape of an arch. It has wide use in the representation of scores and it can also be used in their standardization. Table 6.5 and figure 6.2 show the construction of an ogive. As ours is a small group of only 32 scores, it is best to smooth the curve out a little by omitting some of the points on each side of the line so that the curve provides the best possible fit to the trend.

The first two columns in the table are taken from table 6.4. The third column – the rounded cumulative percentage – is found by expressing the cumulative frequency as a percentage of 32. For example, class interval 32–33 has an entry for the cumulative frequency of 15. Thus,

$$\frac{15}{32} \times 100 = 46.88 = 47\% \text{ approximately}$$

The advantages of the ogive will be demonstrated when the standardization of marks is described in a later section. Note,

Figure 6.2   Ogive constructed from data of table 6.5.

however, that the raw scores could easily be replaced by any quantile points (e.g. percentiles). This would have no effect on the shape of the ogive.

Finding the 'Central Tendency' of the Scores

It is often the case that frequency polygons, ogives or even the elementary histogram depict all a teacher needs to know in order to interpret the scores of children in relation to the group of scores to which they belong. Nevertheless, there are other kinds of information we may require. If we continue to think of the horizontal axis in all our graphs as a number line, we often need to know just where along that line the scores tend to occur. Referring back to the frequency polygon shown in figure 6.1 we can see that the scores tend to bunch together towards the higher values in the range. There is only one major hump corresponding to the class interval 36–37 but the majority of scores tend to occur close to that hump on either side of it. Three measures of central tendency are particularly useful in describing a distribution of this kind: (a) the mode; (b) the median; and (c) the arithmetic mean.

The mode

This is the most *frequently occurring* score. Adopting the mid-point of the interval we would say that the mode of the *grouped* data in table 6.3 is 36.5. Going back to the ungrouped data of table 6.2, the mode is 37. If all scores occurred with equal frequency (a most unlikely event) the group of scores has *no mode*. If two scores which are not adjacent to one another occur with equal frequency we describe the distribution as bi-modal. Sometimes distributions have one *major* mode and several *minor* modes.

The median

This is the score which divides the distribution into halves such that half the scores are greater, half lower than the median. In other words it is the 50th percentile (P_{50}). Inspection of table 6.5 shows that it must occur somewhere between scores 33 and 34 since there are 47% of scores up to and including that interval. As a rough approximation to the median this method of inspection will often be sufficient for descriptive purposes. You can find the median by the method described for the calculation of percentiles but finding P_{50}, not P_{75} as in our example, alongside table 6.4. Using that method – the reader should check – the median is found to be 34.0. The results of the steps:

(1) $0.5n = 16$
(2) $L = 33.5$
(3) $16 - 15 = 1$
(4) $1/4 = 0.25, 0.25 \times 2 = 0.5$
(5) $33.5 + 0.50 = 34.0$

You will get away with less arithmetic if you have an odd number of scores without ties. In this case the median is the middle score when they are placed in rank order: for example, the scores 23, 28, 29, 33, 39 give a median of 29. If the scores are an even number of untied scores the median is half way between the two middle scores when these have been ranked: e.g. for the scores 36, 38, 41, 43, 49, 58

$$\text{median} = (41 + 43)/2 = 42$$

The arithmetic mean

The mean is by far the most useful measure of central tendency. There are in fact several means (arithmetic mean; the geometric mean; the harmonic mean) but we are concerned here only with the *arithmetic mean* more commonly known as the familiar *average*. If we obtain a distribution of a large number (say several hundred) of scores, we shall almost certainly find that the mode (which can be obtained at a glance), the median and the mean are very close to one another. One difference between them, however, is that the mode and median are affected only little by extreme (or 'wayout') scores, whereas the mean is affected by them. This anticipates our need for some measure of variability as well as of central tendency in the full description and interpretation of scores.

The calculation of arithmetic mean poses no problems especially if a calculator is available: it is simply the sum of the scores divided by the number of scores. It is very useful, however, to use symbols to stand for these operations. The formula is:

$$\bar{x} = \frac{\sum_{1}^{n} x_i}{n} \qquad [6.2]$$

where

$\bar{x}$ = arithmetic mean (pronounced 'x bar')

$\sum_{1}^{n}$ = 'sum of'

(the subscript indicates where to start summing, i.e. 1, the first score, and the superscript where to stop, i.e. the nth score. These are normally taken as understood and will be omitted from future examples.)

x_i = the score of child i

n = the number of scores

Applying formula [6.2] to our data in table 6.1 we find that

$$\sum_{1}^{n} = 1052 \qquad n = 32$$

Hence

$\bar{x} = 1052/32 = 32.875$

If our scores are grouped as in table 6.3 a very close approximation can be reached using formula [6.3]:

$$\bar{x} \cong \frac{\Sigma f_i \text{ (mid-point)}}{n} \qquad [6.3]$$

where

$$\bar{x} = \text{arithmetic mean}$$

$\cong$ stands for 'approximately equal to',

$$f_i = \text{frequency}$$

'mid-point' stands for 'mid-point of class interval',

$$n = \text{number of scores}$$

The product of the frequency and mid-points is shown in table 6.6. For table 6.6 the approximation to the mean is very close indeed:

$$\bar{x} \cong 1050/32 = 32.81$$

(compared with 32.87 for the ungrouped calculation).

In general, the greater the width of the class interval (only two points in our example) and the larger the number of scores in each, the poorer will be the approximation to the mean using this method. This is because the method assumes that the scores within an interval are evenly distributed throughout its length, which is never the case.

Let us just pause for a moment to compare the properties of our three measures of central tendency:

mean   takes all the scores into account but is influenced by the (possibly few) very high or very low scores;
median   is to be preferred where an index relatively unaffected by extreme scores is required;
mode   is best where teachers wish to name the single score

Table 6.6 – Calculation of mean-grouped frequency data.

Frequency	Mid-point	f_i (mid-point)
2	42.5	85.0
2	40.5	81.0
4	38.5	154.0
5	36.5	182.5
4	34.5	138.0
3	32.5	97.5
2	30.5	61.0
2	28.5	57.0
3	26.5	79.5
2	24.5	49.0
2	22.5	45.0
1	20.5	20.5
		Σf_i (mid-point) = 1050

which best represents a group's performance. It is, however, very unsuitable in small groups.

A word of warning
It is, of course, possible to calculate mean, median and mode for *any* set of scores or grades. But it is not always terribly informative to do so. We can cite criterion-referenced scores as an example. Suppose we have a ten-item test for the attainment of an objective (with a specified mastery level of 80%). During the course of a few weeks, 20 children were tested for mastery and the scores obtained were found to be distributed as in table 6.7. Notice that the objective was such that children either attained it or they failed to attain it by quite a considerable margin of scores. (Such a distribution is often found in examination of students' mastery of statistics. Those who find it easy, find it very easy; those who do not, find it very difficult!)
Values for the central tendency of these scores are:

    mean   = 5.35
    median = 7.70
    mode   = 8.0 and 1.0 (the curve is bimodal)

Table 6.7 – A distribution of criterion-referenced scores.

Score	Frequency	
10	2 ⎫	
9	4 ⎬	'Masters'
8	5 ⎭	Criterion score = 8
7	—	
6	—	
5	—	
4	—	
3	—	
2	2 ⎫	
1	5 ⎬	'Non-masters'
0	2 ⎭	
	$n = 20$	

It is obvious that the mean and median of these scores tell you nothing very helpful about them. No child scores within two and a half units of the mean in either direction, for example. In this example the mode is probably the most descriptive value since it has two values and enables the recipient of this information to reconstruct a visual image of the shape of the distribution far more easily and accurately than either of the others, which are positively misleading. This is one reason why comparisons between average incomes in various countries in the EEC are not particularly meaningful in the absence of other measures of the shape of the distribution.

The Shapes of Distributions

If we look again at the frequency polygon for table 6.3 and redraw it somewhat idealistically, its general shape is something like the curve shown in figure 6.3 with its approximate mean (33) shown by the broken line.

This distribution is certainly not symmetrical about the line which represents its mean because the scores tended to bunch near the high end of the distribution. Such a distribution is known as a 'negatively skewed' distribution because its distortion is mainly at

Figure 6.3   Smoothed frequency polygon for data in table 6.3.

the low end of the range. Had the test been rather more difficult we might have expected scores to bunch near the low end. The curve would look something like that shown in figure 6.4.

The distribution is described as 'positively skewed' because its distortion is at the high end of the range.

One distribution which has been used extensively in test construction and in the interpretation of data in all branches of science and social science is the so-called 'normal distribution'. Its properties can be described mathematically but it is helpful at this stage to gain a visual idea of it. Its chief feature is that it is perfectly symmetrical about its mean, which also coincides with the mode and median. Its 'cocked-hat' shape (figure 6.5) is familiar to nearly everyone: normal curves belong to a family of curves having similar shape.

PROBABILITY AND THE NORMAL CURVE

A great deal is involved in a full understanding of the properties of the normal distribution and only a brief and intuitive idea can be given here. Nevertheless, teachers should try to grasp its fundamental properties since they are involved in the understanding of a great deal of measurement theory. This section can, however, be treated as a digression and readers may, if they wish, skip the text as far as the section on measures of variation (p. 170).

Figure 6.4   A positively skewed distribution.

Readers will almost certainly have some grasp of the concept of probability. One basic concept is that of sample space. It describes the number of events that could have occurred. For example, a bag containing four white objects and six red objects has ten points in sample space. Every time one object is taken from the bag, a white object or a red object could be retrieved. Thus white objects occupy four points in sample space (out of ten) and red objects six points in sample space (out of ten). Similarly blue, black, purple objects occupy *no* points in that sample space. Other everyday examples of events in sample space could be the number of people in a room (the points being occupied by men, women and children), the number of million passenger miles flown in one year by British Airways, the number of times a pedestrian crossing is used in an average day, and so on.

Formally, the probability of an event is the ratio of the number of sample points which are examples of that event to the total number of points in sample space. Thus the probability of a blindfold person drawing a white object from our bag would be

$$P \text{ (white object)} =$$

$$\frac{\text{no. of white objects}}{\text{total no. of points}} = \frac{4}{10} = 0.4$$

Similarly the probability of drawing a red object

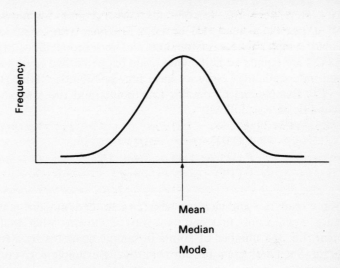

Figure 6.5   A normal distribution.

P (red object) =

$$\frac{\text{no. of red objects}}{\text{total no. of points}} = \frac{6}{10} = 0.6$$

Notice that the probability of drawing *either* a white or red object

P (white or red object) =

$$\frac{\text{no. of white and red objects}}{\text{total no. of points}} = \frac{10}{10} = 1.0$$

In other words, our blindfolded victim is certain to draw an object of one or other of these two colours because there are no objects of any other colour in the bag.

Interest in probability theory, and in particular the calculation of probabilities in gambling, led to the discovery in the late seventeenth and early eighteenth centuries of an equation for a curve which provided a good fit to the probabilities associated with coin tossing. Each time a coin is tossed one of two events takes place (unless, of course, the coin falls down a drain or is otherwise lost): it can be a head (H) or tail (T). Since two events are possible, sample space has two points and both probabilities $P(H)$ and $P(T)$ are equal to a half. What could happen if two coins were tossed independently? Now we have four possibilities: HH, HT, TH, TT. Sample space contains four points and the associated probabilities are as follows:

$$P \text{ (HH)} \qquad\quad = 1/4$$
$$P \text{ (HT or TH)} = 2/4 = 1/2$$
$$P \text{ (TT)} \qquad\quad = 1/4$$

Many readers – and children who have studied 'modern mathematics' – will know that one neat way of showing what could happen (i.e. the number of points in sample space) is by a tree diagram. Such a diagram for our coin tossing example is given by figure 6.6.

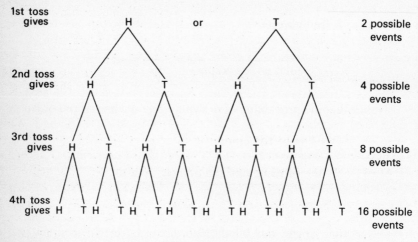

Figure 6.6   Tree diagram for probabilities of obtaining 'heads' and 'tails' in coin tossing.

What could happen if we tossed coins independently (or of course the same coin three times?). There are now eight possibilities (i.e. eight points in sample space). Check that the probabilities are as follows by counting up.

P (HHH)	= 1/8 or 0.125
P (HHT or HTH or THH)	= 3/8 or 0.375
P (TTH or THT or HTT)	= 3/8 or 0.375
P (TTT)	= 1/8 or 0.125

Now we could toss ten coins independently (or the same coin ten times) and graph the probabilities of the possible events (figure 6.7). (There are, in fact, 1024 possible events, that is points in this sample space.) Here just the number of heads is shown.

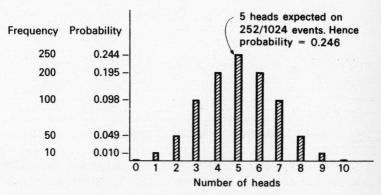

Figure 6.7   Distribution of probabilities of obtaining given numbers of 'heads' in ten tosses of unbiased coin.

A famous mathematician called De Moivre solved the problem of finding an equation to describe the line which nearly fits the tops of the columns. The actual formula is complicated and we shall not examine it here but the reader is asked to visualize the shape of the smooth curve which would fit the diagram. Imagine what would happen if an increasing number of coins were tossed and probabilities of the 'heads' calculated. Gradually the fit of the columns would come closer and closer to the smooth curve. You will, of course, by now have realized that there is no point in doing the actual tossing!

The equation derived by De Moivre yields a normal curve and it is indispensable to statisticians. It is more correct to speak of *a* normal curve than of *the* normal curve since its actual spread could easily be changed by an alteration to its scales. Distributions which are flatter than normal are called *platykurtic distributions*, those which are more peaked than normal are known as *leptokurtic distributions* (see figure 6.8).

Scores

Figure 6.8   Varieties of the normal distribution: A, leptokurtic (small value for spread of scores); B, platykurtic (large value of spread).

This brief digression has been made in order to give the reader some idea of 'where the curve comes from'. To understand its use we have to study measures of variation, however.

Measures of Variation

The range

We have already met the simplest measure of variation: the inclusive range (p. 153). Though informative it can be misleading because its size is determined by just two scores in the group (the highest and lowest). Because of this limitation various other measures of range have been suggested but for some inexplicable reason they are seldom quoted. One is called the *semi-interquartile range*. In our example of quartiles (p. 155) we saw how the complete range can be divided into quarters using three values called quartiles. They are Q_1 (the point on the number line below which 25% of scores lie), Q_2 (50%) or the median and Q_3 (75%). The semi-interquartile (Q) range is given by:

$$Q = \frac{Q_3 - Q_1}{2}$$

[6.4]

Whilst groups of scores which have similar values for the inclusive range need not be similar in any other respect (for example in shape), if two distributions have similar values for Q then they are likely to be similar in many respects. If a distribution is approximately normal then about 50% of the scores lie between the median $\pm\ Q$. Under these circumstances knowledge of Q and the median conveys a lot of information about the scores.

The variance

This is one of the central organizing concepts in the whole of statistics. Recall the computation of the mean using equation [6.2]. The mean uses every score in the group, unlike some of the other measures discussed. Obviously the variation of a *single* score can be determined by finding out how much it differs (known as the 'deviation score') from the mean of the group to which it belongs. Let us propose a small set of scores to illustrate these points: to make the arithmetic simple we shall use the scores of eight pupils on a spelling test whose maximum score was ten (table 6.8).

The second column shows that the sum of the deviation scores is equal to zero. This is always the case because the sum of the positive deviations is cancelled out by the sum of the negative deviations. This provides a check on the calculation of the mean. So merely adding the signed deviations provides no idea of the spread of scores. We could achieve this idea, however, by ignoring the signs and simply adding up the absolute value of the deviation scores. We could then divide by the number of scores and find the *mean deviation*. In our example the sum of the deviation scores regardless of sign is 16 and the mean deviation, therefore, 16/8= 2. This is not entirely useless since a large value for the mean deviation indicates a large spread of scores.

For a variety of reasons, however, the mean deviation is little used as a measure of variation. Instead, the *variance* is greatly to be preferred. If the deviation scores are squared, that is $(x_i - \bar{x})^2$ is found for each score, the values in the final column of table 6.8 are obtained. If these are added over all scores, the sum of the squared deviations is found. In our example

$$\sum_{1}^{8} (x_i - \bar{x})^2 = 44$$

This expression is known for short as the *sum of squares* (or SS).

Table 6.8 – Marks out of ten for eight children on spelling test.

Score	Deviation score	Squared deviation score
8	8 − 5 = 3	9
5	5 − 5 = 0	0
3	3 − 5 = −2	4
4	4 − 5 = −1	1
9	9 − 5 = 4	16
6	6 − 5 = 1	1
2	2 − 5 = −3	9
3	3 − 5 = −2	4
$\sum_{1}^{8} x_i = 40$	$\sum_{1}^{8} (x_i - \bar{x}) = 0$	$\sum_{1}^{8} (x_i - \bar{x})^2 = 44$

$\bar{x} = 40/8 = 5$

Dividing SS by the number of scores we obtain a value which is literally the mean of the squared deviations. This value is called the variance. In our example

$$\frac{\sum_{1}^{8} (x_i - \bar{x})^2}{n} = \frac{44}{8} = 5.5$$

In general

$$\sigma^2 = \frac{\sum_{1}^{8} (x_i - \bar{x})^2}{n} \qquad [6.5]$$

is the formula for the variance, where

σ^2 = variance (pronounced 'sigma squared')

$\sum_{1}^{n}$ = sum of, starting at the first score and continuing to include the nth score

x_i = raw score of ith child

Table 6.9 – Calculation of variance of two groups of scores.

	Group A			Group B	
Scores	$(x_i - \bar{x})$	$(x_i - \bar{x})^2$	Scores	$(x_i - \bar{x})$	$(x_i - \bar{x})^2$
2	$2 - 3 = -1$	1	7	$7 - 3 = 4$	16
4	$4 - 3 = 1$	1	1	$1 - 3 = -2$	4
4	$4 - 3 = 1$	1	1	$1 - 3 = -2$	4
1	$1 - 3 = -2$	4	7	$7 - 3 = 4$	16
5	$5 - 3 = 2$	4	1	$1 - 3 = -2$	4
2	$2 - 3 = -1$	1	1	$1 - 3 = -2$	4
$\Sigma x = 18$		SS = 12	$\Sigma x = 18$		SS = 48
$\bar{x} = 3$			$\bar{x} = 3$		

$\bar{x}$ = mean score
n = number of scores

To reinforce these ideas, examine the two distributions given in table 6.9. They are the scores obtained by two groups of children (A and B) on a given test.

In the first place the means are the same but it is clear that the shapes of the distributions are very different. Whereas the inclusive range of the group A scores is five, that for group B is seven, but this will not make all that big difference. In the second column for each group the deviation scores $(x_i - \bar{x})$ have been found, and in the third the squared deviation $(x_i - \bar{x})^2$. Adding these squares (to get SS) we find they are very different, 12 for group A, 48 for group B. Dividing by six (the number of scores in each group) we find that the variance in group A is only two whereas in group B it is eight. We can now see that the variance of the scores is four times as great for group B scores as for group A scores. Now if we had described each set of scores using only the mean and the range, the magnitude of the difference between the variability in the two sets would not have been so apparent.

Text book examples always involve easier arithmetic than is met in real life scores! In our two examples the mean and therefore the deviation scores are whole numbers. Where means are not whole numbers, however, squaring the actual deviations can involve tedium and accumulate error. A few lines of elementary algebra[2] show that

$$\Sigma (x_i - \bar{x})^2 = \Sigma x^2 - (\Sigma x)^2/n \qquad [6.6]$$

With this formula there is no need to calculate deviations: we can use the raw scores because

Σx^2 = sum of squared scores
$(\Sigma x)^2$ = sum of scores all squared
n = number of scores

Applied to the scores in group A, we get

Scores	Squared scores
2	4
4	16
4	16
1	1
5	25
2	4
$\Sigma x = 18$	$\Sigma x^2 = 66$

Therefore

$$(\Sigma x)^2 = 324$$

and so

$$\begin{aligned}\Sigma (x_i - \bar{x})^2 &= 66 - 324/6 \\ &= 66 - 54 \\ &= 12 \text{ (as before)}\end{aligned}$$

[2]Actually only a slightly more complicated manipulation of $(a - b)^2$.

Thus

$$\sigma^2 = 12/6 = 2$$

Even without a calculator the arithmetic is very simple using the raw score formula for the sum of squares. Combining the final division by n into formula [6.5] to get the variance (σ^2) our formula becomes

$$\sigma^2 = \frac{1}{n}\ [\Sigma x^2 - (\Sigma x)^2/n] \qquad [6.7]$$

or

$$\sigma^2 = \frac{\Sigma x^2}{n} - \bar{x}^2 \qquad [6.8]$$

which is even simpler to use. In the example

$$\sigma^2 = \frac{66}{6} - 3^2$$
$$= 2$$

Readers who find an invitation to use symbols altogether too great a shock can try to visualize the concept of variance. Suppose we think of the scores in group A in table 6.9 as lying along a number line and then express them as deviations fron the mean of the group. If we square the deviation score for the first child (-1^2) we get a square whose size is one square unit. This square can be drawn as shown in figure 6.9. Actually we have four children with deviation scores of one, so we must think of four superimposed squares each of area one square unit on the diagram. The fourth child in the list has a deviation score of minus two so the area of his squared deviation score is four square units. The size of the square for the fifth child in the list is also four square units. So, all told, we have four children with squared deviations of one square unit and two with squared deviations of four square units. The size of the average square, therefore, is two square units: this is the variance, indicated by the shaded area in the diagram. This is a visual demonstration that the variance in test scores is equal to the mean of SS (or average square).

Figure 6.9   Illustration of 'variance'.

The standard deviation

Although the variance is an indispensable measure of variation and figures prominently in studies of overlap between two or more sets of scores, unlike the scores themselves it is a square measure. But we can very easily derive a measure of variation which is on the same linear scale as the scores themselves by finding the positive square root of the variance. Reference back to figure 6.9 shows that the resulting value would equal the base of the mean squared deviation: this is the definition of the standard deviation (σ) or 'root mean square deviation'.

Its formula would obviously be the square root of formula [6.5]. Hence

$$\sigma = \sqrt{\Sigma (x_i - \bar{x})^2 / n} \qquad [6.9]$$

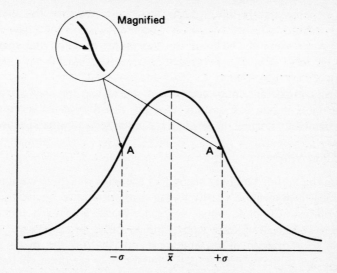

Figure 6.10   Normal curve showing the points of inflexion at $\bar{x} \pm \sigma$.

Readers are recommended to think of the standard deviation as the square root of the variance or as a linear (along a line) measure of the 'average variability' in a set of scores.

One important use of the standard deviation comes from its relationship with scores whose overall distribution is normal, or nearly so. Recall the shape of a normal curve (figure 6.10). If one were to put a magnifying glass on the points ringed one would see that there the shape of the curve changed from being convex to concave (at the point marked A). A change like this is known in mathematics as the point of *inflexion*. If a line is dropped perpendicular from this point to the horizontal axis it corresponds with the points on the scale which are one standard deviation above $(+ \sigma)$ and one standard deviation below $(- \sigma)$ the mean respectively. If the distribution is normal three important properties of the standard deviation apply:

(1)   Approximately 68% of the scores (area under the curve) lie between the mean $\pm \sigma$. Thus approximately 34% of the scores are between the mean $+\sigma$ and 34% between the mean and $-\sigma$.

(2)   Approximately 95% of the scores lie between the mean ± 2σ.
(3)   Approximately 99% of the scores lie between the mean ± 3σ.

Many important inferences about scores can be drawn from these facts if one can assume that the distribution of scores is approximately normal, as we shall see in the section which follows.

Standard Scores

When the author taught in secondary school it was quite common practice to determine yearly overall 'class positions' by awarding first place to the child whose aggregate marks across school subjects was highest. Occasionally, and in order to emphasize the greater importance of mathematics and English, the totals for these two subjects were doubled but little or no other manipulation of scores was undertaken. Some problems arose. In the years prior to the work of the Equal Opportunities Commission boys studied woodwork whilst girls took domestic science (now home economics). Unfortunately for the class list system, marks in woodwork were always much higher than marks in domestic science even where the least dexterous in the one was comparable to the most calamitous work in the other. Adding marks on very different scales of measurement, therefore, was very unfair, to say the least. One way in which the scores on disparate scales could have been compared was through the construction of 'standard scores', or by using the equivalent but slightly more cumbersome device of the 'z-score'. Percentile scores are used by some people for this purpose but their intervals are unequal (there may be as many as, say, nine points difference between the child ranked at the 95th percentile and the child ranked at the 90th percentile but only two or more three marks difference between the child at the 50th and 45th percentile). What is needed, then, is a way of converting scores to a common unit of measurement. This is accomplished by dividing the deviation score by the standard deviation of the group of scores. The effect of this on our woodwork and cooking scores is to translate the scores into deviations from their respective means (thus removing the first effect, i.e. that of the higher woodwork mean) and dividing by the average

INTERPRETATION OF SCORES   179

Table 6.10 – Calculation of z-scores for data in table 6.9.

Group A			Group B		
Scores	$(x_i - \bar{x})$	z	Scores	$(x_i - \bar{x})$	z
2	-1	$-1/\sigma = -0.71$	7	4	1.41
4	1	$1/\sigma = 0.71$	1	-2	-0.71
4	1	$1/\sigma = 0.71$	1	-2	-0.71
1	-2	$-2/\sigma = -1.41$	7	4	1.41
5	2	$2/\sigma = 1.41$	1	-2	-0.71
2	-1	$-1/\sigma = -0.71$	1	-2	-0.71
SS $= 12$			SS $= 48$		
$\sigma^2 = 12/6 = 2$			$\sigma^2 = 48/6 = 8$		
$\sigma = \sqrt{2} = 1.41$			$\sigma = \sqrt{8} = 2.83$		

variability, thus adjusting for the differences in the spread of the scores.

This operation as a formula becomes:

$$z = \frac{x_i - \bar{x}}{\sigma_x} \qquad [6.10]$$

where the symbols have the same meaning as before. Applied to our two groups of scores (A and B in table 6.9) it yields the results shown in the table 6.10. We can see that the z-scores for groups A and B are now directly comparable. Thus the child who scores two in group A has a score which is 0.71 of a standard deviation below the mean; the child who scores seven in group B has a score which is 1.41 standard deviations above the mean, and so on.

Because the percentages of scores corresponding to different areas of the normal curve are known and z-scores are in units of the standard deviation one type of score can easily be translated into the other using figure 6.11.

One difficulty in the use of z-scores is that they involve decimals and negative signs. In practice in most published standardized tests in Britain, scores are given on scales which have a mean of 100 and standard deviations of 15. These are called *standardized scores*. To obtain them simply multiply the z-score by 15 and add 100. Thus a

Figure 6.11   The normal curve and types of scale.

Source: H. G. Seashore, 1955. Methods of expressing test scores. *Test Service Bulletin 39*. New York: The Psychological Corporation.

z-score of 1.0 becomes $100 + (15 \times 1) = 115$; a z-score of -3.0 becomes $100 + [15 \times (-3)] = 55$, and so on. There is nothing sacred about these particular values for the mean and standard deviation: any value could be chosen. But by convention values of 100 and 15 have been widely adopted for published tests. With published tests the scores are first *normalized*, that is, the scores of large numbers of pupils which form the norms are transformed in order to smooth out the irregularities which occur in actual frequency distributions, to make them 'normal'. A brief explanation of how this can be done is provided later in the chapter.

Classroom teachers will not usually wish to bother to normalize their scores but may, instead, translate the actual scores obtained into what is known as 'stanines'. These are a type of standard score closely related to z-scores. It is a nine-point scale with a mean of five and a standard deviation of two. Stanines are shown in the second bottom line of figure 6.11 and are preferred by many people since they do not imply too great precision in scoring yet are sufficiently differentiating between pupils and easily understood by parents and children. On this scale, pupils whose stanine scores are four, five or six are found within the band captured by one standard deviation above and below the mean. A stanine score of eight or nine would be obtained only by about the 'top' 12 or 13% of pupils, and scores of one or two by a similar percentage 'at the bottom'. Readers may also come across a related scale known as 'T-scores'. They are on a scale with a mean of 50 and standard deviation of ten. Thus a z-score of +1.0 corresponds with a T-score of 60, a T-score of 35 with a z-score of −1.50, and so on.

Readers should study figure 6.11 carefully. Providing the assumption that the scores are normal, or nearly so, can be made, it shows how a score on any scale can be interpreted in terms of where it occurs on a normal curve. It demonstrates that the norm-referenced assessment of pupils gives meaning to a score only in terms of the scores obtained by a large number of similar pupils. The normal curve is also very important in probability theory and is closely bound up with deciding whether a particular observation – say the result of an experiment – is a 'chance' or 'real' occurrence.

The assumption that the normal curve represents a good approximation to the real life occurrence of biological data – such as height – is deeply embedded in Western science. It is the case that where a large number of observations of natural phenomena are made their distribution is often near normal. But while scores in scholastic tests often provide a reasonable fit to this curve it is very easy indeed to alter the distribution to achieve a different shape by the inclusion of items of different characteristics. By including a large number of easy items the curve can be 'shifted upwards' – that is, it can be negatively skewed – while, by the same token, a number of difficult items will produce a curve which is positively skewed. Near-normal curves are known to result from tests whose items have a facility level (see chapter 4) of around 0.5; that is items which are answered correctly by about half the respondents. Obtaining such a distribution does not of course show that the *abilities* which are assumed to be responsible for the obtained scores are themselves normally distributed! Scaling the scores so that they are normal is done for convenience of interpretation only. As the first objection in chapter 3 argues, what is done for convenience should not be allowed to assume the properties of a natural law – not, of course, that any such laws have been identified in the social sciences!

Modern intelligence test scores (still, perhaps misleadingly, called 'IQs') are normalized standard scores: they have been constructed to correspond to the normal distribution and with mean 100, standard deviation 15 (16 in the case of the Stanford–Binet test). It is, therefore, nonsense to claim that they *demonstrate* the normal distribution of intelligence. Classical intelligence test interpretations used the concept of IQ first put forward by Stern for the comparison of scores obtained by Binet's famous tests. It is not the purpose of this section to go into detail about these developments since there are already many excellent accounts (e.g. Karmel and Karmel, 1978) but since much confusion about the IQ still exists we shall just point out that IQs (intelligence quotients) *used to be found* using the formula

$$IQ = \frac{\text{mental age (MA)}}{\text{chronological age (CA)}} \times 100 \qquad [6.11]$$

If a child is nine years old and achieved the average score for nine year old children on the test then his IQ was 100:

$$IQ = \frac{9}{9} \times 100 = 100$$

A second child, also nine, whose score was as high as the average for 12 year olds, however, had an IQ of 133, and so on

$$IQ = \frac{12}{9} \times 100 = 133$$

One of the problems with this method lay in the unfortunate misinterpretations which became attached to the concept of 'mental age'. Firstly it is merely a ratio of a score on a test to age and describes only a comparison between the testee and the average of a number of other testees at a similar or different ages. Although it is still common for some criminals to be described at their trial as having a 'low mental age' it would be wholly misleading to assume that their accumulated experiences and mental lives were in any way comparable to those of the young children with whom their performances on the solution of a few abstract puzzles was being compared. For statistical reasons, too, the classical method of obtaining the IQ has given way to use of the normalized standard score. Unfortunately, the terminology has not been standardized! Wechsler intelligence scales (WAIS, the adult scale and WISC, the children's scale) employ the term 'deviation IQ', but this is merely a way of retaining a link with its historical antecedents whilst adopting the modern practice of using standardized scores. It is not anticipated that teachers will have much use for intelligence tests but the moral is clear: make sure the manual of any published tests being used is explicit in its description of the type of scale being used and the inferences about the norm-referenced description of a child's performance permitted by it.

Normalizing Scores

The relationships we have been discussing between the various types of scales apply only when the distribution of raw scores is normal. The construction of published tests of ability and achievement takes great care to ensure that the raw scores on which the norms have been based have been normalized from a large sample of children. When using standardized tests (mean 100, standard deviation 15) teachers can be confident that a score of 130 indicates that the child's performance is at a level which would be exceeded by less than 2½% (2.27% precisely) of similar children, and so on. In interpreting a score in a class of, say, 30 children it is often convenient to translate it into a z-score (or one of its derivatives) and to report this score as if it were a member of a normal distribution. Obtaining some sort of standard score is, of course, necessary in all cases where overall class lists based on the summation of several scores are required. But with a class of the size usually met in schools a normal distribution is extremely unlikely, to say the least. With such a small group there would be little point in normalizing them because, amongst other reasons, there would be far too few children near the tails of the distribution (i.e. very high or very low scorers) to provide the necessary information.

An approximate and simple method of normalizing is illustrated in table 6.11 using the data of table 6.2. Although one would not normally bother to normalize only 32 scores the method is applicable to larger distributions. The steps in the normalizing procedure are:

(1)   Record the raw scores in descending order and tabulate the frequencies (columns one and two).
(2)   Record the cumulative frequencies upwards (column three).
(3)   For each raw score, record the cumulative frequency *below* the score and add half the frequency in the row corresponding to the raw score. Place the result in column four. For example, the cumulative frequency up to (i.e. below) raw score 33 is 13. The frequency of score 33 is two: therefore the entry in column four is $13 + (\frac{1}{2} \times 2) = 14$.
(4)   Express the cumulative frequency in row four as a proportion of the total number of scores. Record the result in column five. For example, the cumulative frequency up to and including raw score 37 in column four is 22.5. There are 32 scores, therefore the proportion is $22.5/32 = 0.7031$.
(5)   Consult the table of areas under the normal curve for given z-score values (see appendix) to find the value corresponding to the proportions. For example, the proportion corresponding to raw score 40 is 0.8906. This means that 0.8906 of the normal curves area is below the value for z. Since the normal curve is symmetrical *half* the area (0.5000) is below the mean – which is z-score 0.000. Therefore the area *between* the mean and 0.8906 is $0.8906 - 0.500 = 0.3906$. Inspection of the table shows that 0.3906 corresponds with a z-score of 1.23. (Actually 0.3907 corresponds to a z of 1.23, but go to the nearest value.) It is a little trickier to read the table for negative z-scores but the logic is the same. For example, the proportion corresponding to raw score 26 is 0.1719. We are now dealing with that half of the normal curve which is *below* the mean since 0.1719 is less than half (0.5000). Therefore the proportion of the area between the mean and the z-score which contains 0.1719 of

Table 6.11 – Calculation of normalized scores from data in table 6.2

Raw score	f	Cumulative f	Cumulative f below score + ½f	Proportion	Value of z in normal curve	Rounded T-score (10 × z) + 50	Standardized score (15 × z) + 100
43	1	32	31.5	0.9844	2.15	72	132
42	1	31	30.5	0.9531	1.68	67	125
41	1	30	29.5	0.9219	1.42	64	121
40	1	29	28.5	0.8906	1.23	62	118
39	2	28	27.0	0.8438	1.01	60	115
38	2	26	25.0	0.7813	0.78	58	112
37	3	24	22.5	0.7031	0.53	55	108
36	2	21	20.0	0.6250	0.32	53	105
35	2	19	18.0	0.5625	0.16	52	102
34	2	17	16.0	0.5000	0.00	50	100
33	2	15	14.0	0.4375	−0.16	48	98
32	1	13	12.5	0.3906	−0.28	47	96
31	1	12	11.5	0.3594	−0.36	46	95
30	1	11	10.5	0.3281	−0.45	46	93
29	1	10	9.5	0.2969	−0.53	45	92
28	1	9	8.5	0.2656	−0.63	44	91
27	2	8	7.0	0.2188	−0.78	42	88
26	1	6	5.5	0.1719	−0.95	41	86
25	1	5	4.5	0.1406	−1.08	39	84
24	1	4	3.5	0.1094	−1.23	38	82
23	1	3	2.5	0.0781	−1.42	36	79
22	1	2	1.5	0.0469	−1.68	33	75
21	1	1	0.5	0.0156	−2.16	28	68
	32						

the score is $0.5000 - 0.1719 = 0.3281$. The nearest entry in the table to this value is 0.3289: it gives -0.95 as a value for z. Place the entries in column six.

(6) The z-scores are now normalized. To remove the negative signs decide which scale is required and use the appropriate formula at the top of the column. Column seven shows T-scores (mean 50, standard deviation ten) column eight standardized scores (mean 100, standard deviation 15).

Inspection of the resulting standardized scores or the T-scores shows that normalization has compressed the scale in some places but elongated it in others. We can see the disadvantages of having only a small number of scores. In the middle of the range a difference of one between raw scores yields a corresponding difference of only two in the standardized score whereas a difference of one in raw scores at the extremes of the range yields a difference in standardized score of seven at the top and four at the bottom end of the distribution. For this reason published tests standardize their scores by using much larger samples and more sophisticated methods of normalization at the extremes. The method described, however, should be sufficient for most purposes where teachers wish to normalize scores. Ideally, scores on two distributions are only directly comparable where both are normal and have the same standard deviation.

Use of Norms

Following the method will give some insight into the construction of norms. Clearly standardized scores in our sample of 32 children are totally inadequate to constitute worthwhile norms for interpretation. But what makes norms adequate? The purpose of norms is to provide a reference frame by which to compare the scores of our children with scores by similar children elsewhere. Mere size of the standardizing sample is not the only attribute to look for: if the sample was very different in composition from the children using the test little would be learnt. Tests which are sold for wide geographical use may not quote meaningful national norms. An enormous sample of children in the south-east of England would not be a 'national sample', for example, so teachers should look to the manual to see whether a full description of the sample is given. Schools could well be recommended to develop local norms especially in relation to achievement tests which reflect local teaching objectives. These could be revised from time to time. Careful study should also be made of the year in which the norms were produced. Thère is an inevitable timelag between original publication and use, such that some may be so much out of date as to be inapplicable. Teachers should also ask themselves whether they have need of norms at all: in some instances, say where the ablest children in the group are to be identified, norms are unnecessary.

Karmel and Karmel (1978) have listed nine things to look out for in the manual by which to judge whether the normative data are adequate. They are (Karmel and Karmel, 1978, 96–7):

(a)   the scales used for reporting the scores should be thoroughly explained;
(b)   standard scores should be used for reporting raw scores;
(c)   conversion tables should be provided;
(d)   norms should be published in the manual at the time of distribution;
(e)   the normative group should be clearly defined and described;
(f)   standard scores should reflect the distribution of scores in a reference group that is appropriate for the comparison you wish to make;
(g)   the method of sampling school and pupils which constitute the norms should be fully reported;
(h)   achievement test norms should report the number of schools as well as the number of children tested;
(i)   variance in scores because of such variables as age, sex and amount of education should be reported.

Very few manuals consulted by the writer pass muster on all these aspects. In the past there has undoubtedly been what Seashore and Ricks (1950) have called the 'lumping together of all the samples secured more by chance than by plan', but standards of sampling have improved. Nevertheless, if test constructors do not provide all the information required by the nine principles above teachers may, with justice, adopt a sceptical attitude to the value of the norms presented.

Measurement of Relationships

The product–moment correlation

Many occasions arise in which measurement of the relationship between two sets of scores obtained by the same group of children on two different forms of the same test as is often necessary, as we shall see in chapter 7, in the study of *reliability*. Similarly, we might be interested in finding the relationship between a test and a criterion test taken much later. One obvious instance of this is where an examination taken at age 11 was held to predict later performance in school. This relationship needs to be examined in studies of the validity of the test (see chapter 8). An equally important application would be in studies of how well a test which claims to measure 'attribute X' overlaps in the information it provides with a second test which also claims to measure the same attribute. A still more complicated application is in the study of the relationship between several sets of scores in an attempt to identify and name a smaller number of 'underlying abilities' responsible for the performances – for example a number of tests which appear to require the mental manipulation of shapes to see whether the performances can be explained in terms of a single ability which could be labelled 'spatial visualization'.

Teachers will almost certainly have tried to intuit relationships between variables. Some are convinced that pupils better than average in one school subject or activity are also better than average in another. Some may claim to have recognized a tendency for pupils of certain 'home backgrounds' to do better than pupils from others. Still more may expect higher achievement scores from pupils whose parents have attained higher educational standards. We are not concerned here with the validity of these impressions but merely to point out that they are examples of relationships which teachers suspect may exist. The purpose of calculating correlations, however, is to replace subjective impressions of this kind with more precise indices which actually measure the strength of the relationship.

Before the advent of computers, the first step in the examination of a correlation between two variables was to display the relationship on a type of graph known as a 'scatter diagram'. If numbers are not too large this method still repays study. Suppose a teacher has obtained scores for ten children (we shall keep the numbers small for simplicity's sake) on two tests of, say, com-

Table 6.12 – Scores of ten children on two tests of comprehension: perfect positive correlation.

Child	x	y
A	28	23
B	25	21
C	22	19
D	19	17
E	16	15
F	13	13
G	10	11
H	7	9
I	4	7
J	1	5

Figure 6.12   Scatter diagram for data of table 6.12.

prehension. Following convention we shall label one test 'X', the other 'Y': the scores, denoted by x and y respectively, are given in table 6.12. These scores are then plotted to form a scatter diagram (figure 6.12, with x on horizontal, y on vertical axis, by convention).

The relationship between the two sets of scores is a perfect one as shown by the straight line which joins the points. Moreover it is *positive* because the highest score on X is paired with the highest on Y, the second highest on X with the second highest on Y, and so on through the list. Mathematically its strength is $+1.0$.

Suppose these two lists had been inversely related: that is the *highest* score on X is paired with the *lowest* score on Y, the second highest on X with the second lowest on Y and so on. Once again the relationship would have been perfect and all points would be on a straight line but this time the line would have been sloping from top left to bottom right. In this case the relationship is described as being 'perfect negative' and mathematically its strength is -1.0.

Now the relationships between two sets of scores in real life are never perfect, either positive or negative. More often test scores in school subjects are paired something like the relationship shown in table 6.13. Figure 6.13 shows the relevant scatter diagram.

It is obvious from this scatter diagram that the relationship is far from perfect, but if one were to draw the line which best represents the plot it would tend to run from top right to bottom left. This shows that whilst there are individual exceptions, the tendency in the scores in the group as a whole is for higher than average scores on X to be higher than average on Y. In fact the correlation calculated from these data is $+0.57$. We would call this a positive relationship but only of moderate strength.

We shall not bother to quote actual sets of data for figure 6.14. Figure 6.14(a) shows no relationship between X and Y since one finds as many children who are 'high on X, low on Y' as one finds children who are 'low on X, high on Y'. This scatter diagram illustrates a zero-order relationship, correlation 0.00. Figure 6.14(b) shows a definite relationship but it is certainly not one that can be described by a single straight line. Although the actual measurement of the correlation is zero we would not wish to say there is no relationship since it is curved (more properly, 'curvilinear'). It is typical of the theoretical relationship between test performance (Y) and anxiety (X) since performance improves with a moderate amount of anxiety (up to anxiety score 12 to 15) but decreases thereafter.

Readers will have gathered from the above that a correlation can be thought of as the closeness of the fit between the points and

Table 6.13 – Scores of ten children on two tests: moderate positive correlation.

x	y
28	21
25	13
22	23
19	13
16	15
13	21
10	12
7	17
4	11
1	9

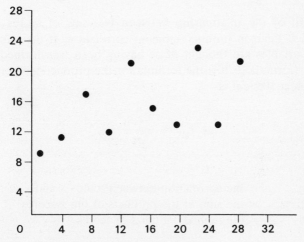

Figure 6.13   Scatter diagram for data of table 6.13.

a *straight* line. Perfect correlation is said to exist when points fall *on* the straight line which can slope positively or negatively. The further the points lie away from a straight line the smaller the correlation until, where the points make a roughly circular pattern, the correlation is zero.

Provided the scatter plot does not indicate a curvilinear relationship, the device which provides the most useful index of the

Figure 6.14   Scatter diagrams showing two reasons for zero correlation: (a) no relationship between X and Y; (b) curvilinear relationship between X and Y.

strength of the relationship between two sets of scores is the so-called Pearson product–moment correlation. If the scores on both variables are thought of as having been transformed to z-scores (formula [6.10]) the formula for the product–moment correlation coefficient is

$$r_{xy} = \frac{\Sigma z_x z_y}{n} \qquad [6.12]$$

where

r_{xy}	=	the correlation between scores x and y
$\Sigma z_x z_y$	=	the sum of the products of the z-scores
n	=	the number of pairs of scores

In practice this formula is rarely used since it is computationally clumsy and can yield rather a lot of error if the two sets of scores run to several places of decimals. Many moderately priced calculators provide a direct computation of the product–moment correlation but a fairly convenient raw score version of formula [6.12] can be derived by simple algebra. It is:

$$r_{xy} = \frac{N\Sigma xy - (\Sigma x)(\Sigma y)}{\sqrt{\{[N\Sigma x^2 - (\Sigma x)^2][N\Sigma y^2 - (\Sigma y)^2]\}}} \qquad [6.13]$$

where Σxy = the sum of the products of the raw scores
         Σx = the sum of the x scores
         Σy = the sum of the y scores
         $(\Sigma x)^2$ = the sum of the x scores 'all squared'
         $(\Sigma y)^2$ = the sum of the y scores 'all squared'
         Σx^2 = the sum of the squared x scores
         Σy^2 = the sum of the squared y scores

Use of this formula in calculating r_{xy} is demonstrated in table 6.14.

This correlation is positive but low. If we square 0.368 we get the proportion of the variance in mathematics scores which can be predicted from the English scores (0.135). This can be interpreted to mean that only 13.5% of what is measured by the test of English enters into performance in mathematics. Using these English scores would not make a very good job of predicting mathematics achievement; in fact, because we had only 12 pupils in our example the correlation is *not significantly different from zero*. If you plot the scattergram you can see that the points provide a very poor fit indeed to a single straight line. In fact the value for the correlation where only twelve pairs of scores are involved would have to reach ± 0.57 before a statistician would claim that the correlation was significantly different from zero. Notice that a correlation of − 0.57 indicates the same *strength* of relationship as a correlation of + 0.57 but differs only in direction. Notice, too, that a correlation of 0.80 is not indicative of a relationship that is twice as strong as a correlation of 0.40. In fact the correlation of 0.80 allows 64% of the variance in one test to be predicted from the other (0.80^2), whereas only 16% is possible for the correlation of 0.40. From this point of view, then, the strength of the relationship is proportional to the *square* of the correlation coefficient.

It is not the purpose of this section to provide any more detail about correlation coefficients than is necessary for an understanding of basic measurement theory but one common misconception about the inferences that can be drawn should be pointed out here. In a nutshell it is: correlation does not indicate causation. All that the correlation coefficient tells us is the strength and the direction of the linear relationship between the two sets of scores, not that one variable causes the other.

The rank order correlation
Where the two sets of scores are on an interval scale the method

Table 6.14 – Calculation of the product–moment correlation between an English and a mathematics test.

Pupil	English test x	Mathematics test y	x^2	y^2	xy
A	38	30	1444	900	1140
B	25	18	625	324	450
C	35	26	1225	676	910
D	22	17	484	289	374
E	40	17	1600	289	680
F	42	26	1764	676	1092
G	41	16	1681	256	656
H	41	37	1681	1369	1517
I	37	21	1369	441	777
J	30	16	900	256	480
K	31	37	961	1369	1147
L	41	37	1681	1369	1517

$n = 12$ $\Sigma x = 423$ $\Sigma y = 298$ $\Sigma x^2 = 15415$ $\Sigma y^2 = 8214$ $\Sigma xy = 10740$

Using formula [6.13]

$$rxy = \frac{(12 \times 10740) - (423 \times 298)}{\sqrt{\{[12 \times 15415 - (423)^2][12 \times 8214 - (298)^2]\}}}$$

$$= \frac{128880 - 126054}{\sqrt{[(184980 - 178929)(98568 \times 88804)]}}$$

$$= \frac{2826}{\sqrt{(6051 \times 9764)}}$$

$$= \frac{2826}{7686.48}$$

$$= 0.368$$

described above is appropriate for measuring the strength of the relationship. But we have already seen that rank orders can be used to indicate the relative position of children in a list and it is easy to correlate two sets of ranks using Spearman's rank order correlation (usually abbreviated ρ (rho) and sometimes r_S) if formula [6.13] or one of its variants is used.

A very simple formula is used to calculate ρ. It is

$$\rho = 1 - \frac{6\Sigma d^2}{N(N^2 - 1)} \qquad [6.14]$$

where

Σd^2 = the sum of the squared differences between ranks
N = the number of pairs of ranks

The use of this formula is illustrated for the data in table 6.15 but here ranks have been substituted for the raw scores. Assigning 'one' to the highest on each test, 'two' to the next highest and so on to rank 12 and giving the mean of the ranks covered in cases of a tie occurring, we have data as shown in table 6.15.

Notice in the above list that a considerable number of tied ranks has occurred especially in the mathematics test (which was not a terribly good discriminator between pupils' achievements). When tied ranks occur, the resulting answer is not a particularly good approximation to r_S. In this event it is probably simplest to calculate a corrected r_s using the formula for the product–moment correlation r_{xy} (formula [6.13]) but replacing the scores by the ranks assigned. Readers should check that the summary data for computation of r_{xy} from table 6.15 are as follows:

$$\Sigma xy = 551.5$$
$$\Sigma x = 78$$
$$\Sigma y = 78$$
$$\Sigma x^2 = 648$$
$$\Sigma y^2 = 646.5$$

By substitution into formula [6.13] we get

$$r_S = \frac{(12 \times 551.5) - (78 \times 78)}{\sqrt{[12 \times 648 - (78^2)][12 \times 646.5 - (78^2)]}}$$

$$= \frac{6618 - 6084}{\sqrt{[(7776 - 6084)(7558 - 6084)]}}$$

Table 6.15 – Calculation of the rank order correlation, ρ.

Pupil	Rank order on English test X, R_X	Rank order on mathematics test Y, R_Y	$^dR_X - R_Y$	$(^dR_X - R_Y)^2$
A	6	4	2	4
B	11	8	3	9
C	8	5.5	2.5	6.25
D	12	9.5 =	2.5	6.25
E	5	9.5 =	−4.5	20.25
F	1	5.5 =	−4.5	20.25
G	3 =	11.5 =	−8.5	72.25
H	3 =	2 =	1	1
I	7	7	0	0
J	10	11.5 =	−1.5	2.25
K	9	2 =	7	49
L	3 =	2 =	1	1

$$\Sigma d^2 = 191.5$$

$$\rho = 1 - \frac{6 \times 191.5}{12\,(12^2 - 1)}$$

$$= 1 - \frac{1149}{1716} = 1 - 0.6696$$

$$= 0.330$$

$$= \frac{534}{1682.98}$$

$$= 0.317$$

Notice that the presence of ties tends to inflate the correlation coefficient but that the correction exerts only a relatively small effect. Generally, correlation between ranks tends to be a lower estimate of the strength of the relationship than the product–moment correlation between the raw scores on which the ranks are based.

At this point it is necessary only to point out that there are other types of correlation coefficient for use with different types of data. Most of the teachers' needs in dealing with test results are met by one or other of the two methods described. Note, however, that there is no such thing as *the* correlation between two tests and that the use of different methods produces different values. Tables have been prepared and are included in most basic statistics text books which give the probability that an obtained result is a chance occurrence. By convention, two cut-off points, or levels of significance, have been adopted by which to decide these probabilities. These are the 0.05 and 0.01 levels of significance. The former indicates that the result you have obtained would be expected by chance in only five cases out of 100, the latter only once in 100. Thus in the first instance you are taking the risk that five times out of 100 you will report a chance difference as a real one, and so on. The sample size is important. For example, if you have a sample of 20 pairs of scores the product–moment correlation has to reach ± 0.43 and ± 0.55 to be declared significant at the 0.05 and 0.01 levels respectively.

SUMMARY

In this chapter the reader has been introduced to some of the basic 'statistical' ideas in the use and interpretation of tests. If topics of a similar nature to those in chapter 4 are also included you should by now be conversant with the following principal ideas:

(1)   If measurement is defined as 'the assignment of numbers to objects or events according to rules', two main types of scale are achieved by most assessment in education: these are the *interval scale* and the *ordinal scale*. In interval scales, distances between scores can be interpreted whereas in ordinal scales only the order of scores can be interpreted. Most measurement in physical sciences is on *ratio* scales which have a zero point as well as order and interval. Sometimes a number is nominally assigned to a characteristic of a person, '0' for male '1' for female. This is occasionally known as a *nominal* scale but it has neither order, interval nor zero point.

(2)   Because scores in education have no zero point they can be interpreted only in relation to a larger number of scores obtained by a group of children.

(3)   How to tabulate frequency distributions, and how to find and use some very simple summarizing indices such as the *inclusive range, quantiles* (percentiles, deciles, etc.); how to construct and use an *ogive*.

(4)   The characteristics of *three measures of central tendency* – mean, median and mode – and their general *lack* of applicability to criterion-referenced scores.

(5)   The distribution of scores for large groups can be described by a smoother curve almost fitting the tops of the histogram or smoothing out the frequency polygon. The resulting shapes can be skewed negatively or positively, can have a single mode, several modes or no mode, and vary in their degree of similarity to the normal distribution.

(6)   Two sets of scores may have similar means but very different shapes. The need for the measurement of the amount of variation in a set of scores (individual differences in the scores) is met by the calculation of the *variance* (a squared index) and the *standard deviation* (a linear index). Methods of calculation of these values have been demonstrated.

(7)   Where a distribution of scores is normal the percentages of scores which fall between the mean and units of the standard deviation along the horizontal axis are known.

(8)   Where the standard deviations of distributions are different no meaningful comparison can be made between a raw score on one distribution and a raw score on another. For this reason standard (or 'z') scores may be calculated.

(9)   In a normal distribution, a direct conversion between various types of standard scores (including percentiles, stanines and 'T-scores') can easily be made (figure 6.11).

(10)   Because percentages of scores in various segments of a normal curve are known, distributions which are not normal can easily be normalized.

(11)   Published norms are often of variable quality. Because of this, certain fundamental questions about the appropriateness of norms to the children tested by the teacher need to be asked.

(12)   The use and interpretation of two types of coefficient of correlation (the Pearson product–moment coefficient for interval scores and the Spearman rank-order coefficient for ordinal scores).

7

Reliability of Assessments

This chapter presents one of the most important concepts in assessment theory. It is rather technical and requires that the reader understand some pre-requisites. These have in fact been dealt with in chapter 6 so readers should make certain that the concepts of *mean, variance, standard deviation* and *correlation* have been grasped if they are to make intelligent use of the material in this chapter. Other important ideas about measurement will be introduced in contexts which teachers will recognize as familiar classroom applications.

Basically, the chapter attempts to deal with the problem of consistency of an assessment. The first section examines the concepts of errors of measurement and shows that the results or scores of a test vary both within an individual at different times as well as between individuals. Some sources of variance in test scores are identified and a distinction drawn between 'true' and 'error' variance. The problem of estimating reliability is seen as that of differentiating these types of variance, and several methods of doing so are described with examples. Readers are then shown how to use these results in the estimation of a child's true score and the size of the error in the estimate as well as how to decide whether scores by two children on the same test represent a real or a chance difference in the ability measured. Some special problems in the reliability of open-ended or essay type assessment are discussed in this chapter and a method of estimating the reliability of criterion-referenced tests is described. Finally, the importance of the concept of reliability for teachers who construct their own tests or use those of others is summarized.

ERROR IN TEST SCORES

The essential problem in the study of reliability is to determine the extent to which test scores are in error. Suppose a test which claims to measure reading comprehension has been given to a class of children. On the test, which has a mean of 50 and a standard deviation of ten, John scored 48 and Mary 52. From the raw scores (the scores actually obtained following marking) it is obvious that Mary's score was the higher, but not by a very large amount. Before teachers conclude that Mary's reading comprehension (which is slightly above average) is better than John's (which is only just below average) they will need to know how much error is present in the measurement for it is quite possible that on a second testing occasion John's score would be higher than Mary's, thus reversing the conclusion if hastily made. The important point is that error is *always* present even when we measure the same attribute several times, but the results of a test are of little use to us unless we find some consistency in them. It really would not be at all helpful to have to conclude that Peter's arithmetic *ability* was average for his age on Wednesday, outstanding on Thursday, but well below average on Friday even though we expect *some* fluctuations in performance! Even where we are measuring an attribute known to be fairly unstable (for example a pupil's motivation) we ordinarily expect a certain amount of consistency if we are to make any use of the results of the assessment. We normally estimate the reliability of a test using correlation and we can think of the result as indicating the degree to which a test would be expected to give a similar result on a number of occasions.

INTRA-INDIVIDUAL VARIABILITY

An understanding of reliability can be gained by examining what would be expected to happen if John and Mary took the same test of reading comprehension a number of times. We would, of course, expect the scores to vary from occasion to occasion for all children (unless, of course, the test was so easy that John, Mary and the other children got every answer right each time, but even here boredom might set in so that they made careless mistakes). The very fact of John and Mary taking the test would alter their performance, but if we were to imagine that they took it 50 times then 50 estimates of what is known as their *true score* would be obtained. These estimates could be plotted on a graph, one for

John and one for Mary, and would probably resemble an approximation to the normal curve. Each curve would have a mean value and a spread of scores around it. Because we would think of that mean as being the best single estimate we could obtain of the true score we would interpret the curve as indicating the *error* in the scores. As before, the positive square root of that variance would be the standard deviation of the error. A similar example of variation in scores would apply if we were to draw the distribution of results when 50 children independently measured the length of the top of teacher's desk. Notice, however, an important difference. In our example of the reading comprehension test the variability we are measuring occurs in the scores obtained by a *single* child (John or Mary). For this reason we are measuring an *intra-individual* variation. This is expressed as a standard error of measurement and is explained in a later section.

INTER-INDIVIDUAL VARIABILITY

For obvious reasons the same test cannot be administered a large number of times to the same pupil but, fortunately, classroom use of tests is often satisfied by an alternative approach to the estimation of reliability. Methods of doing so will be explained more fully later in the chapter but it is useful to get an overall view here. Whereas the first approach described above implies that a reliable test is one which gives a similar score for a child on a number of separate occasions, the second approach assumes that a test is a reliable one so long as it places a *group* of children in a similar rank order each time it is used. One way of estimating this is to obtain two measures for each child in the group and to compare the two sets of scores obtained. If we assume that any similarity between the two *sets* of scores obtained is because of the relatively stable differences between children in the attribute (reading comprehension) being measured, the variation between the two rank orders is assumed to result from the other sources ('chance'). The amount of variation then indicates the size of the errors due to chance. Unlike our first approach where we are concerned with the variation in scores of single children on repeated testings, here we are examining the size of the variation *between* children: in other words our approach to reliability is now by studying *inter-individual* variation.

Whichever approach is adopted it should serve to remind the teacher that raw scores are not precise. In order to interpret them intelligently we *must* be able to estimate the size of the error inherent in the score. Even where tests are claimed by publishers to be exceptionally reliable (for example, intelligence test scores), the conclusion should be a tentative one with a stated margin of error attached to it. One of the reasons for the decline and near death of selection at 11 years of age was that mistakes were inevitably made in placement particularly at or near the cut-off point. Given that no test is completely reliable, an intelligent choice will be to select the one which provides the most dependable estimate of the ability or performance the teacher seeks to measure. Although no teacher would wittingly use a test whose reliability is little better than zero, teachers are frequently using tests whose reliabilities are unknown.

THE SOURCES OF VARIANCE IN TEST SCORES

There are several methods for estimating the reliability of a test but their usefulness depends upon the type of test used and the purpose to which it is put. For example, if teachers wish to assess a child's performance in its own right, to diagnose the child's strengths and weaknesses or to identify the amount of learning that has taken place over a period of time they will probably have little interest in comparing one child with another. In such a case a criterion-referenced test (chapter 5) will probably be used. The ideas about reliability discussed in the next sections are not particularly helpful in estimating the reliability of that type of test, however. This is partly because a criterion-referenced test which gave all children the same score might, in some circumstances, be useful but there would be no variance in the scores obtained. If the teacher is interested in making differentiations between pupils (either for placement or in the end-of-year assessment) a test which spreads the children out over a number of score values is obviously required. But not all the variance in such scores is of equal interest since it arises from a number of sources only some of which refer to the abilities or performance being assessed.

The sources of variance in scores may be classified into six main types. Briefly, they are as follows.

Stable and General Features of Children

This refers to the more or less permanent and general characteristics of the children taking the test. They include the level of ability on general traits needed for performance in a number of tests (e.g. the ability to read), general test-taking skills (contrasting the 'test-wise' with the 'test-naive' child) and the ability to comprehend and execute instructions.

Stable but Specific Features of Children

This refers to the more or less permanent but specific features of the children. They include the ability specifically required by the test and any peculiar to actual test items (e.g. the child's familiarity with certain facts but not others).

Unstable and General Features of Children

This source refers to temporary but general characteristics of the child. These are the features associated with the child's state of health, motivational level and anxiety which affect his performance throughout the test.

Unstable but Specific Features of Children

This source refers to temporary but specific characteristics of the child. For example, the ability to 'catch on' in items where particular tricks may lead to the correct solution. They also include brief fluctuations in memory or attention ('careless errors') which frequently occur during test taking.

Features Outside the Child during Assessment

Systematic or chance fluctuations which affect the administration of the test are meant here. These include the conditions of testing, the clarity of the tester's instructions, freedom or otherwise from distraction, the presence of disruptive children or any features of the administration which interact with the children taking the test. (The sex or race of the tester may be relevant here.)

Other Sources

These refer to chance variance (that is, variance not accounted for by any of the five sources above). The most pervasive source of this type of variance is probably guessing.

It is an obvious problem to decide which of the above sources of variance are of chief interest to the test user. Although guessing seems a relatively pure form of error variance teachers may not object to its contamination of the raw scores, on the grounds that pupils whose general level of ability (first source) is high are likely to be better guessers than others. Most users of tests would probably argue that the first and second sources are of special interest in the measurements they wish to make and that these, therefore, properly constitute 'true' variance. The size of these components can be minimized. For example, differences in the comprehension of instructions and in test-wiseness (first source) may be partly overcome by careful instructions and the use of practice items which provide an opportunity for all children to get the 'feel' of the tests. Nevertheless, other sources of variance would not be acceptable as being of systematic interest; for example, if the particular format or layout were a source of error in measuring the attribute in question (fifth source). In practice, most test manuals quote coefficients of reliability which help the user distinguish the true only from the undifferentiated error variance. Quite recently Cronbach and his colleagues (1972) have produced methods by which the error variance may be differentiated, that is, separated into a number of different components. The next sections are devoted to the basic problems of obtaining, using and interpreting reliability coefficients in published and teacher-made tests.

WAYS OF ESTIMATING RELIABILITY

Although a child's obtained score will vary from test to test and from time to time on the same test, his or her true score on the attribute in question would remain the same provided the occasions are close together. Cattell (1973) has described this reliability as the *dependability* of the test. It is applicable if the testings are close enough together (say, about one month) for a little or no change to be expected by learning or maturation. Any variation in actual score, therefore, is by definition 'error'. Cronbach (1971) has pointed out, however, that the meaning of error depends upon the purposes of testing. If the purpose is to assess a child's temporary condition at the time of testing then scores which vary are the goal of the assessment. However, where the score is obtained as a measure of a relatively stable attribute such as an ability, transient variation is undesirable. This raises the obvious question , already referred to: 'Which sources of variance in scores are properly regarded as error variance?' The answer is, of course, implied above: 'It all depends on the purpose of the assessment'. Given that the concern of the book is to deal with assessment within the cognitive domain, especially of ability and learning performance, it is fairly clear that we are interested in the assessment of relatively stable attributes of the child which inform our decisions in an educational context. Instability from occasion and test to test is, therefore, properly thought of as error. If teachers are interested in a systematic study of the change or growth in pupils' abilities, then a test–retest design will be adopted with a large enough interval between testings for growth to be observable. Periods of less than one year are not likely to be of much interest in this connection.

In theory we could construct a large number of forms of a test all designed to measure the same attribute. If we then gave all these forms to a group of children, we would assume that for a single pupil his or her true score for the attribute would be the same on every form of the test. The difference between the true score and obtained score would vary from test form to test form but would always constitute the error. As we make no attempt in this approach to reliability to differentiate the types of error we can write the equation (for each pupil):

$$x_i = T + e \qquad\qquad [7.1]$$

where

x_i = obtained score by the ith child
T = the unknown true score
e = the error score, which can be positive or negative

It is then assumed that for any one child the mean error over *all* forms of the test is zero. In other words, though the error on some forms of the test will be positive (i.e. will inflate the score above the true score), on other forms it will be negative. We further assume that the size of the error in one form of the test is uncorrelated with the error in another. Under these conditions the child's true score is *estimated* simply as the mean of his or her obtained scores because the error scores will cancel one another out to give zero for the error for each child.

Think of the entire group of children taking the test. Since each child would have his or her own 'personal equation' (equation [7.1]) the variance of the obtained scores can easily be shown by simple algebra to be the sum of two component variances, true variance and error variance. As a formula:

$$\sigma^2_o = \sigma^2_t + \sigma^2_e \qquad [7.2]$$

where subscripts o, t and e stand for obtained score, true and error scores respectively. Formally, the reliability coefficient is given as the proportion of obtained (total) variance which is true variance, that is

$$r = \frac{\sigma^2_t}{\sigma^2_o} \qquad [7.3]$$

Unfortunately for our formula σ^2_t is by definition unknown and unobservable! The difficulty, however, is a minor one. From equation [7.2],

$$\sigma^2_t = \sigma^2_o - \sigma^2_e$$

so formula [7.3], by substitution, becomes:

$$r = \frac{\sigma^2_o - \sigma^2_e}{\sigma^2_o} \qquad [7.4]$$

By now the reader will probably have had enough of these abstract ideas and we turn to ways in which the reliability coefficient (*r*) can be estimated. Before doing so, however, we must distinguish the reliability *index* (*r*_i) from the reliability *coefficient* (*r*) although these terms are often (incorrectly) used interchangeably. The reliability *index* is the correlation between the true scores and the obtained scores. The reliability *coefficient* is the proportion of variance in the obtained scores which is predictable from the true scores. In words, the relationship between the index and the coefficient is that the square root of the reliability coefficient is equal to the reliability index. As a formula, $\sqrt{r} = r_i$ or

$$r = r_i^2 \qquad\qquad [7.5]$$

The two fundamental types of reliability and their various methods of estimation are shown in table 7.1. For type 1 in table 7.1, the difference in emphasis between dependability and stability has been pointed out by Cattell (1973) although both are obtained by the test–retest method. *Dependability* refers to the test–retest correlation obtained from two occasions which are close together whereas *stability* applies to the test–retest correlation obtained after a longer time (say more than one month) has elapsed between the two occasions. This distinction is made to differentiate between the various sources of fluctuation that would be expected to occur over the longer period but which would be absent from the shorter.

At first sight this may appear confusing. Yet it is to be expected. The sources of variance which overlap to give the correlation between the two halves of the same test (type 2(i)a in table 7.1) will be different from those responsible for the correlation between scores obtained on the same total length test used on two occasions (type 1a). This is illustrated in figure 7.1 for a dependability coefficient obtained from two administrations of the same test taken seven days apart and a consistency coefficient of the split-half type. To simplify we classify the sources of variance as 'general', specific, 'permanent' and 'temporary' variance and can see from the diagram that the dependability coefficient includes as true variance different portions from those included in the consistency coefficient.

All these methods yield coefficients which are expressed as numbers which range from 0 to 1.0. A test with perfect reliability

Table 7.1 – Types of reliability coefficient.

Type	Name	Description	How obtained
(1) Dependability or stability	(a) test–retest coefficient	Estimates stability of scores over time	By correlating scores obtained on same test administered twice to same group of children
(2) Consistency	(i) *Internal equivalence or homogeneity*		
	(a) split-half coefficient	Estimates agreement between scores on two halves of a test	By correlating scores obtained on the two halves of a test
	(b) Kuder–Richardson coefficient	Estimates agreements between all items within a single test	By calculating proportion passing and failing each item and total test variance
	(ii) *Parallel forms equivalence*		
	(c) alternative forms coefficient	Estimates agreements between two equivalent measures of the same ability	By correlating scores obtained on two equivalent forms of a test

would obviously yield a coefficient of 1.0. By definition (formula [7.3]) the coefficient expresses the proportion of variance in the obtained scores that is attributable to differences in true scores. Thus a value for the reliability of 0.89 means that 89% of the differences in obtained scores occurs because of differences in true scores. A reliability of 0.64 means that 64% is true variance and so on. Quite obviously the error of measurement is given by the simple formula

$$\text{error} = 1 - r \qquad\qquad [7.6]$$

A reliability of 0.89 indicates 11% error of measurement and 0.64 an error of measurement as high as 36%.

Figure 7.1   Sources of true variance in the types of reliability estimate.

The Test–Retest Estimate

This is probably one of the easiest to obtain since it involves only two administrations of the same test to a given group of children. Each child obtains a pair of scores (X, Y) which are then used to calculate the correlation coefficient as already described in chapter 6. This correlation is then the reliability estimate. If the value is high it confirms that a child high in the ability tends to be highly placed on both administrations of the test, and vice versa. Referring to figure 7.1 it can be seen that temporary factors, especially the child's health and motivational level, may serve to lower the reliability estimate obtained in this way because they are not sources of true variance. Quite obviously this estimate will also vary with the time interval separating the two administrations. If it is short, the child may recall earlier answers and reproduce them; this may inflate the coefficient. If it is long, the tester will not know whether the reliability is low because of measurement error or whether there are genuine individual changes due to learning or maturation in the ability being assessed by the test. Herein lies the value of Cattell's distinction between dependability (symbolized r_d) from immediate retest and the stability (r_s) from retest after a month or two. The *constancy* of the attribute being measured (r_c) is given by the formula

$$r_c = \frac{r_s}{r_d} \qquad [7.7]$$

This has proved a most helpful formula in demonstrating the size of the fluctuations which can occur in traits which, it used to be thought, change comparatively little during a person's lifetime, for example in intelligence (see second objection in chapter 3).

The Split-half Estimate

This is calculated in exactly the same way as the test–retest coefficient only this time the x and y scores for each child are the scores on the two halves of the test. Teachers will probably find this the most convenient to calculate since only one form of the test has to be used. A test can be split into two halves in a number of ways. It is usually accomplished at random or by taking half-tests composed of odd and even items. If several items together make up a unit (as would be the case where more than one question refers to the same paragraph or to the same map) it is preferable to divide the test into odd and even *units* rather than odd and even items within units, since the latter are likely to involve some of the same response elements and may inflate the reliability coefficient. Having obtained a score for each pupil on the two subdivisions (X, Y), they are then correlated as before. Notice, however, that each subdivision of the test is only half as long as the complete test. In order to estimate the reliability of the full test, therefore, the Spearman–Brown prophecy formula is used:

$$r_{ft} = \frac{2r_{\frac{1}{2}t}}{1 + r_{\frac{1}{2}t}} \qquad [7.8]$$

where subscripts ft and ½t stand for full test and half-test respectively. Suppose a test consisting of 20 items has a reliability of 0.82, what reliability would be expected if 40 items had been used? Using formula [7.8]:

$$r_{ft} = \frac{2 \times 0.82}{1 + 0.82} = 0.90$$

Kuder–Richardson Estimates

This is really a family of methods which do not involve a division of the test or the calculation of a correlation. It assumes that each item in a test measures the same general ability and requires that each item be scored as a dichotomy, that is either 'right' or 'wrong'. The easiest to use is usually known as 'formula 20'. It is

$$r = \frac{n}{n - 1}\left(\frac{\sigma_o^2 - \Sigma pq}{\sigma_o^2} \right) \qquad [7.9]$$

where

n = number of items in a test
p = proportion passing (1) an item
q = proportion failing (0) an item
σ_o^2 = variance in test scores

Its underlying argument is a little difficult to describe. The term Σpq is the sum of the variances of all items and σ_o^2 is the total test variance. The difference between the two (technically the sum of the covariances) can be thought of as indicating how much agreement or overlap there is between scores in the items. Since overlap between items is assumed to be because of the same general ability, this is where the true variance is to be found. This definition then fulfils the requirements for a coefficient of reliability. Its calculation is shown using the scores of ten children on a ten-item test with items arranged in order of difficulty as an item-score matrix (table 7.2) following Guilford and Fruchter (1973, 411). The reader should check that the variance of the scores (σ_o^2) is equal to 8.41 and the standard deviation 2.90. Substituting in formula [7.9]

Table 7.2 – Item-score matrix for ten children on a ten-item test.

Child	|				Item						|	Total	Odd score	Even score
	|	1	2	3	4	5	6	7	8	9	10	|			
A	|	0	0	0	0	0	0	0	0	0	0	|	0	0	0
B	|	1	0	0	0	0	0	0	0	0	0	|	1	1	0
C	|	1	0	1	0	0	0	0	0	0	0	|	2	2	0
D	|	1	1	0	0	1	0	0	0	0	0	|	3	2	1
E	|	0	1	0	1	0	0	1	0	0	0	|	3	1	2
F	|	1	1	1	0	1	0	1	0	0	0	|	5	4	1
G	|	1	1	1	1	1	1	0	0	0	0	|	6	3	3
H	|	1	1	1	1	0	1	0	0	1	0	|	6	3	3
I	|	1	1	1	1	1	1	0	1	0	0	|	7	3	4
J	|	1	1	1	1	1	1	1	1	1	1	|	10	5	5
Total	|	8	7	6	5	5	4	3	2	2	1	|	43	24	19
Proportion of ones (p)	|	0.8	0.7	0.6	0.5	0.5	0.4	0.3	0.2	0.2	0.1	|			
Proportion of zeros (q)	|	0.2	0.3	0.4	0.5	0.5	0.6	0.7	0.8	0.8	0.9	|			
pq	|	0.16	0.21	0.24	0.25	0.25	0.24	0.21	0.16	0.16	0.09	|	$1.97 = \Sigma pq$		

$$r = \frac{10}{9}\left(\frac{8.41 - 1.97}{8.41}\right) = 0.85$$

When all the items are of roughly equal difficulty we can get an approximation to the value for the reliability using an even simpler formula. It uses only the number of items (n) the mean $(\bar{x})$ and the total test variance (σ_t^2):

$$r = \frac{n}{n-1}\left(1 - \frac{\bar{x}(n - \bar{x})}{n\sigma_o^2}\right) \qquad [7.10]$$

Since the mean score is 4.3, substitution in formula [7.10] gives us:

$$r = \frac{10}{9}\left(1 - \frac{4.3\,(10 - 4.3)}{10 \times 8.41}\right) = 0.79$$

The reason why the values of r obtained from formulae [7.9] and [7.10] differ is that the items in our test were of different degrees of difficulty, the easiest being item one and the hardest item ten. Even here, however, the approximate method yields a quite similar value to that using 'formula 20' (equation [7.9]). Where items are not scored dichotomously (as right or wrong), the coefficient α (alpha) developed by Cronbach may be used. It is very similar to the Kuder–Richardson (KR) 'formula 20' (equation [7.9]):

$$\alpha = \frac{n}{n-1}\left(1 - \frac{\Sigma s^2}{\sigma_o^2}\right) \qquad [7.11]$$

The meaning of the symbols is as before, but Σs^2 is the sum of the variances of the single items. It yields exactly the same result as formula [7.9] if applied to the dichotomous data of table 7.2.

It is interesting to see what would have happened if we had calculated the reliability coefficient using the split-half (odd–even) method. Total test scores have been appropriately subdivided to the right of table 7.2 and the correlation, calculated using what by now will be a familiar method, is 0.72. This estimate is lower than the higher KR coefficient because it is based on only one of the many ways in which the test could have been subdivided.

Alternative (Parallel) Forms Estimate

This method is more difficult for the teacher to carry out since it requires the construction of two tests which have similar content. It is difficult in practice to fulfil criteria by which tests may be considered parallel. They should, however, contain the same number of items designed to cover the same content, be of similar difficulty and be arranged in the same format. Instructions and conditions of administration should be comparable. Although it has certain disadvantages (for example, scores are susceptible to practice effects as in test–retest reliability) the parallel forms method can, unlike the other methods described, be used to estimate the reliability of speed tests (a speed test is one which is made up of relatively easy items which most children would be expected to get right but for the fast conditions under which they are administered). The parallel forms reliability coefficient is simply the correlation between the scores obtained by the same children on two different forms of the same test. The correlation, of course, is calculated as shown in chapter 6.

STANDARD ERROR OF MEASUREMENT

This is the most useful concept in reliability theory to the teacher. Formula [7.3] reminds the reader that reliability is defined as the ratio of true variance and obtained variance:

$$r = \frac{\sigma^2_t}{\sigma^2_o} \qquad [7.3]$$

Use of the most elementary algebra shows that formula [7.2] in this chapter can be rewritten for σ^2_t as follows:

$$\sigma^2_t = \sigma^2_o - \sigma^2_e \qquad [7.12]$$

If we substitute [7.12] into [7.3] we get:

$$r = 1 - \frac{\sigma^2_e}{\sigma^2_o} \qquad [7.13]$$

This is another expression for the reliability.

Now the standard error of measurement is actually the standard deviation of the error, so we want to derive a formula for the latter. This can easily be done by rearranging formula [7.13] and taking the square root. Solving [7.13] for σ_e we get:

$$\sigma_e = \sigma_o \sqrt{1 - r} \qquad [7.14]$$

We have now get a simple formula for the *standard error of measurement* (σ_e). This is usually indicated by the symbol SE_m which we shall be adopting from now on.

Some Uses of the Reliability Coefficient

(a)   If two tests have approximately equal standard deviations the one with the higher reliability coefficient gives the better estimate of a child's true score.

Example

Suppose we have two English tests each having mean 50 and standard deviation ten. Test A has a reliability of 0.96 and test B one of 0.64. Suppose Mary scored 56 on test A and Tony 56 on test B. How closely do these lie to the true scores? We can obtain a fair approximation of the answer to this question as follows.

Using the general formula for the standard error of measurement (formula [7.14]) we can now see its value.

Mary's score on test A (r = 0.96)

Steps in the argument are as follows:

(1)   If 0.96 is the reliability estimate (the proportion of true variance), then $1 - 0.96$ (4%) is error variance.

(2)   The standard error of measurement is, therefore, $\sqrt{0.04} = 0.2$ of the standard deviation of the obtained scores (i.e. $0.2 \times 10 = 2$ points).

(3)   Since roughly two-thirds (68%) of scores lie between true score ± one standard deviation (see section in chapter 5 on the normal curve) the odds are two to one that Mary's obtained score would not exceed 56 plus two nor fall below 56 minus two points on repeated testing.

(4)   If we want to be more confident we can use the fact that 95% of scores lie between the mean and ± two standard deviations. In this case the odds are roughly 19 to one that Mary's obtained score would not exceed 60 nor fall below 52 points. These are sometimes known as the 95% confidence intervals for the true score. To be strictly accurate, the 95% confidence interval is the obtained score ± 1.96 SE_m but it is easier to remember to use two for most practical purposes.

Tony's score on test B (r = 0.64)
Using the same argument the standard error of measurement for test B is 0.6 of the standard deviation (i.e. six points). The 68% confidence interval, therefore, is from 62 to 50 points (compared with from 58 to 54 for Mary) and the 95% interval from 68 to 44 points (compared with 60 and 52).

Notice that the measurement error is a function of the reliability and the standard deviation of the test. To give you some idea of their interdependence look at table 7.3. The body of the table shows the value of the standard error of measurement for different standard deviations and reliabilities. Notice that standard errors for the test with high reliability (5% error variance) are less than half as large as those for low reliability (25% error variance).

The interpretation of the standard error of measurement
The most helpful way of using the standard error of measurement to apply to an individual child is to think of it as the standard deviation of the child's distribution of test scores on a large number of administrations. In figure 7.2 curve A shows the distribution of scores for *all* children taking the test, curve B shows the distribution for *one* child over several occasions. In our example the standard deviation of the large curve is ten but the standard deviation of the small curve is only two when $r = 0.96$.

Although this method applied to an individual's score gives us a reasonably approximate answer to the question: 'What are the limits within which Mary's or any individual's true score is ex-

Table 7.3 – The relationship of standard error of measurement to the standard deviation and reliability estimate.

Standard deviation	Reliability		
	0.95	0.85	0.75
30	6.7	11.6	15.0
20	4.5	7.7	10.0
10	2.2	3.9	5.0

Figure 7.2   The distribution of an individual child's test scores (B) with that of all children taking the test (A).

pected to lie?', it is not a strict interpretation. It would be more correct to conclude that 68% of *all* true scores are likely to be within the limits $\pm$ SE$_m$ and 95% within $\pm$ 1.96 SE$_m$ of the obtained score. In other words, 32 out of 100 children or only five out of 100 children taking this test would be expected to have true scores *outside* these respective intervals rather than that any *one* child's true score would be inside these intervals 68 or 95 times in 100 testings.

(b)   The higher the reliability coefficient the closer the obtained score to the true score.

When we know the reliability in a group of children we can *estimate* a child's true score using the simple formula:

$$T = \bar{x} + r\,(x_i - \bar{x}) \qquad\qquad [7.15]$$

where

T = true score
$\bar{x}$ = group mean
r = reliability coefficient
x_i = raw score of ith child

This formula assumes that the true scores have a linear relationship with the raw scores and it is known as the 'least squares equation' (see Lord and Novick, 1968).

Example
Suppose Peter scored 48 on a science test (reliability 0.89) on which his year group's mean was 40 and standard deviation eight points. His estimated true score is:

$$
\begin{aligned}
T_{Peter} &= 40 + 0.89\,(48 - 40) \\
&= 47.12 \\
&\cong 47
\end{aligned}
$$

(c)   The higher the reliability the more confident we can be that the difference between two scores in the same group of children is real.

Suppose John and Helen were among the age group of 120 pupils who took the above science test and they scored 42 and 46 marks respectively. Is the difference between these scores large enough to be considered real, i.e. unlikely to have arisen by chance? Steps in the argument are:

(1)   Standard error of measurement is

$$
\begin{aligned}
SE_m &= \sigma\sqrt{1 - r} \\
&= 8\,\sqrt{1 - 0.89} \\
&= 2.65
\end{aligned}
$$

(2)   We now know that 2.65 is the estimated size of the standard deviation which would be expected in John's and Helen's

scores if they each took the test a large number of times. But we need to know what would be the standard deviation of the *differences* between a number of *pairs* of scores (one for John, one for Helen) if these were obtained. A formula for this value, known as the *standard error* of the difference (SE$_d$), is given by

$$SE_d = \sqrt{2SE_m{}^2} \qquad [7.16]$$

Thus

$$SE_d = \sqrt{2 \times 2.65^2}$$
$$= 3.75$$

(3)   When we express the ratio of the difference between the scores and the standard error of their difference we get what is known as a *t-ratio*. Obviously the larger the difference between two scores compared with the standard error of their difference, the more confident we can be that the difference is a real (as opposed to a chance) one. We find the *t*-ratio, using the formula:

$$t = \frac{x_1 - x_2}{SE_d} \qquad [7.17]$$

Thus

$$t = \frac{46 - 42}{3.75}$$

$$= 1.07$$

(4)   Now see if the value for *t* equals or exceeds the value in table 7.4. The obtained value for t_{120} (1.07) is less than 1.98. This means that a pair of scores whose difference is four (Helen scored four marks more than John) could have occurred by chance *more often* than five times in 100. We have no grounds for concluding that the difference is *unlikely* to have

Table 7.4 – Values for *t* required for significance.

		Significance level	
	Size of group	5%	1%
	20	2.09	2.85
	30	2.04	2.75
	40	2.02	2.70
	60	2.00	2.66
Look for group size minus 1	120	1.98	2.62

occurred by chance. For all practical purposes, therefore, John and Helen do not differ in science ability as measured by this test.[3]

We can extend the above ideas to calculate how large the difference between two scores must be for it to be unlikely to have arisen by chance. To have occurred by chance only five times in 100, the value for *t* must be equal to or greater than 1.98 (see table 7.4). Hence.

$$1.98 = \frac{\text{size of difference}}{3.75}$$

therefore

$$\text{size of difference} = 1.98 \times 3.75$$
$$= 7.25$$

On our test, assuming no fractions of one in the scoring and with this size of group, therefore, a difference between any two scores of about seven points would need to exist before we could conclude that the odds were 95:5 (19:1) in favour of this being a real, rather than a chance, difference. (Notice that in all these calculations the *reliability, standard deviation* and *group size* are needed.) In all these applications we have used the same estimate for the

---

[3] Full tables for *t* can be found in most basic statistical texts, usually in an appendix.

standard error of a given test by which to interpret and calculate confidence intervals for each child's score on that test. This is probably what all teachers will be able to do for their home-made tests, but it can be shown that the actual value for the standard error of measurement varies at different points along the test's range. If the reliability is calculated for a very large group of children, then different standard errors at different score points can be presented. Some published tests do indeed report different standard errors for different obtained scores. If a really crucial decision were to be taken about the confidence intervals for a given score, a teacher could use an alternative procedure proposed by Lord (1957) which enables the computation of intervals for each child. The formula is

$$SE_m \cong \sqrt{\frac{1}{n-1} x_i (n - x_i)} \qquad [7.18]$$

In this formula

SE_m = the standard error for an individual
x_i = the obtained score for that individual
n = the number of items in the test

The methods described so far are applicable to finding the reliability of tests for which scores are available. Rather different problems are experienced with essay type tests, and it is with these that the remainder of this chapter is concerned.

RELIABILITY OF ESSAYS

Essays are open-ended examinations in the sense that the titles or questions set require the writers to recall, organize and present material selected by them as relevant in answering the question. No right or wrong answers to this type of test exist (except, of course, in the factual content of the essay). Unlike standardized tests, in which the score for each child may be regarded as a value on an interval scale, essays or open-ended ratings are on an ordinal scale only. Quite erratic variation in the scoring often occurs when teachers mark essays but some of the ways in which greater agreement can be obtained by reaching consensus, before marking, as to the number and nature of the criteria to be employed in the assessment were described in chapter 4. Nevertheless, so long as methods of assessment which permit the individual differences between markers to influence results continue to be used, there is always certain to be less than perfect agreement amongst even the most well-intentioned and conscientious of judges.

The problem of the reliability of such marks can be investigated in three ways.

Method 1

We can think of the true score on an essay type examination as the mean of the assessments of all qualified raters and the reliability of the assessment as the mean correlation between the marks given by the teachers rating the essays. This value could be called the coefficient of concordance (between the examiners).

Method 2

We can construct two equivalent forms of the essay and administer it to all the children with a suitable time interval to prevent boredom. Each rater would read all the answers to both forms and a correlation between grades on the two forms would constitute an estimate of reliability. This is obviously similar to the parallel form estimate (type 2c in table 7.1) already discussed and is the method preferred by Cureton (1966).

Method 3

We can estimate the *self-consistency* of individual raters. Each teacher would be asked to mark the same essays twice with a time interval between them and the correlation between the two sets of marks calculated. This exercise is often salutary for the marker concerned but a high correlation could indicate only that the examiner is consistent in his prejudices. The 'mark–remark' or 'self-consistency' coefficient obviously yields no information whatever as to how close each mark is to the true score and is, therefore, of limited use.

Only method (2) corresponds with the reliability estimates for objective tests already discussed in table 7.1. The other two

Table 7.5 – Marks given by three raters for ten children's essays.

Child	Marker		
	1	2	3
1	10	8	13
2	3	5	16
3	12	4	9
4	5	11	17
5	7	17	15
6	14	6	9
7	11	12	10
8	9	14	14
9	16	9	11
10	4	15	13
Total	91	101	127
Mean	9.10	10.10	12.70
Standard deviation	4.11	4.20	2.72

methods refer to the consistency between *markers* or within a *single marker* on different occasions. In them the error attached to the ratings refers to the variability between raters or within a single rater whereas true reliability refers to the variation in the ability or attribute being assessed. Because of this it is somewhat misleading to group the three types of coefficient under the single heading of 'reliability' although this is frequently done. We shall distinguish them by describing them as: (1) coefficient of concordance; (2) coefficient of reliability; (3) coefficient of self-consistency, respectively. Whilst each has its value, the teacher should note that it is their meaning and, therefore, the inferences that can be made from them which differ. It is only using method 2 that one could defensibly calculate a standard error of measurement, for example.

We illustrate below a simple method for obtaining an estimate of the reliability in the sense of method 1 of essay type examinations which avoids making very strong assumptions about the nature of the measurement made. It follows Lord and Novick (1968) who propose that the most effective way of studying essay marks is to transform all observed scores into rank orders and to

Table 7.6 – Marks in table 7.5 transformed to rank order.

Child	Marker			Sum of ranks
	1	2	3	
1	5	7	5.5	17.5
2	10	9	2	21
3	3	10	10	23
4	8	5	1	14
5	7	1	4	12
6	2	8	9	19
7	4	4	8	16
8	6	3	3	12
9	1	6	7	14
10	9	2	5.5	16.5

see how consistently a number of markers agree as to the relative merits of the children's work: that is, to obtain an estimate of concordance. The layout in table 7.5 illustrates the marks given (out of 20) by three hypothetical markers for ten children.

Unfortunately these teachers had failed to agree their marking criteria beforehand such that child two, who is an appalling speller, is penalized by markers one and two but evaluated highly for content by marker three who is indifferent to spelling deficiencies! Notice also that the markers are using different implied scales. Not only are the mean values different but, more importantly, so are the standard deviations. Marker three is most generous and also makes less differentiation amongst individual children than the other two markers. It would clearly make no sense to claim that the mean of the three scores for each child estimates the true score if the three markers are using different scales.

In table 7.6 each marker has placed the scripts in rank order. These values can now be used to calculate the correlations between each pair of markers (r_{12}, r_{23}, r_{13}). Using the procedure described in chapter 6 we find the following values:

$$r_{12} = -0.32$$
$$r_{23} = +0.38$$
$$r_{13} = -0.81$$

Thus the average correlation, $\bar{r}$, is given by

$$\bar{r} = \frac{-0.32 + (+0.38) + (-0.81)}{3}$$
$$= -0.25$$

Remember that a positive correlation indicates that there is a tendency for children who receive an above-average mark from one rater to receive it from the other. A negative correlation shows the tendency for children rated above average by one marker to be rated below average by the other. The more cases there are of the former, the higher the concordance between the two raters. Marker one is obviously employing very different criteria from the other two markers. In fact, if marker one rates a child as above average, the other two seem more likely to rate his score lower than average: this is suggested by the negative correlations. Markers two and three have achieved some agreement, but it is not very strong. If a result such as this was obtained, it would be very difficult indeed to know what meaning could be attached to the scores given and the teachers clearly have a lot of collaboration to do before marks are given in the future for this kind of work!

It is not very likely that teachers will find time to have the work graded by more than three independent raters. In this case only three correlations and their average need be calculated. There is, however, a similar technique available which provides a measure of the *overall* agreement between a number of judges: it will be illustrated briefly using the same data.

Some understanding of how this method works can be given by thinking of what would have happened if the raters had been in perfect agreement – a most unlikely event! In this case they would each have ranked the ten children in exactly the same order: one would have received three ranks of one, a second child three ranks of two, and so on. The 'top' child would have obtained one + one + one = three, the 'second' child two + two + two = six and the 'bottom' child ten + ten + ten = 30. Notice that these constitute a series as follows: number of raters; two × number of raters; . . . number of children × number of raters. If we say we have k raters, our series will be $k, 2k, 3k, 4k, \ldots, 10k$. It is obvious from our data that we get nothing like this series. In fact our lowest sum of ranks (child five) is 12, and highest 23 (child three). Now we know what the average sum of ranks per child is. The sum of the ranks is given by

$$k\left(\frac{n}{2}(n + 1)\right)$$

and in this case $k = 3$ and $n = 10$. Thus the sum of ranks is

$$3\left(\frac{10}{2}(10 + 1)\right) = 165$$

and so the average sum of ranks is $165/10 = 16.5$. It is very easy therefore to find the variance in the sum of the ranks exactly as we find the variance in any other set of scores. Refer back to table 6.8 where you will see that the deviation for any child is given by the difference between the child's score and the mean of the group. Therefore the deviation for child one in table 7.6 is given by $(18 - 16.5)$, for child two $(21 - 16.5)$ and so on. Squaring these values, summing over all ten children and dividing by the number of children therefore gives us the actual variance in the ranks (s^2). This is then expressed as a proportion of the variance which would be the case if perfect agreement were obtained, actually equal to $1/12k^2 (n^3 - n)$. The coefficient of concordance (W) which indicates the strength of the overall agreement between three judges can now be obtained. It is given by:

$$W = \frac{s^2}{1/12k^2 (n^3 - n)} \qquad [7.19]$$

$$= \frac{124.5}{1/12 \, 3^2 (10^3 - 10)}$$

$$= 0.17$$

Notice that we use W where the concordance is measured between *more than* two raters, r where it is between only two raters. W is closely related to the average correlation between judges ($\bar{r}$) already obtained. To be exact, the relationship between them (W and $\bar{r}$) is given by:

$$\bar{r} = \frac{k\,(W) - 1}{k - 1} \qquad [7.20]$$

W can take only values ranging from 0 to $+1$ whereas the correlation can, of course, take values ranging from -1 to $+1$. To check that formula [7.20] holds substitute $W = 0.17$ and $k = 3$ from our example:

$$\bar{r} = \frac{3\,(0.17) - 1}{3 - 1} = -0.25$$

which agrees with the value already obtained.

There are other methods of assessing the reliability of essays depending upon the purpose of the marking, but these are not referred to here. Examples of reliabilities obtained for essay marking have been given by Gosling (1966). A large number of rating scales and procedures have been adopted so it is difficult to compare the results obtained. A selection of values reported is given in table 7.7.

It is clear from table 7.7 that interest has persisted for a very long time and that values of the coefficients vary with the procedure adopted. It is possible by careful preparation of marking schemes, the training of examiners and the use of multiple marking that is both analytical and impressionistic to increase the reliability of the essay as a technique for the evaluation of learning. Teachers are unlikely to have the time or resources for such elaborate schemes and will probably come to rely more heavily on alternative tools of assessment where more objective standards may be achieved.

It is instructive for teachers to examine the coefficients listed in table 7.7 to see whether much value can be gained from such results. In the first place, only the type of estimate made by Finlayson would permit the teacher to estimate the size of the error component in each grade awarded. To do this, the standard deviations would also be required. But a coefficient as low as 0.60 would indicate that a large margin of error is present. The other coefficients are of concordance (agreement between markers) and of self-consistency (agreement between the same marker on a number of occasions on which the same answers were marked). To take the latter first, consider

Table 7.7 – Some examples of reliability of essay tests.

Situation	Value of coefficient	Type	Source
(a) British university scholarships	0.51	concordance	Hartog and Rhodes (1936)
(b) School compositions	0.25 to 0.59	concordance	Cast (1940)
(c) School certificate essays	−0.04 to 0.95	self-consistency	Hartog (1941)
(d) American university qualifying exam	0.55 to 0.83	concordance	Stalnaker (1934)
(e) School exam	0.66	self-consistency	Philips (1948)
(f) Grammar school entrance	0.72 to 0.88	self-consistency	Nisbet (1955)
(g) Primary school	0.60 to 0.80	parallel forms	Finlayson (1951)
(h) Students	0.55 to 0.77	concordance	Vernon and Millican (1954)
(i) Australian university students	0.60 to 0.89	concordance	Dunstan (1959)
(j) O-level biology	0.64	concordance	Head (1966)
(k) Biology exam (Australia)	0.35 to 0.79	self-consistency	Lucas (1971)

situations (c) and (k). They demonstrate that very large discrepancies can exist within a single marker. Such fluctuations may be so large that it would be most unwise to draw conclusions about the children from them, not to say grossly unfair! The best use that teachers can make of this coefficient is to check their own consistency and correct it if necessary. Though the high values suggest that greater self-consistency can be attained they do not show that it is objective or even fair. For this reason it is recommended that these types of estimate are used to check the marking procedures and only indirectly to draw inferences about children's work. In any case essays are almost always so unreliable that their proper place seems to be as part of a programme of assessment, but always marked by more than one teacher, among other alternative assessment techniques.

To turn to the concordance estimates which are all, in fact, average correlations rather than values for W, and as such show the average agreement amongst pairs of markers. Notice that even the highest (0.89) reveals considerable disagreement. A correlation of 0.71 between the sets of marks by two judges indicates that only 50% of the individual differences in one marker's list can be predicted from the other's list! Knowing that the same teacher's marks vary from time to time and that different teachers' marks vary is 'common sense', but quantification of the error will often emphasize the dangers inherent in educational decision making on the basis of essay marks. It is not possible to specify a cut-off point by which to decide whether to accept or to reject the marks as meaningful. But if the teachers concerned have agreed on a marking schedule, have practised its use and are satisfied that the essay is a valid method of assessment, any set of results which yields a mean correlation between markers of less than 0.80 must be regarded as unsatisfactory, and deserves the report 'could do better'!

RELIABILITY OF CRITERION-REFERENCED TESTS

It must by now be clear that the concept of reliability discussed so far can be applied only to tests in which variance exists. Given the definition of reliability, it is obvious that if a test failed to distinguish between children (say if all children in a group got the same mark) it would be impossible to differentiate zero variance into true and error components! Although such a test would be useless as a norm-referenced instrument it is not entirely valueless in the assessment of criterion-referenced learning. Remember from chapter 3 that the purpose of criterion-referenced testing is often to classify learners into 'masters' or 'non-masters' of an objective so that the teacher may decide whether a pupil is ready to move on to the next objective or whether it would be advisable to spend longer on related learning in order to overcome the deficiency identified. In this usage teachers would ordinarily be delighted to find that all children in a group exhibited mastery of a given objective! In such a case the facility of the item would be 1.0 whereas we saw in chapter 4 that items with facilities of around 0.5 may be expected to maximize the variance.

Because criterion-referenced tests are designed to assess how closely a child's performance approaches the objective there is little point in determining the variance of the mean score as this would only give us an idea of the relative performance of the pupils. Instead we need to know how many individuals achieve mastery of the given objective where mastery has been defined in terms of a prescribed score (say 80 or 90%; the decision is arbitrary) on the criterion test. The methods of estimating reliability for norm-referenced tests which depend on the existence of variance, therefore, are not entirely applicable to criterion-referenced tests since their purpose is different. Because of this, there is as yet no universally agreed method for estimating the reliability of criterion-referenced tests. However, some people have attempted to obtain a reliability coefficient for criterion-referenced tests which is analogous to those for norm-referenced tests. Livingston (1972), for example, has provided a formula recommended by some writers (e.g. Mehrens and Lehmann, 1978, 107). In practice this method has been found to be unsatisfactory because it yields higher criterion-referenced reliability the greater the distance between the criterion score and the mean score. For theoretical reasons, too, the coefficient obtained in this way cannot be used to estimate whether or not a true score falls below or above a given criterion value and is of limited value.

If measurement theorists, then, are unable to provide a satisfactory method for estimating the reliability of criterion-referenced tests what can teachers do to improve the reliability of those they have constructed? Perhaps the best and simplest advice that can at present be offered is to reinterpret the concept of reliability for criterion-referenced tests in terms of the consistency with which a test makes a decision about the 'mastery state' of the pupils taking it. Normally a criterion-referenced test programme contains a number of objectives and a number of items per objective. If the objectives are relatively independent of one another there is no reason to suppose that a child who achieves the criterion score on one will necessarily achieve it on another. In this sense, then, there are as many reliabilities as there are objectives within a test. Suppose, however, as will ordinarily be the case, a given objective

Table 7.8 – Pupils achieving mastery state on two administrations of the same test.

2nd administration			
1st administration	Masters	Non-masters	Total
Masters	33 (a)	2 (b)	35
Non-Masters	7 (c)	8 (d)	15
Total	40	10	50

is assessed using a number of items, these items will constitute a test in its own right. Following a single administration, children would be classified as masters or non-masters of that objective. Let us suppose, in order to make the arithmetic easy, that 50 children take the test (not necessarily all at the same time) and as a result 35 of these reach the criterion score. In other words 35/50 are classified as masters, 15/50 as non-masters. On a second testing with the same items the corresponding numbers are 40/50 and 10/50 respectively. By plotting a simple table like table 7.8 the teacher can compare the numbers of children classed as having the same or different mastery status by the two administrations.

Quite obviously the size of the entries in cells (a) and (d) relative to those in cells (b) and (c) indicates the agreement between the two administrations. From these a simple index of *consistency of classification* can be stated. Using the symbol k (to remind ourselves that its interpretation is different from that of the usual reliability coefficient) it is:

$$k = \frac{P_o - P_e}{1 - P_e} \qquad [7.21]$$

where

P_o = the observed proportion of agreement
P_e = the expected proportion of agreement

To calculate this coefficient we must change the numbers in the cells to proportions as shown in table 7.9. In cell (a) 33 out of 50

Table 7.9 – Data of previous table as proportions (expected proportions in brackets).

1st administration	2nd administration		
	Masters	Non-masters	Total
Masters	0.66 (0.56)	0.04	0.70
Non-masters	0.14	0.16 (0.06)	0.30
Total	0.80	0.20	

pupils were classified as masters on both occasions and 33/50 = 0.66, and so on for all cells and totals in the margin. The observed proportion of agreement (P_o) is, therefore, the sum of the proportions in cells (a) and (d), i.e. $0.66 + 0.16 = 0.82$.

Calculation of the Expected Proportion of Agreement

Since the proportion of masters on the first administration was 0.7 and on the second occasion 0.8 the proportion expected to be masters on both occasions is the product of the separate probabilities, i.e. $0.7 \times 0.8 = 0.56$. By the same argument the expected proportion of non-masters on both administrations is 0.06. The sum of these probabilities (P_e) is, therefore, 0.62. Substituting in formula [7.21]

$$k = \frac{0.82 - 0.62}{1 - 0.62} = 0.53$$

We now have a single number which indicates the consistency with which a test classifies a group of children into masters and non-masters. This approach has been described as *decision-theoretic* approach to reliability. It provides a useful index of the consistency of the test but it cannot be used to estimate the child's true score nor the standard error of the measurement.

By experience and use the teacher can gradually accumulate criterion-referenced items for a single objective which exhibit high consistency of classification. These can then constitute the test of that objective. If the degree of consistency is not examined there is a danger that the test items will be measuring different things and the resulting test will thus be an unreliable one.

IMPLICATIONS FOR TEACHERS OF THE STUDY OF RELIABILITY

This section attempts to draw together the importance of reliability for teachers' assessments of children.

(1)   Assessment is both time-consuming and potentially dangerous (chapter 2). Assuming that it is undertaken to provide information which will be used to evaluate and make decisions about children, we need to know how much confidence can be placed in the results. Estimating the reliability of the test or essay is one method of obtaining this information. If an assessment results in measurement (as in a test), in which pupils can be placed in rank order, or in a practice by which pupils are allocated to the next stage in learning, then the means exist for estimating how well our methods accomplish these ends.

(2)   A study of the reliability of an assessment alerts the teacher to its degree of consistency. Inconsistency (error) is inevitable: it results from many sources which teachers need to know if they are to interpret a result intelligently.

(3)   When choosing a published test or considering its adoption, teachers are helped if they understand how to place confidence intervals around the score obtained by any child. This can be accomplished only by using the standard error of measurement. All other things being equal the test with the highest reliability is the most useful.

(4)   There are many ways of estimating reliability (table 7.1). Each permits a different conclusion. In reading test manuals the teacher is helped by knowledge of the features of the reliability quoted. (Tests produced by the National Foundation for Education Research normally quote Kuder–Richardson coefficients.)

(5)   The construction of tests is time-consuming. There is little point using one whose scores contain a great deal of error. If the interpretation of those scores is to be used to make

important decisions about children's learning a check on the test's internal consistency can easily be conducted and requires only one administration of the test. Reliable tests can be retained for later use, unreliable tests can be discarded.

(6) Estimation of the reliability of an assessment makes its degree of error explicit. Through a study of reliability greater accuracy of assessment can be achieved: this is an important aspect of professional accountability.

(7) Knowledge of the concept of reliability helps to assess the consistency with which markers carry out their task. Estimates of reliability of essay type tests show how the opinions of teachers differ and how the opinions of a single teacher about the same piece of work change over a period of time. Without knowledge of reliability no method of improving the consistency of an assessment can be adopted.

8

Validity of Assessments

Having constructed or obtained a reliable test one is now faced with a question crucial in deciding whether it should be used. The teacher may have concluded that if the test is a reliable one then it is a good one: but this is not so. One can obtain highly reliable assessments, yet these can quite easily remain of little or no use in the appraisal of children. Indeed, probably the most important problem in the use of assessment – and one which, unfortunately, teachers often have too little time to examine – is whether the test measures what it is supposed to measure. It really is of little significance if we can say of a test: 'it yields obtained scores which deviate only by a small amount from the corresponding true scores but I really haven't much idea what the test measures, and therefore, what I can infer about a child from the score obtained'.

Some examples may clarify this point. Whereas at one time it was widely agreed that intelligence test scores indicated a child's 'innate general cognitive ability' (Burt, 1955), today there is far less agreement as to what can be inferred from them. Vernon (1979) has presented a summary of recent changes in the interpretation of intelligence test scores. In clinical work and in child guidance, for example, intelligence tests (which are certainly reliable in the sense discussed in chapter 7) are often used in determination of brain damage or in the identification of children who seem to need remedial or special education. One could say that the tests are valid for these latter purposes, but not in the determination of the genetic potential for learning, though this was widely held to be the case 30 years ago (Cronbach, 1975) and is still apparently believed to be true by some. In similar fashion, the author was involved with a colleague some years ago in the use of a test designed to assess the child's style of thinking (Satterly and Brimer, 1971). It proved to have satisfactory reliability in distinguishing certain qualitative differences in approaches to a task, but subsequent work has failed to show that the test correlates with any criterion of behaviour or performance in school. This suggests that the test scores have failed to check against some other observation and that the test is, therefore, of little identifiable external merit. These two examples should serve to emphasize the most important aspect of test validation; namely, that one cannot meaningfully talk of an *assessment* or *test* being valid or invalid, but only its *interpretation* as valid or invalid for *some specified purpose*. In the general sense, however, we can think of the test measuring whatever causes, or enables, some individuals to get high but others low scores on that test.

`The truth of Cronbach's (1971, 445) statement, 'validation of an instrument calls for an integration of many types of evidence' must already be apparent. It will become clear that no teachers are going to be able to conduct many of the studies that are relevant to the establishment of the validity of a given test: they are going to have to take on trust, or not, as the case may be, what is claimed by test publishers. A classroom teacher who constructs his or her own test or other instrument for assessment of the outcomes of a new course on, say, child care, may be prevented by lack of time from carrying out a systematic study of its properties. And yet it is invaluable for this teacher to know of the problems in validity if only to recognize the limitations of the assessment. But such knowledge is also necessary if teachers are going to exercise an intelligent judgement as to whether the evidence for validity presented by a test's publisher is adequate – or even downright unsatisfactory! In one sense, then, there is continuity in the twin concepts of reliability and validity. Although separated for convenience, they are both important in examining claims that any test or other method of assessment should be adopted and used.

TYPES OF VALIDITY

Assessments are made for variety of purposes (chapter 1). The study of validity is, therefore, the study of how well these purposes are fulfilled. Each type of purpose requires a different method of investigation. To simplify this problem, a threefold classification of validities is usually adopted:

(1)   *content* validity;

(2)   *criterion-related* validity;
(3)   *construct* validity.

The teacher can investigate all these aspects, if necessary. Each type of validity poses a different question about the assessment as shown in table 8.1. In the sections which follow we shall provide examples of these types of validity and show, briefly, how teachers can obtain information on which to base decisions about the inferences that can be drawn from the results of the assessment.

Face or Faith Validity?

Before discussing the three types of validity listed above brief reference must be made to the concept of 'face validity'. Some writers fail to distinguish this type from content validity but they are not the same. Whereas claims for content validity are substantiated by evidence that the test measures what it claims to measure, face validity claims are unsubstantiated.

A fairly recent example of tests which gained widespread credibility amongst psychologists and educators on claims for face validity is provided by the so-called tests of creativity. These tests were devised to sample rather trivial but measurable components of the kind of thinking apparently characteristic of creative people. These included originality and novelty of response, fluency in suggesting new solutions to old problems and freedom from the restraints and inhibitions which characterize most (non-creative) people. Though these may well be global descriptions of what is involved in some types of creativity, the tests themselves (use of objects; making up titles for stories, etc.) have failed to correlate highly with one another, have not been shown to correlate substantially with external criteria of creativity, and have tended to trivialize the concept. The only claims for validity as tests of creativity, therefore, have come from the opinions of test constructors and users. For this reason Cattell has justifiably renamed the concept 'faith validity'.

Content Validity

A common use of classroom tests is to ascertain to what extent the children have learned what they have been taught or expected to learn under guidance. This might be because the teacher or school

Table 8.1 – Types of validity and their purpose in education.

Type	Question asked	Purpose
(1) Content	Do the items and the observations they permit actually sample the domain of tasks the assessment is intended to measure?	To ensure that children are assessed by items which cover the objectives of teaching in proportion to the importance attached to them
(2) Criterion-related (a) predictive ability	Does the assessment predict the performance of children on an educationally meaningful criterion?	To decide if the assessment should be used to draw inferences about future performance in selection of pupils, or for placement in instructional alternatives according to the result
(b) concurrent validity	Does the result of the assessment agree with the present status of children on some independent external criterion?	To decide if the results of the assessment generalize to another made at the same time
(3) Construct	Does the test measure what it claims to measure? Is the psychological or educational theory behind the test sound?	To see if the inferences drawn from the results are in agreement with theory and other evidence

wishes to evaluate a curriculum, because the teacher believes that the test provides a goal which motivates pupils or because the teacher is required to provide an order of merit for the class. In each case there is need to know how well the items or problems which make up the test match the objectives of the curriculum and the actual content of the teaching and learning experiences. Content validity is an especially important concept for achievement tests and requires that the teacher or test constructor builds into the test not only the topics which were covered but also items which demand the application of the skills and concepts in the manner in which they are presented and exercised during learning.

In chapter 4 we saw how, by the use of a specification grid, the teacher can map the objectives of the teaching and the contexts in which they were learned onto the content of the assessment. Drawing these up, it will be remembered, is principally to ensure that the test adequately represents the teaching and learning that have gone on. Here the teaching and testing are under the teachers' control. If an external test is used (one set either by an external testing agency, such as the examination boards or a standardized achievement test), it will have content validity only insofar as its contents represents the teaching goals of those teachers using it.

Quite obviously from the above, it is meaningful to think of a given test as having validity for the work and assessment by one classroom teacher but not for another. The problem facing test constructors and test publishers, therefore, is to try to develop a test which reflects the generally accepted aims of teaching over a wide area – a task notoriously difficult to achieve in view of the variations that exist in an educational system free from central control. This is one of the reasons why it is often difficult to compare the effectiveness of schools since no two schools teach to an identical syllabus nor accord equal status or time to the learning of skills and concepts. Although test constructors make sterling efforts to build tests of wide validity through the inspection of innovations in the curriculum, the dangers inherent in allowing external tests to dominate the curricula have already been pointed out in the fifth objection in chapter 3. The arguments presented there encourage teachers to construct their own instruments for assessment if they wish to ensure a test's validity for their particular course of study. We conclude this section by summarizing the guidelines in the evaluation of the content validity of external tests:

(1)   Look at the test manual or publisher's blurb to see if the

content and sampling are described. For example, does a test of mathematics describe the items, the range of subject matter, the age group for which it is suitable and the relative balance between the mathematical operations and concepts it includes?

(2) Does the manual give details of who made the decision as to what is included in the test and how these decisions were made?

(3) If the test was designed to measure the objectives of a particular curriculum (say, the 'Science 5–13' curriculum) are its limitations (i.e. lack of generalizability for other curricula) expressly stated?

Courses of study, teaching methods and children's interests change. These changes may limit the lifespan of a test's appropriateness. (Note that one reading test constructed 30 years ago is still in widespread use in primary schools despite the change in the conception of reading from decoding or 'barking at print' to reading for meaning.)

The measurement of content validity
There is no way in which the content validity of a test can be measured. As Cronbach has pointed out, ensuring that the test contains homogeneous items (i.e. those which correlate highly with one another) does not ensure content validity. A test designed to contain items representing a relatively homogenous set of teaching objectives or area of knowledge (such as knowledge of the symbols for the chemical elements) is sometimes known as a domain-referenced test. If, however, the domain (i.e. all the items that would have to be devised in order to test *all* the objectives) is itself heterogeneous, then high inter-item correlation would mean that the test did *not* represent it! Unlike criterion-related validity (see below) the correlation between the items and an outside criterion is of no help in establishing content validity. Cronbach gives, as an example, the fact that knowledge of the highway code does not correlate highly with a miles-without-accident criterion. This does not indicate that the test of knowledge of the code is invalid (Cronbach, 1971, 455).

Criterion-related Validity

(a) *Predictive validity*

All tests predict imperfectly and some teachers, mindful of the dangers inherent in the attempt to predict, may prefer to restrict their interpretations of an assessment to a description of a child's achievement at that point in time. Nevertheless, there are occasions on which teachers are concerned with the usefulness of predicting some *future* performance even if these occasions are kept to a minimum. For example, some comprehensive and middle schools use tests to 'band' pupils of similar ability to share a common teaching and learning environment. Though this purpose is ostensibly to produce relatively homogeneous groups it contains an implicit prediction about future performance – relatively high or low achievement in the subject at a later stage in school career. In this case, a test taken now which predicts a later criterion effectively is said to have high predictive validity. All selection tests require this property.

There are obvious difficulties. In the first place, if we are looking for a test with high predictive validity for 'success in school' we need a criterion of that success. In the United States, grade point average (GPA) has become an almost universal criterion despite its acknowledged deficiencies. In Britain some have employed a weighting system which uses the number and level of examination successes (five points for an A, four for a B, so on: the assumptions here are too obvious to require enumeration). A firm which employs apprentices might be interested in the predictive validity of an aptitude test for achievement in engineering, or the staff of an assessment centre might value a measure of the personality of the offender as an index of suitability for alternative forms of treatment. These, too, are instances of the need for predictive validity. Unfortunately, however, if the assessment does not correlate very highly with the criterion we do not know which of three possibilities is the case. Either the assessment is a poor predictor of the criterion, or the measure of the criterion is unreliable, or both! Reliability and validity are required of both predictor and criterion, of course. In fact, although one can attach a number to the predictive validity of a test using the correlation between predictor (X) and criterion (Y), there is a mathematical limitation on the size of that correlation which is imposed by the reliabilities of both X and Y. Thus the correlation between predictor and criterion (r_{xy}) cannot be larger than the square root of the product of their separate reliabilities. Here and later in this chapter we use capital letters X, Y when referring to tests and lower case letters x, y when we mean the scores in tests X, Y respectively. As a formula:

$$r_{xy} \leqslant \sqrt{r_{xx} r_{yy}} \qquad [8.1]$$

where $\leqslant$ stands for 'is less than or equal to',

$$r_{xx} = \text{reliability of predictor}$$
$$r_{yy} = \text{reliability of criterion}$$

In this formula r_{xy} is sometimes known as the validity coefficient.

It is unlikely that many teachers are currently assessing the predictive validity of their assessments over a long period of time. In checking on the short-term predictive validity of a test, however, there is a possibility that a teacher's assessment of the criterion is distorted by memory of the score awarded to a child on the predictor. This would create a spurious impression of predictive validity. For this reason different teachers should be involved in the two assessments. A practical and simple method for determining criterion-related validity, but not as a coefficient, will be discussed following a brief consideration of concurrent validity since the method is applicable to both.

(b) Concurrent validity

Little need be said about this because the only operational difference between it and predictive validity is that the two measurements or assessments are made at or near the same time. For example, if the teacher wished to develop a questionnaire which measures 'boredom with school' the results ought, at the very least, to differentiate children who are independently rated as 'bored' or 'not bored' on everyday school behaviour. The extent to which it does so the (correlation between the two) is an index of its concurrent validity.

The measurement of criterion-related validity

One obvious way is to report the validity coefficient (the correlation) between predictor and criterion. Suppose a school uses a mathematics test (X) to help organize the sets or bands into which children are grouped, and reports the correlation of scores from this test with later success in GCSE mathematics (Y) as $r_{xy} = 0.45$. This indicates a moderate relationship between predictor and criterion. A more helpful interpretation is to find the coefficient of determination using the correlation, i.e. finding $(r_{xy})^2$. This would be interpreted as showing that 20.25% $((r_{xy})^2 = 0.2025)$ of the eventual success in mathematics can be predicted from the scores in the school test.

Example

Suppose Peter scored 59% on our mathematics test in a group of children where the mean was 42% and standard deviation ten. If the predictive validity of the test is 0.45 what score would he be expected to get in GCSE mathematics (the criterion) assuming a criterion mean of 38% and standard deviation of 12 points?

The equation used is

$$\hat{y} = r_{xy}\left(\frac{\sigma_y}{\sigma_x}\right)(x_i - \bar{x}) + \bar{y} \qquad [8.2]$$

where

$\hat{y}$ = the predicted criterion score (GCSE)
r_{xy} = correlation between test and GCSE marks
σ_x = standard deviation of test scores
σ_y = standard deviation of GCSE scores
x_i = score test
$\bar{x}$ = mean of test scores
$\bar{y}$ = mean of GCSE scores

Hence for Peter:

$$\hat{y} = 0.45\left(\frac{12}{10}\right)(59 - 42) + 38$$
$$= 47\%$$

If we wish to go further we can employ a procedure analogous to that of formula [7.14] by finding what is known as the standard error of the estimate (or prediction on the criterion $(S_{\hat{y},x})$. Thus

$$S_{\hat{y},x} = \sigma_y \sqrt{1 - (r_{xy})^2} \qquad [8.3]$$

where

$S_{\hat{y},x}$ = the standard error of the estimated value for y from a given x

σ_y = standard deviation of the criterion
r_{xy} = validity coefficient

Applied to Peter's score:

$$\begin{aligned}
S_{\hat{y},x} &= 12\sqrt{1 - 0.45^2} \\
&= 12 \times 0.893 \\
&= 10.72 \\
&\cong 11
\end{aligned}$$

This may then be interpreted as described in chapter 7. The odds are roughly two to one that Peter's score in GCSE mathematics would not exceed 58 (i.e. $47 + 11$) nor fall below 36 (i.e. $47 - 11$). The reason for this large margin of error, of course, is the low value for the correlation between predictor and criterion.

Normally, of course, teachers would not have knowledge of the actual external test scores by which to measure predictive validity in the way just described. In this case grades will be available and a very simple method – using an expectancy table – can be adopted (table 8.2). This is illustrated by the results of a school test in geography and GCSE grades received but its use with any two tests (provided one is the predictor, the other the criterion) would be appropriate. In the left hand column of table 8.2 are the school test scores (arranged in intervals of ten) and across the top the GCSE grades. Entries in the table are the percentages within each grade. Thus 59% of those who scored between 40 and 49 received grade C in the GCSE exam, and so on. No statistical expertise is required to interpret this table. The test has predictive validity in that all highest scorers (over 70 on the test) achieved grade three or better, whereas 80% of the low scorers (under 29 on

Table 8.2 – Expectancy table to calculate the predictive validity of test scores for exam success.

Test scores	GCSE grades						Total %
	F	E	D	C	B	A	
70–79				10	10	80	100
60–69			5	10	55	30	100
50–59		3	5	28	64		100
40–49		1	22	59	18		100
30–39	5	8	19	68			100
20–29	3	32	45	20			100

the test) achieved no better than a grade D. Obviously the predictive validity of the test varies at different points in its range. We can state that the probability that children who score over 70 in the school test will get a grade one is 0.8; the probability that they will get a grade two or higher is 0.9, and so on. The two principal disadvantages of the expectancy table, however, are that the number of cases from which percentages can be calculated is often small and one cannot derive a meaningful overall coefficient of validity other than the correlation from the data.

If an assessment is made and a criterion score available, then predictive or concurrent validity can be obtained by these methods. Remember, validity is not an all-or-none affair, and there is no fixed point at which a test becomes valid. But a validity coefficient which fails to attain significance at the 5% or 1% levels (see chapter 6) is not likely to be of much practical significance to a teacher.

'False positives' and 'false negatives' in prediction
There are probably few occasions on which irrevocable decisions about children are made on the basis of test score information. Nevertheless, those few areas of the country where 11+ selection persists, the decisions are inevitably subject to two kinds of error. We saw in chapter 3 that verbal reasoning tests taken at age 10–11 years do predict *some* of the variance in achievement at age 15–16 years although this can be explained in a variety of ways, including use of the self-fulfilling prophecy. Selection at 11+ years or at any

other age, therefore, involves error. In general, predicting 'success' when 'failure' results is known as a 'false positive' and predicting 'failure' when 'success' would have occurred, a 'false negative'.

No attempt is made here to examine the assumptions inherent in selection at 11 years, or at any other age for that matter. The point is that no assessment for selection is free from the two kinds of error. Mehrens and Lehmann (1978, 124-5) present a useful discussion of the costs of faulty decisions. Some of these can be assessed. But the psychological effects of 'failure' seem incalculable. Clearly some tests can be shown to commit more errors in selection than others, but the use of a single test *alone* (however valid) in making a decision is indefensible.

Construct Validity

This is conceptually different from the other two types of validity. Whereas content validity is concerned with the correspondence between the objectives of teaching and what is assessed, and criterion-related validity with the relationship between the test and outside criteria, this type of validity is concerned with establishing the meaning of the scores or identifying the construct which is theoretically responsible for the difference between children on that test.

Psychological theory is structured around a system of constructs. For example, when, early in this century, Spearman found that the scores of groups of people on a number of mental tests tended to correlate positively he sought an explanation for this overlap in terms of the construct of 'g' or general intelligence. When constructors of personality questionnaires found that those people who experienced irrational fears also claimed to be easily swayed by their feelings they borrowed the construct of neuroticism to account for, or to summarize, this correlation. Psychological theory abounds with constructs; others with which the reader will be familiar are anxiety, extraversion, self-concept, achievement, motivation, and many more. Some of these are used in education and in the everyday organization of experience. But whenever teachers ask what tests are *really* assessing or measuring they are asking for information of the validity of the construct.

The best discussions of construct validity to date are provided by Cronbach and Meehl (1966) and Cronbach (1971). The sections which follow are based upon them. At first sight it may appear to be obvious what a test measures (i.e. it may be 'face valid'). If an author claims that his test measures 'reading comprehension' and its format consists of a set of paragraphs or extracts followed by questions then, clearly, this is what it does indeed measure and further discussion is unnecessary. But if 'counter hypotheses' can be advanced and the test's author has not shown them to be false or less defensible alternatives, other names for the construct can be a distinct possibility. In the first place the test is probably subject to a time limit: then *speed* of reading may contribute to the variance in responding. If the author has not established by investigation the time limit necessary for all children to respond then he has not eliminated the possibility that speed, as well as comprehension, is being measured. (One well-known test of reading, widely used in Britain, derives a measure of accuracy, speed and comprehension from the same set of paragraphs, so the example is not far-fetched!) Secondly, the questions set may emphasize recall of factual information in the text. This places too much stress on memory, not enough on understanding, for it to be construed as assessing reading comprehension. Thirdly, the passages could well contain words of differential familiarity to the children. If so, is the test also measuring vocabulary? Finally, many of the passages appear to be 'cooked up' for the reading test and to have little or no literary merit or interest for the children in the age group. If so, are the passages so boring that readers, able to read the extracts, nevertheless lack the motivation to do so? The important point here is not that a test can be a 'pure' measure of a single construct but that in a study of validity the competing claims for other explanations should be minimized. Indeed, all tests used in education will tap motivational components but it is part of a long process to establish just how much of test score variance is attributable to constructs other than the one the test ostensibly claims to measure.

Any performance by a child is determined by an unknowable combination of the characteristics of the test, the child, the test situation and so on. No one is more aware of this than the person who has tried to establish the construct validity of an instrument! Nevertheless, marketed tests are usually presented as if an interpretation of scores in terms of a single construct were intended. The processes of construct validation are the means whereby claims for a single interpretation are investigated.

Before we look at these processes one or two other words of caution are in order. Suppose one hypothetical test of comprehension contains information with which some respondents are already familiar. If they can answer the questions without careful reading of the passage than the test is not measuring *their* reading comprehension. In other words a test may be a valid measure of construct X for some pupils but not for others! Quite obviously, too, if the material of the test is familiar to pupils from one culture but not to those from another, the test may be valid for the children in one group but not for the other. This is one reason why statements about the differences between racial groups in mental test scores should be viewed with the greatest caution.

How, then, may construct validity be investigated? Basically, three methods have traditionally been adopted. Some will be beyond the scope of most teachers but all should be understood by teachers who aim to make an informed choice of tests, or to construct their own.

Correlation methods

Although this is established practice it is somewhat circular. The test constructed by the teacher (or the newly constructed published test) is correlated with tests with an established reputation for measuring the trait being examined. For example, if the new test were of reading comprehension, then construct validity would be claimed if it correlated substantially with an existing test of the same trait name. In the validation of group administered intelligence tests, the Stanford–Binet intelligence test has been used as the criterion for many years. Understandably, some critics have objected to the logic of this method. In the first place, it relies on the construct validity of the criterion itself and assumes that it measures what it claims to measure. Secondly, because construct validity is claimed for the new test if it does indeed correlate highly with the reference test, then the new test will yield almost the same information about individual differences as the one against which it is being validated. If this is so, why bother to construct a new test? One answer to this question is, of course, that the 'new' test may be more convenient to use and to score and cheaper to produce than the criterion test. But it is small wonder that one critic has described this process of construct validation as 'finding out what we know already'. Given that the arbitrary specification of one test as *the* criterion for a construct suffers from these deficiencies it can be seen that test validation does not end with this type of demonstration. Other types of evidence will also be needed. Merely to show high correlations between the test under study and other tests is of comparatively little interest in itself.

Methods of factor analysis

These are mathematically quite sophisticated. Basically, the techniques analyse the interrelationships among a *number* of tests (say a dozen at least) and try to account for them in terms of a smaller number of constructs. These underlying (or source) traits (or factors) are assumed to be responsible for the overlap in variance among the actual tests and can be used to show how much of the variance in each test can be explained by more than one construct. Each test receives a correlation (known as 'loading') with the construct and those with the highest loadings are assumed to be the best measures of that construct. In this way, an investigator can gradually build up a picture of what a test measures. If it repeatedly receives a high loading along with other tests on a single factor, examination of the content of the tests should enable the investigator to identify what they have in common and hence name the construct. This account is too brief to give more than a rough idea of the procedure but interested readers could refer to a clear introduction to factor analysis by Child (1970). Unfortunately factor analysts invariably disagree as to which is the most appropriate technique amongst many and no teacher untrained in their use is likely to be in a position to re-examine one solution in the light of the alternative solutions from other techniques.

There are other difficulties in the factor analysis of educational tests. When scores obtained by children on a number of tests of achievement are factorized one typically finds that they can be accounted for by very few factors (Cronbach, 1971). This suggests that tests which have high 'face validity' (i.e. appear to be testing an easily definable attainment, separable from other attainments) nevertheless appear also to be measuring much the same thing as one another! To the teacher, this merely signifies that pupils best in one subject are also among the best in others, but it presents some difficulties for this method of construct validation.

In general, then, the results of factor analysis help to add one kind of information about what a test measures which must be considered alongside other information in a lengthy process of establishing test validity.

Deliberate attempts to alter test scores

These techniques are based on a simple rationale. If a test constructor claims to know what his tests measure he should be able to predict the effect upon them of a logically related treatment. Although this is unlikely to be a great deal of use in educational tests of cognitive outcomes it has been employed with psychological tests which are of interest to teachers. Karmel and Karmel (1978, 109) cite as an illustration the case of a test of anxiety. One would expect such a test to be susceptible to the influence of stress which, if the investigator did not have ethical objections, could then be experimentally administered, and its effects on scores examined. Jacobs (1966) has carried out a study which might serve as a model for investigations of this kind using educational tests. He studied the effects of coaching on test scores. Provided the coaching is in the use of those techniques which the test is designed to assess, a demonstration (with suitable experimental control) that scores are influenced by this coaching would strengthen the author's argument that the test does indeed measure what it claims. Given that *all* educational tests involve motivational components as well as those it is intended the tests should measure, it is possible to estimate the degree to which scores depend on motivation by experimental manipulation. This could be done using instructions and techniques to enhance the motivation of some groups of children drawn up at random but to depress it amongst others.

Which method?

Teachers are likely to find correlational techniques the easiest by which to check the validity of their tests. Factor analysis requires computing facilities and some mathematical expertise. Increase in test scores as the result of coaching in the relevant skills is corroborative evidence of validity, but only mildly so. But always remember to check the validity data presented by publishers when using standardized tests.

SUMMARY

The process of validating tests is a long and never-ending investigation of the behaviour of tests in a variety of contexts and for a variety of purposes. Information comes from judgements of how closely they match what has been taught, how well they correlate with a criterion in the present or future and how successfully they measure what they claim to measure. Teachers can contribute to this information, although establishing construct validity presents considerable philosophical as well as methodological problems. The teacher as teacher is unlikely to play an extensive part in the statistical analysis of a test's relationship with other tests, nor in the development of a theoretical network which helps to explain the inferences that may be permitted by a test's scores. Readers interested in this topic could refer to an excellent discussion of this aspect of validity ('nomological networks') by Cronbach (1971, 475–84).

The fact that a test has been used by teachers for a very long period of time and has come to be accepted by them as valid is, in itself, no particular recommendation. The longevity of a certain reading test, now 30 years old, whose validation studies were not impressive and which provides only limited inferences, testifies to the truth of this comment. Such is the inertia in school assessment that more recent and technically superior tests which measure a number of components in reading skill are slow to be adopted.

Although no universally acceptable answer to the question: 'What does this test measure?' is easily found it is, nevertheless, a question that every test user and everyone who makes use of a score as part of an assessment needs to ask constantly. We have described the sort of answers to look for insofar as criterion-referenced and content validities are concerned. The teacher interested in the construct validity of a published test should set the following as a standard interrogation of the manual or publishers' claims (these are based on pp. 29–31, 46–8 of *Standards for Educational and Psychological Tests* 1974, published by the American Psychological Association):

(1) If the test is to measure a theoretical construct, it should *define* that construct in terms of the chief kinds of evidence that the test will provide. For example, if the test claims to be a test of the development of children's mathematical concepts, the concepts should be stated and the contexts in which they are to be tested described.
(2) The manual should summarize the evidence available to substantiate the above interpretation.

(3) Any evidence available concerning the relationship of the test scores to other established, conceptually linked, tests should be given.

(4) The age range for which the test is valid should be explicitly given. Any restrictions on its general use must be fully explained.

9

Setting Standards

HOW CAN STANDARDS BE SET?

One of the objections to assessment advanced in chapter 2 was that tests can become the objectives of teaching. Standardized tests are, of course, chiefly used in norm-referenced assessment and are designed to maximize the variance within a representative group of respondents. This is achieved by the deliberate construction of tests composed of items of known and, usually, increasing levels of difficulty. Although the items are carefully constructed by writers who, from experience, have a reasoned expectation of their suitability for the children in the relevant age range, the inclusion of such an item as part of a test is based upon an empirical study of its characteristics. Although tests may become standards over time, no particular questions of standards are raised during their construction and development since any item which discriminates among its respondents is potentially useful. Criterion-referenced assessment, on the other hand, raises serious problems of standard setting, in particular the specification of the criterion or cut-off score.

Readers will recall that criterion-referenced assessment is designed to describe an individual's performance in relation to a standard held to indicate mastery of the objective. In general it is not necessary for a pupil to achieve a 100% correct score on an objective for him or her to be classified as a master of that objective. Instead a score of say, 80 or 90% is held to be appropriate. If the objective is one which forms part of a hierarchy where later objectives are logically dependent upon earlier pre-requisites then the problem of specifying a minimal acceptable level of performance arises. Critics of this process have argued that specification of the criterion score is inescapably arbitrary and that because of error of measurement and the unpredictable nature of future performance no assessor can know with confidence the score which is necessary for success or readiness for the next objective. So great is this problem that an entire issue of the *Journal of Educational Measurement* was devoted to the issue of standards and criteria (Volume 15, Winter, 1978).

Glass (1978) has identified six techniques by which criterion scores have been determined. They are presented in the following section.

Techniques for Determining Criterion Scores

Study of the performance of a large group of comparable children

This is an extension from norm-referenced testing. In order to determine what is a reasonable level of expectation for a group the *median* score for pupils of the same type (who had the best teaching available) is taken as the most appropriate single reference point for establishing the criterion score.

Counting backwards from 100%

Mastery does not indicate perfection. Teachers and other experts in the relevant subject area try to reach agreement and decide how far a master shall be allowed to fall short of perfection. This decision is, obviously, arbitrary and the criterion score will depend upon how tough or lenient the 'experts' are prepared to be.

Study of the performance of established masters

In this method a study is undertaken of the performance of established masters on the items which test the attainment of objective. Their performance is then taken as the criterion score. Glass calls this 'bootstrapping on other criterion scores'.

Judging minimal competence

This is the method recommended by Ebel (1972). Experts (teachers) study a test or an item and then declare that a child with minimal competence should be able to achieve such and such a score. The basis for the expert's judgement may well have been acquired from knowledge of the results of the first three methods, of course.

Two kinds of objection can be offered to this method. In the first place, empirical studies have shown surprisingly large disagreements between experts. One example that can be cited is

from the field of medical education where, one hopes, clinical
teachers will have clear ideas as to what are the minimal levels
required for the successful practice of medicine! Nevertheless,
Meskauskas and Webster (1975) found that one group of experts
specified 68% competence on a set of items as indicative of
minimal competence, whereas another placed the level at only
49%. The second objection to this method is that it implies a
degree of knowledge on the part of the experts of the dependency
of the whole performance on mastery of the elements. The nature
of this difficulty may be clarified by use of an analogy. It is possible
to analyse the act of playing an off-drive in cricket into a number of
logically related structural elements having a natural order: grip-
ping the bat is a pre-requisite of back-lift, back-lift is a pre-requisite of a pendulum-like movement, a pendulum-like movement is
necessary to impart momentum to the ball using the full face of the
bat and so on. And yet slow-motion photographic analysis of the
greatest batsmen in action invariably reveals lack of mastery of
some of these elements. Thus, although many intellectual tasks
also yield themselves to this kind of analysis and instructional
psychology has benefited greatly from Gagné's work on the structure of task hierarchies (Stones, 1979), psychological studies have
provided no grounds for the belief that experts can specify minimal
competence with any dependability.

Decision-theoretic approaches
These were touched upon when the problems of reliability and
validity of criterion-referenced tests were discussed in earlier
chapters. They are potentially time-consuming because they involve the determination of scores on an external criterion of
mastery as well as on the criterion-referenced test itself.

Quite obviously, a criterion-referenced score which separates
masters from non-masters ('sets the standard') should differentiate
levels of competence in the performances on other tasks it is
designed to predict. It is often easier to find an example from other
branches of education and training than schools. One would
expect one apprentice who has achieved a criterion score which
classifies him as master to outperform another who has not yet
been dubbed master, in a range of other engineering tasks. If the
criterion scores so used are plotted against an objective assessment
of performance on these tasks for a group of apprentices, as shown

Table 9.1 – The relationship of criterion-referenced test scores to performance on an external criterion.

Criterion-referenced test scores \ External criterion	High performance	Low performance
Masters	P_A	P_B
Non-masters	P_C	P_D

in table 9.1, the problem of setting the standard is simply that of adjusting the criterion score to *maximize* the value of the expression:

$$f(c) = (P_A + P_D) / (P_B + P_C)$$

where c is the criterion-referenced score, P_A the number of apprentices who are masters on the criterion-referenced test and high performers on the external tasks and P_D the number who are non-masters and low performers. The rationale for this approach is obvious: the higher $(P_A + P_D)$ relative to $(P_B + P_C)$ the more effective is the prediction using the criterion score.

So far as the writer can judge there are few, if any, studies in schools which seek to determine a minimal acceptable standard (i.e. the value for the criterion score) necessary for later success although there are, in principle, no reasons why they should not be undertaken.

Operations research methods
Glass (1978) cites the work of Block (1972) as an example of this approach. Minimal standards are determined by dividing a population of learners at random into equivalent groups and teaching them until they achieve pre-determined levels of proficiency on a criterion-referenced test, say 10, 15, 20% and so on. Given that an external measure (that which one is trying to predict) is available, a graph which relates level of mastery on the criterion-referenced test to performance on the external criterion is plotted. Inspection of the graph provides a guide to the identification of the criterion-referenced score above which little or no increment in perform-

Figure 9.1   Hypothetical curve: criterion-referenced test scores and scores on external criterion.

ance on the outside criterion is obtained. The hypothetical curve relating criterion-referenced score to the external criterion is shown in figure 9.1. This method then determines the point along the horizontal (x) axis beyond which the curve of performance on the external criterion 'flattens out'. This is then established as c. Although there might well be small rises after c, it would be a matter for the professional judgement of teachers whether the time and effort needed to increase the value for c were worthwhile in the light of improvements in performance on the external criterion.

A practical, if global, application of this technique would be where a teacher attempts to determine the cut-off or criterion score on a reliable assessment to decide whether a pupil is 'ready' to progress to a more difficult topic within a hierarchically organized curriculum or to attempt a higher grade in grade-related examinations.

NEED STANDARDS BE ARBITRARY?

One of the difficulties inherent in the type of standard setting which involves labelling children as masters/non-masters is of course the imposition of two categories on achievements which actually vary from 'no-performance' to 'perfect performance' (or 'near-perfect performance'). Labelling theorists would insist on the dangers inherent in the practice. Though writing about 'deviance' as a label the words of Erickson (1962) could just as easily apply to the use of the label 'master':

> Deviance is not a property *inherent* in certain forms of behaviour: it is a property *conferred upon* these forms by audiences which directly witness them.

No doubt the implication of this statement (for mastery) is to avoid the use of the term altogether or to turn attention to the assumptions which underlie the practice of those who find it necessary to use this term.

But it is difficult to see how accountability could conceivably work in practice without some dependency on the idea of performance standards, at least implicitly. The essence of the argument therefore, seems to be not how can we take the arbitrariness out of standards altogether, but how can our standards (though to a certain extent arbitrary) be useful and facilitate individual and group learning, rather than remaining a dead hand on educational development.

Recent events in the United States – where by March 1978, 33 states had taken action to mandate the setting of minimum standards of competency in elementary and secondary schools (Pipho, 1978) – and in Britain through the setting of national curriculum attainment targets show that some form of standard setting is politically acceptable. The problems in the two countries are to a certain extent different, of course, in that there are no nationwide examinations in the US. But it would be far too simple-minded to believe that the very existence of a number of examination boards ensures that standards are maintained or remain comparable from year to year in Britain.

One fashionable view of how to avoid arbitrary standard setting is embodied in the concepts of 'functional skills' (Burton, 1978). This argues for the identification of minimal levels of functioning in everyday skills and concerted efforts to ensure that all children attain these levels. The approach can be attacked on the grounds that it sometimes embodies a very insulting model of the future lives of children. One frequently hears views of the kind: 'All these children need to be able to do is to fill in football pools, read the *Sun,* handle their wage packets and know how much change to expect when shopping.' Granted that there are notional levels of competence in, say, reading and writing, needed to enable pupils to go further, no one in his or her right mind would be likely to specify the potential limits of a pupil's future exercise of these skills. And this view, that the purpose of schooling is to transmit the minimal levels of skill and knowledge to prepare the child for adulthood, is predicated on agreement as to what sort of adult functioning is appropriate. In a wry comment on this way of conceptualizing the child's survival skills, Bowles and Gintis (1976) point out that survival in a capitalist society is more likely to be ensured by mastery of subservience to authority, a submission to motivation by extrinsic rewards and through exceptional toleration of routine and repetitive tasks. Given that all these seem to be required, would schools be correct in regarding them as competences? Much earlier, Dewey questioned the moral basis for the belief that schools should prepare pupils to live in a corrupt society.

It seems very unlikely, therefore, that standard setting through the identification of minimal competency for adult functioning will give a clear guide to schools. (Folklore is rich in stories of scrap metal millionaires who can neither read nor write.) Nevertheless, a high level of performance in basic skills enlarges the choice that children can eventually make in adult society but those who hold conceptions of minimal requirements (employers, for example) constitute only one set of participants in the standards debate.

The most recent attempt to set standards as part of the national curriculum is through the statement of attainment targets in maths, English and science. Such statements attempt to specify what every pupil should 'know, understand and be able to do' at the four ages where reporting is required by the Secretaries of State, namely 7, 11, 14 and 16. These statements, if agreed, follow the recommendations of expert working groups (including teachers) set up by the Secretaries of State and carry far-reaching implications for teaching and assessment.

Standard setting seems likely to be a continuous process of revision as curricula, norms and the expectations and requirements held by different audiences change with time. Although schools cannot afford to be insensitive to concepts of the 'country's needs' they are unlikely to gain clear guidance for standard setting from those who have such conceptions. Institutions like schools have a tendency to enshrine the technologies of yesterday and present them as cultures for today. The teaching of Latin for the proper conduct of church services (technology), only later became a mental discipline of intrinsic value (the culture). This is a case in point. It may be a cause for some regret that shop assistants of today are unable to add up long columns of figures and reach a correct answer for the shopping bill but modern electronic tech- nology renders such skills largely redundant in that context. (There are better reasons for an understanding of numbers that the conduct of commercial life, of course!) Similarly, although it is widely claimed that growth in a modern industrial society depends upon its educational system, this remains an untested assumption of popular political platforms.

CONCLUSIONS

In summary, we have seen that a distinction can be drawn between standards (the characteristics of the performances held up as models against which judgements are to be made) and levels of performance (that is, what pupils actually achieve). We have argued that there are three chief approaches to standard setting:

(1) the pragmatic approach – trying to lay down minimal levels of competence which a child needs to achieve in order to 'function effectively' in adult society;
(2) the scientific approach – the systematic examination of adult competences and the setting of performance standards be- cause they have been shown to have high predictive validity (chapter 7); and
(3) the norm-referenced approach – an examination of the levels of attainment of large representative groups of pupils to find out what can reasonably be expected of those at various positions of the normal curve of attainment in that subject.

Each poses problems and has serious disadvantages. In all cases, however, the methods seem applicable only to those problems that have a small definable set of possible solutions. 'Laying down basic standards', though an intuitively appealing notion, will have to take far more factors into account than are apparent in the public pronouncement of those who have vested interests in the maintenance of the structure of society, or in its complete upheaval. From the point of view of the individual learner, however, standards serve as goals without which learning activities cannot be organized and learning potential be harnessed (Gagné, 1974). From this perspective many standards will be relative to the child's competence and current status as a learner. Meanwhile, a standard which is too low for a given child can encourage boredom or complacency, one which is far too high defeatism and low self-esteem. With these potentially deleterious psychological effects in mind, the setting of standards which act as appropriate goals for the individual learner must be approached with a subtlety and ingenuity absent from the appraisal by those whose chief interest in educational standards is politically motivated.

Profiles and Records of Achievement

Discussion about how to report results of assessment has been dominated over the last five years by talk of 'profiles' and 'records of achievement'. Just what these terms mean is not clear, even to experts:

> . . . while there is widespread agreement about the need to develop 'profiles' and 'records of achievement' for all pupils, considerable confusion about what these terms mean exists. A 'record of achievement' for some is a catalogue of a wide range of different achievements including a 'profile' of personal qualities and skills. For others, paradoxically, it is simply one element in a broader 'profile' of skills and attainment in all aspects of the curriculum. (Broadfoot, 1987b, 6)

One of the original distinctions was that a 'profile' would describe a number of intellectual features of the child as a statement of his or her relative strengths and weaknesses whereas 'records of achievement' (ROAs) would portray only the positive features, that is those for which credit can be given. This distinction has become blurred, however, by a recognition that only positive achievements should receive acknowledgement in both types of assessment.

In early discussions the concept of profile was restricted to the description and evaluation of pupils' abilities and performances (analogous to that of the 'personality profile') whilst records were to express broader details of the pupils involvement in curricular and extracurricular activities. Thus the DES (1984) suggestions envisaged three components for the latter: externally assessed successes (such as exam results), internal and continuously assessed work and extracurricular details. However, since confusion is so widespread and since considerable variation exists in profiles and records of achievement in practice, we shall follow the recommendation of Brown and Black (1988) in using the terms more or less interchangeably.

A more serious disagreement amongst experts is whether profiles and ROAs are a method of assessment or not. Bray seems to see them as a method: 'Profiling is. . . the main assessment *technique* (my emphasis) in most vocational training. . . ' (1986, 141). However, Brown and Black argue (correctly in the writer's view) that it 'does not, in principle, imply that any particular means of assessment is used nor even that the assessments are criterion-referenced rather than norm-referenced' (1988, 72–3).

Some idea of profiles and ROAs can be gained by an examination of any of the nine pilot schemes supported by government funding and of the many other initiatives. Although there is great variation, their common feature appears to be a format for recording, cumulatively, in-school achievements, aptitudes, competences, and capabilities; knowledge and understanding; skills; learning experiences; personal qualities and interests and out-of-school activities where relevant, but in varying proportions. The entire profile or ROA forms a document which can be taken on leaving school or college as a 'rounded picture' of the candidate for jobs or courses (DES, 1987a, 1).

Despite the current variation in profiles, substantially similar ideas have informed their development:

(1) Traditional examinations have been defective in representing across-the-board achievements and experiences of pupils especially for those who used not to obtain O-level or CSE certification. Even the new GCSE offers little or nothing by way of incentive, nor adequate acknowledgement of the worth of 'less able' pupils.

(2) Traditional examination results and grades, in aggregating performance across components, submerge the features of a pupil's learning into an overall statement, thus hiding the specific nature of what has been achieved.

(3) Traditional assessments and reports of results have been made *by* teachers and examiners rather than *between* assessors and pupils. This excludes the learner from participation in assessment and evaluation. Profiles and records provide an opportunity for negotiated and self assessment, with advantages for pupil motivation.

(4) Profiles and records are compiled cumulatively and are more helpful to formative assessment than end-of-term or yearly reports.

(5) Profiles and records are the best way of informing parents and others of what the child has achieved. Potentially they permit greater consultation than other data do between the main parties with an interest in the education of the pupil and his/her subsequent career.

(6) In emphasizing only positive achievement, records acknowledge both in- and out-of-school activities which are resistant to or absent from conventional conceptions of what should be assessed. This, in turn, encourages teachers and pupils to think in terms of broad educational aims as well as the attainment of 'targets'.

(7) Records are sufficiently flexible to incorporate the results of external examinations and conventional assessments alongside those which educators have paid only lip service; for example, the development of personal qualities such as initiative and attitudes.

(8) Records encourage the making of assessments by teachers and pupils which are relative to the pupil's own development and previous performance ('ipsative assessment') instead of being mere comparisons with the performance of other pupils.

Some of the above are clear statements of a reaction to what are held to be undesirable features of the traditional examination system. Some of these defects are potentially overcome by the new GCSE examination which will, of course, face its own problems, and does not overcome the comparisons between pupils, which are invidious to many educators. However, the 'shock' to the system of the GCSE introduction may leave little collective energy for large-scale ROA introduction. Not all teachers who have been involved in the initiatives have been enthusiastic despite the theoretical advantages of profiles and ROAs. Indeed, their enthusiasm has varied as widely as that of pupils for self assessment. Some doubts about the co-existence of ROAs and GCSE have already been expressed by Goldstein and Nuttall (1986).

It is not the purpose of the chapter to review the history of ROAs, or to detail the contribution of individuals and groups in

Swindon, Scotland or the City and Guilds Institute. There will be no detailed examination of the Certificate of Prevocational Education (CPVE), Technical and Vocational Education Initiative (TVEI), and Youth Training Scheme (YTS); nor of developments in the government sponsored areas and LEAs over the trial period of 1985–88. With so many and disparate contributions the great variation in practice is easily understood.

VARIATION IN PROFILES AND ROAs

The work of PRAISE (1987) and Brown and Black (1988) has helped identify six 'dimensions' along which current practices vary:

Pastoral Emphasis vs Academic Emphasis

This dimension contrasts self recording, diary keeping, pupil–teacher interviews, social education and 'life skills' experiences as subjects for records with those which emphasize achievement in school subjects or in cross-curricular skills. Self assessment has been more prominent in the pastoral than in the academic context so far.

Whole School Schemes vs Departmental Schemes

This is self-explanatory. Seeking a profile or record which commands respect and applicability to the entire school requires careful coordination and tends to be limited to profile components which receive a large measure of agreement. Departmental schemes develop from the specific intra-subject focus of the teachers and may be more finely tuned to the intellectual characteristics fostered by the subject matter, and the ways of thinking it encourages. Profile comparability is very difficult to obtain under the latter conditions.

External Schemes vs Within-school Schemes

Some schools have adopted entirely, or with modification, records which have become well known either because of publication, pressure from the LEA (or its advisers and working party members) or because teachers themselves are preparing pupils for wider schemes of award. In many cases the outside body 'endorses' or 'validates' the record thus ensuring greater respectability for the document. Other records have developed from working party recommendations or head or senior teacher's influence within the school. These can respond to any peculiarly local characteristics which are perceived to be influential, for example, suggestions from prominent local employers.

Records based on Structured Criteria or Attainment Targets vs Open Records

Some records and profiles use structured criteria exclusively when reporting pupil achievement; others prefer to leave the choice of record or statement 'open-ended'. Other models have employed a mixture of both types often in deference to the beliefs about assessment held by the more influential teachers involved in ROA development. Since both have advantages and disadvantages the balance between them is usually determined procedurally rather than from theoretical precept.

Formative vs Summative Profiles

This decision seems to reflect differences in emphasis as to the purpose of profiles and their intended audience. Teachers who wish to maximize the importance of assessment in informing and motivating learning tend to encourage cumulative profiling which is formative. Undoubtedly the greatest efforts of 'profilers' have gone into attempts to realize these purposes. Less effort has been made to develop records to sum up achievement for the purposes of comparison, selection, or helping future employers choose their candidates. Major problems of comparability of profiles and records undoubtedly arise in relation to summative profiles where comparisons between pupils may be made on their basis. Very many 'profilers' have been indifferent to these technical difficulties, preferring instead to emphasize the formative functions. Readers interested in some of the technical issues can consult Goldstein and Nuttall (1986).

Selective vs Comprehensive

Some schools and departments have 'gone the whole hog', as it were, and have incorporated all assessments made into the record

of achievement. The obvious consequence has been a quite vol-
uminous document. Others have restricted profiles to recording
only selected aspects of a pupil's performance and experiences (for
example, in the core areas of the curriculum) or have proposed to
do so in respect of the attainment targets which are to form the
principal 'entitlements' of the national curriculum. The distribution overlaps somewhat with the 'pastoral' and 'academic' emphases above.

FORMATS FOR PROFILES AND ROAs

From the diversity of forms of profiles and records it is not possible
to predict which will emerge as a recommended or standard
format, even if such were desirable. There are many ways in which
assessments may be presented clearly and informatively and each
has its proponents and detractors. The complete profile or record
will probably be made up of a number of components or permutations and combinations of types of format. It is likely to consist of
statements against criteria of pupil achievement (perhaps formulated in relation to the national curriculum's targets), various types
of record, some 'closed' by choice from a bank of descriptors,
others entirely open-ended. These will be teacher assessment,
pupil's self assessment, and negotiated assessment. Some may
contain norm-referenced, others only criterion-referenced components. External as well as internal results will probably be included. In keeping with the guidelines set up in the DES pamphlet
(1987a), 'all records should contain only factual and potentially
verifiable material on pupils' experiences and personal achievements'. It will be extremely difficult to achieve consensus as to the
relative balance between these kinds of components and it would
be foolish to argue that a single best solution to the problem exists.
However, fitness for purpose requires that the aims of the profile
must be clear and confusions as to the intended recipients of the
record resolved. It is highly unlikely that specific recommendations for the format of records will emerge from the various
research groups currently evaluating the data from the government sponsored initiatives. Given the diversity of teacher-driven
initiatives and the often quite passionate adherence of some of the
schemes they have nurtured, no single format is likely to command

respect unless and until it is guided either by examination boards (who have yet to determine how to incorporate records into their GCSE examination procedures) or specifically required by the national curriculum.

Broadly speaking, five types of profile format may be identified as in current use but receiving different degrees of support.

Grid Profiles

Basically these consist of lists of characteristics being assessed (competences, skills, abilities, knowledge, cross-curricular skills) arranged down the left-hand side (as rows) gradually increasing in difficulty if this can be determined. Across the top (the columns) grades are arranged from lowest to highest with model descriptions in the intersection of row and column (the cells). Some arrangement is made – often a small box beneath each description – for recording which of the descriptions most closely describes the pupil's performance.

The major objection usually offered to grids is that the descriptions force the assessment into a standard form leaving little or no scope for recording any of the individual's special performance characteristics. Secondly, critics have objected to the ambiguity, in the absence of a standard frame of reference, of certain key words (for example, 'simple', 'complex') frequently used in describing various grades of competence in the areas specified by the rows of the grid. Thirdly, the adequacy with which the various grades of description (left to right) cater for the complete ability range has also been questioned. However, there is general agreement that the descriptions need to be accompanied by clear statements of the criteria which are to be met before a pupil's performance is judged to have deserved the description. Quite clearly, a large number of desirable areas of attainment do not lend themselves to this arrangement and a great deal of work has had to be done in stating and refining descriptions and criteria, as well as in establishing the extent to which school work can be arranged hierarchically (in order of difficulty) to form the rows of the grid.

Cumulative Grid Profiles

The layout of cumulative grids is similar to the above but the left to right axis (the columns) progresses in a stepwise manner which expresses the development of the attainments and competences as 'desirable' stages in learning. Thus there is assumed to be a clear and smooth sequence in which learning proceeds as pupils move from early and elementary levels towards later and more complex attainments. Boxes beneath the cells permit the date on which the pupil is assessed to have reached the stage or level to be recorded and a cumulative record built up. Such grids are difficult to construct and useful only where what is being learned can be arranged on a continuum as discernible stages of progress. The objections to other types of grid apply equally here.

Scale Profiles

These are the two main types. The *polar opposite type* requires that pupils are rated, one characteristic at a time, on a (usually) five-point scale with only the opposite poles (1 and 5) described. Suppose a languages department wishes to assess and report the attitudes of the pupil towards use of the language laboratory: here the polar opposites might be (1) Has made little or no attempt to use the language laboratory, and (5) Has made full use of the opportunities for study in the language laboratory. Intermediate points are undefined and the record is simply a ring around the number held by teacher or negotiated with pupil to be appropriate. Without some idea of the reliability of scores given we do not know how big a difference between any two scores has to be in order to be statistically significant. The straightforward *rating-scale type* is very familiar. Here the scale (usually over five points) has each of its values labelled using a form of words judged appropriate for the characteristic being assessed, often but not always with an implicit norm-referenced frame. Thus, for example, the form of an assessment of a pupil's participation in discussion might take the form of Example A in table 3.2 (see page 58), though the given meaning of the statements would be unacceptable to many devotees of ROAs.

Comment Bank Profiles

Here banks of comment found to have been useful by teachers in reporting assessments in given areas of the curriculum or in relation to 'personal qualities' are compiled, on computer if available. Teachers, either alone, in pairs, or with their pupils can consult these banks and select those which, by agreement, express a just assessment of the target characteristic. There is obvious potential of 'speeding up' the process of computing the profile and record provided the bank of descriptions is agreed by users and is open to the deletion of comments which are found by experience to be unhelpful, and to addition or modification of items.

Free Comment Profiles

Here the principal decision is as to which elements constitute the profile and what aspects ('ability', 'effort', 'experiences') are to be assessed. Agreement having been reached, teachers are free to generate comments as appropriate – after negotiation with pupils in the best profiling tradition. Apart from the participation of pupils such a profile differs in only minor respects from the report books which cumulatively accompanied the pupil throughout secondary schooling during the writer's childhood.

The books by Garforth and Macintosh (1986) and Broadfoot (1987a) are excellent sources for the types of profile format most extensively used to date.

PROBLEMS OF PROFILES AND ROAs

A number of good accounts of the issues involved in implementing profiles and records have been prepared, including contributions from those who have been most active in evaluation of the innovation (for example, Broadfoot, 1986, 1987a; Hitchcock, 1986; PRAISE, 1987). The government funded evaluation reported in the last named is cautious and circumspect and it remains to be seen how the vague principles described in the 'Statement of Policy' (DES, 1984) are to be realized in practice in the records which, according to the 'Interim Report' (DES, 1987a), should be in the possession of all school leavers by 1995. During the intervening years a number of forces may encourage coherence among the variations which, understandably, exist in the pilot schemes. 'Good practice' will gradually be distinguished, and models for more widespread adoption may receive official support.

It would be very easy indeed to show the many uncertainties and contradictions that exist in the thinking about profiles and records. By contrast, it is very difficult to determine what might be in the minds of the Secretaries of State when their views are expressed in DES documents such as those above. Even where a recommendation is made, ministerial (or civil service) aptitude for ambiguity is notable. For example, in arguing the inclusion of 'lists of achievements prepared jointly by teachers and pupils, to which others sometimes contribute as well' (DES, 1984, 5) this apparent clarity is immediately clouded by the requirement that the list should be 'factual or largely factual' (partly fictional, perhaps?). Nonetheless, a number of substantive issues may be recognized and seek resolution. These can be commented on only very briefly here.

Content and Comprehensiveness

Although there are hints that profiles and self assessment may lead to the identification of relative lack of strength in pupils, there seems overwhelming agreement that the document should recognize and reward only 'positive achievement'. If the achievements rewarded are to be 'absolute' (entailing CR assessment) rather than 'relative' (NR assessment) in written, oral and practical work then some pupils may, unfortunately, present thinner records than others. Nevertheless, an attempt to incorporate everything which might show the learner in his or her 'best light' would be time-consuming and lead in some cases to an extremely weighty document. Although decisions as to what to include have still to be made we may hazard a guess that the following will receive attention: results of any externally accredited examinations, the attainment of 'core criteria', attainment of the national curriculum targets, lists of participation in 'educational activities' for which reporting is more important than assessment and assessments of 'personal qualities'. These will be accompanied by description of the conditions under which the assessments were made and interpreted, in relation to the opportunities the pupil has received. An optional portfolio of supplementary data may also be compiled.

Confidentiality

Most writers are of the opinion that the record should belong to the pupil who is then free to offer it for inspection by training agencies or employers. This confidentiality, it is argued, is essential if an honest appraisal of personal qualities is to be undertaken. Insofar as the record will contain details of successes in externally validated examinations these elements will, of course, already be public, but one is bound to guess how 'free' a pupil will feel in withholding his or her record from a potential employer who has asked to see it.

Credibility

In 1988 there was what appeared to be a carefully orchestrated attempt to establish the credibility of the new GCSE exam in the eyes of pupils, schools, parents and the outside world. It was even claimed that standards had been raised. All innovations, especially where they involve radical departures from established and ostensibly well-understood practices, are faced with this problem and the incorporation into ROAs of assessments which are radically different from traditional examinations presents special difficulties. Assessments which may have validity in the motivation of learners are not necessarily those which command respect amongst those wedded to norm-referenced comparisons. Considerable efforts, then, must be made to convince those who select for further training and employment that the processes of assessment and recording are dependable and valid. How far this can be ensured by exclusively within-school procedures is debatable.

Special difficulties are faced in establishing the credibility of elements which do not receive the respectability conferred by external examining bodies. Pilot schemes have involved participation by the LEA (for example, in the case of the OCEA – Oxford Certificate of Educational Achievement) and by consortia (such as the Northern Partnership for Records of Achievement) in conjunction with examining associations (who send an assessor to inspect the evidence) and with in-school validation bodies.

It is unlikely that sums of money will be made available to set up extensive validation and accreditation bodies. In all probability some elements will tacitly be seen as having higher status than others. Some control over the credibility of *courses* may be exercised through the national curriculum, and efforts must continue to be made to show that the actual processes of assessment and their results are dependable and valid. This, even if successful, would not guarantee the credibility of the document or record. To do that, records would have to receive some sort of imprimatur: that is, be accredited by a body in whom all participants in education can have confidence. Just how this can be achieved is likely to emerge in the next few years.

Comparability

One of the reasons why external examinations have survived for so many years is that they offer at least an appearance of 'fairness' and comparability. Although a principal aim of profiles and records has been formative, occasions arise where they will be used summatively. In this case, if the present range of profile contents and forms persists, potential users will conceivably lack the ability to compare either profiles or those who are profiled. Some technical aspects of comparability between assessments even within a given form and content have already been suggested by Nuttall and Goldstein (1986) where, without knowledge of the reliability of the assessment, no one can tell whether a pupil receiving, say, a scale score of 3, differs beyond the limits of measurement error from one achieving 4 on the same element. Such problems have not, so far, disturbed the thinking of many 'profilers' but they will be exacerbated if a need exists to compare two school leavers with profiles and rewards which contain little in common. If profiles and ROAs cannot resolve issues of comparability then, paradoxically, this may lead to enhanced respect for those very assessment methods (external examinations) whose perceived inadequacies have largely inspired the strongest proponents of the new approaches.

Comprehensiveness and Coordination with Other Assessment Systems

Schemes at present vary from those which attempt to provide as comprehensive a record of school experience and achievement as is possible in the time available, to those which restrict the record to aspects of a pupil's career which complement more traditional assessments. In these latter cases the record is additional evidence to externally validated and accredited results; in the former, the problem is raised of how far profiles should incorporate the principle of GCSE assessment. If communication to parents is a prime concern, then expecting them to familiarize themselves with a number of assessment frames will not help. For example, schools which adopt literal grades for expressing the results are congruent with the reporting of GCSE, whereas schools which use numerical grades have the additional difficulty of explaining their meaning to readers. Thus, deciding on the relationship of ROAs to external examinations may influence the acceptability of the former. Even so, the singular features of ROAs and those which distinguish them from external examinations (pupil participation, negotiated assessment, elements of self assessment) will be difficult to harmonize in a single document if its parts are to be seen to be equally worthwhile.

Coping with Pupil Differences

There seem to be two aspects to this problem. First, there is the way in which profile and ROA demands on children can be matched to their capabilities. At a simple level of analysis one would expect older children to be able to participate more fully in the making of negotiated statements than younger children – especially after some years' experience. Closely related to this is the extent to which different curricula and organizations typical of older and younger pupils not only prepare them for recording and assessment but also provide opportunities for the development and exercise of the skills and abilities which form the profile component.

In all probability, the suggestions for profile components within the national curriculum which have already been made by maths and science groups will strongly influence the way teachers conceive of domains within their subjects (the science panel has recommended four components with associated attainment targets: exploration and investigation, knowledge and understanding, communication, and science in action (DES, 1988c)). This, together with the principle of differentiation of performance by outcome (that is, by documentation of the different ways in which pupils can illustrate their understanding and skills to given tasks and not by the presentation of different tasks to pupils of different ability level) seems to suggest a profile format and ROA of as wide an application as possible. Thus we shall see that the rejection of differentiated provision of learning activities has its counterpart in a rejection of differentiation by form of record and profile. It also seems certain that the TGAT ten-point scale for reporting performance (DES, 1987b, 11) will be adopted for the inclusion in the record of achievement with the definition of each level by state-ments of attainment. Nevertheless, experience already suggests that pupils of lower than average ability have met difficulty in compiling their records and require additional help from their teachers.

Combining Recording and the Curriculum

There is widespread belief that the compilation of ROAs has had such desirable effects and become such an integral part of im-proved teaching and learning that the distinction between record-ing and assessing on the one hand and teaching on the other has lost much of its validity. Nevertheless, recording is time-consum-ing and many teachers have already expressed frustration at not being able to do justice to the new recording elements in the time available (PRAISE, 1987).

One response to these difficulties has been a tendency to re-organize the curriculum into specific (roughly half-term) units of work, each having its own criteria and attainment targets which constitute the objectives for teaching and the framework for assessment and recording. A second response has been to change the emphasis of the curriculum to incorporate more independent learning in order to make time for teacher–pupil discussion in record keeping. A third response has been to search for 'whole-school' assessment policies to integrate agreed recording proce-dures into the timetable.

The final part of this chapter has concentrated on some of the substantive problems in the development and use of profiles and ROAs. Guidelines are urgently needed if curbs are to be placed on diversity and a working consensus reached. But there are other types of problem – those concerned with training teachers, and with the management by senior staff of the innovations within schools – which are not of concern here. Paradoxically, Scotland, where much of the pioneering work has been done has 'no national position either for or against the development of profiles' (Brown and Black, 1988, 78). Given the governmental statement of policy, development in England and Wales seems likely to come to fruition but its precise nature is still uncertain. Discussion of profiles and ROAs has contributed immeasurably to the debate about what is to be assessed, how the processes may motivate and acknowledge the varied efforts of all pupils, and has helped to embed the processes and results of assessing more explicitly and productively into teaching and learning. But its contribution to the technical issues in assessment theory has been less marked, even to the point of denial by some proponents of the relevance of traditional concepts of reliability and validity. Many problems remain to be solved and more are being identified as experience is gained. For an up-to-date, frank and amusing appraisal, readers should consult the chapter in Hargreaves et al. (1988). Other useful sources include Balogh (1982), Goacher (1983), Stratton (1986) and Stansbury (1984).

Self Assessment

Self assessment is often discussed as an aspect of records of achievement or 'profiling', yet the idea of helping children reflect on and evaluate their own performance merits consideration in its own right, whether or not results are incorporated in personal records or profiles. The purpose of this chapter is to examine some of the issues raised when children are encouraged to assess their own progress or to comment on their own achievements in schools.

THE MERITS OF SELF ASSESSMENT

Many schools have tried to encourage a more active participation on the part of pupils in learning activities by the development of schemes for self assessment. Self assessment takes many forms varying from a scrapbook collection or diaries of personal experiences (more properly thought of as 'self report' or part of a 'record of experience') to formal judgements by the pupils of their degree of attainment and effort using either teacher- or pupil-generated criteria. Teachers who have used such schemes point to a number of theoretical advantages. Many see self assessment as encouraging more active interest on the part of children, as more informative during learning than summative statements, as less destructive of morale – especially for pupils in the middle and low 'ability range' – than traditional tests and examinations, and as helping pupils understand reasons for their own educational performance. Others have argued that use of self assessment has helped teachers develop greater respect for pupils' feelings and points of view about schooling, and has provided insights into the effects of teaching programmes hidden from other methods. It is also claimed to have encouraged an 'individualized approach' to assessment which, in turn, enhances motivation and supports the development of self-directed, self-monitoring young people who might not otherwise reach a realistic appraisal of their own skills and abilities.

Such claims are difficult to susbstantiate. Indeed, there are conceptual and practical problems involved in the notion of self knowledge in which the 'self' is both the agent and object of the processes involved. Undeterred by such difficulties, however, proponents have incorporated self assessment to varying degrees in schools. On the face of it, common sense suggests that pupils know better than their teachers about certain aspects of learning: how hard they have tried, what they were attempting to do, how far they see themselves as successful in their efforts to achieve personal goals and, in the case of records of experience, how they have spent their time in worthwhile activities in and out of school. On the other hand, it is teachers who might be expected to know better than pupils what constitutes acceptable standards of performance in areas of the curriculum and in the criteria that are to be applied to academic attainment. Self assessment, then, can be thought of as supplying information from the perspective of the learner to be used in its own right or to be placed alongside that of an outside observer, thus constituting the starting point for a discussion (or a 'negotiation' as the jargon has it) to reach a just assessment of the processes and products of learning.

In considering what kind of scheme for self assessment is to be introduced into a classroom teachers need to consider three fundamental and overlapping questions:

(1) What features can learners be asked to assess?
(2) Are teachers' or pupils' criteria to be used in the assessment?
(3) In what format are the assessments to be made and recorded?

Each question will be taken in turn.

What can the Learner himself Assess?

We can use the traditional psychological distinctions here. Responses of pupils may be classified as: *cognitive* (the mental processes and products of learning, remembering and understanding, including knowledge); *affective* (interests, attitudes and feelings); *psychomotor* (principally skills in which movements play a major part; and *conative* (motivation and effort). We shall see that existing self assessment schemes have emphasized affective and conative aspects of behaviour, presumably because these, being subjective, appear to be more easily assessed by pupils than the cognitive which involve the application of objective and inferential criteria. But schemes, for example OCEA, have attempted self assessment of selected cognitive outcomes of learning. Existing schemes for self assessment require us to add *'personal qualities'* to this list. This is a ragbag category including individual and social characteristics such as 'social skills', 'relationships', 'initiative', 'reliability', sense of responsibility and so on.

This classification is by no means the only one which could be applied to responses to schooling. A similar scheme has been very influential in conceptualizing the possible content of records of achievement. Records initiated in schools in the Inner London Education Authority (soon to be abolished) distinguish four aspects: I: Knowledge and understanding assessed by traditional examinations (this corresponds roughly with the cognitive category); II: practical skills and skills involving the application of knowledge (a mixture of the cognitive and psychomotor); III: personal and social skills; and IV: motivation and commitment (conative aspects).

Psychological theory suggests that children develop greater understanding of 'the self' as they grow older and typically use different criteria by which to explain their successes and failures in schools. This is known as attribution theory for which good introductory references are Weiner (1980) and Child (1986a, b). At all ages of schooling most children appear to draw on four principal types of explanation or factors affecting learning; these are ability (a cognitive factor internal to the learner); effort (a conative factor internal to the learner); task difficulty (an external factor); and luck (a wide category in which all chance factors are included). Even children as young as five years of age appear to understand that high ability can compensate for low effort and extra effort can make up for low ability. The concept a child has of his or her own ability appears to originate principally in his or her comparisons with other children's attempts to learn and in what his or her teacher signals to him openly by ways of evaluation and, more covertly, in the expectations the teacher sets for him. The explanations for success and failure become more sophisticated as children get older, coinciding with what has become known as 'metacognition'; that is increasing knowledge of how one's own learning takes place and how memory 'works'. One might expect, therefore, that the validity of self assessment increases with age, and that it may be encouraged by settings in which pupils and teachers discuss and elaborate on pieces of work from two complementary perspectives (i.e. as pupils learn more about themselves), but that it is more easily accomplished in certain domains (affective/conative) than in others (cognitive and 'personal').

One of the problems when reading the scattered literature on self assessment is that many people have included the act of recording experience as part of the 'records of achievement' which are gaining steadily in popularity. Rather than attempting an exclusive definition of self assessment we may include self report which consists of descriptions, or what some have called 'have done' statements, but without evaluation: these provide material for self assessment. Pupils experience little difficulty in completing records of their responsibilities and involvement in school functions, membership of societies inside and outside school, their interests and aspirations; the question which arises here is not so much whether children can do this, but rather what should be recorded and, possibly, incorporated into a profile at a later date. When pupils are encouraged to engage in this form of descriptive self assessment they are potentially alerted to the kinds of school career and attitude likely to find favour with future employers and provided with a concept of positive achievement which can be striven for at a level appropriate to their ability. Factual accounts of experience and achievement, then, are relatively easy to elicit from active pupils. If these are compiled during a pupil's career many teachers have testified that motivation and learning are enhanced, though the evidence is mostly of a subjective kind.

Pupils experience greater difficulty when asked to assess and evaluate cognitive perfomance against criteria which require analysis and inference in their application. Part of the problem lies in the nature of the learning itself. Not only is it extremely difficult to identify mental processes by introspection but a pupil just may not know, for example, whether an argument is logical, whether his mathematical proof is correct or elegant, whether the line of reasoning he is pursuing in problem solving is potentially productive, whether his apparatus is up to the task, whether his interactions in a group suggest an awareness of the needs of others. In others words, some of the most valuable educational goals and objectives will require the assistance of teachers or other experts in making a fair assessment. In such cases pupils together with their teachers can formulate usable and objective criteria with which to make the assessment, but existing schemes to date appear to have made comparatively limited and sporadic attempts towards self assessment in the cognitive domain. At present, even as experienced a scheme as OCEA has self assessment within only few of the units of study.

No explicit reference to self assessment has been made by either of the two reports on the national curriculum to date (DES, 1988a, c), but a number of tentative conclusions about the kinds of responses that can be assessed by pupils of secondary school age can be reached.

(a) Records of personal experience and activities undertaken (sometimes known as 'have done' assessments) can be prepared with comparative ease by motivated pupils. Since there is a possibility of faking it is a good idea for teachers as well as pupils to sign their initials or tick the activity if they agree that it has been satisfactorily performed. This type of recording of experience and achievement can be undertaken in a number of ways, including the prior specification of activities or experiences, both within school subjects and cross-curricular areas and outside school. Gaps in such lists (unsigned or unticked items) suggest lack of involvement or may imply negative achievement; they can be a starting point for discussion between teacher and pupil. Signed items provide the raw material for compilation of summative statements which will then recognize only positive experience and achievement in keeping with the Statement of Policy (DES, 1984).

Self-assessed records of achievement may also be compiled by inviting free comments under standard headings. Typical headings include (for a unit of study): planning the work; preparation; difficulties experienced; and specific questions like: Did you redraft your work before submission? and so on. Experience suggests that this kind of approach (even when posed in the form of direct questions) often leads to pupils' responses which do little more than reflect socially desirable answers to the questions ('I organized my work well and redrafted my essay before I handed it in'). Nevertheless, such lists provide a check on pupils' study habits and alert them to important questions as they assume greater autonomy for learning.

(b) Self assessment presents greater difficulty where pupils are asked to reach judgements as to the quality of their cognitive or intellectual characteristics, within school subjects. A great deal of work needs to be done to determine the extent to which pupils of different abilities can use criteria which define either the various grades of achievement or fit different descriptions of levels of competence in attaining a criterion. One scheme which has attempted this but only in certain subject areas is OCEA. Attainment targets have been specified within subject units but this practice has been opposed by some on the grounds that targets restrict the curriculum and constrain the form in which pupils' knowledge, skills and understanding are to be expressed (compare objection 5, chapter 2). If agreement can be reached on what constitutes desirable 'objectives', 'targets' or 'goals' at given levels of the educational system (and it has been the role of government sponsored task groups, e.g. the Kingman report on English (DES, 1988b), to produce targets for four age levels: 7, 11, 14 and 16 years) it should be feasible to give examples of how these may be stated, preferably within given contexts against which the performance of pupils may be compared. Perhaps some of these could receive sufficiently precise description to permit pupils to select the one which is most apt for their own attainments after discussion with their teacher in that subject. By way of example let us suppose that an agreed target objective within mathematics for, say, 13 year olds is stated in the following form: understanding and carrying out multiplication of powers. To avoid the obscurity of many levels per objective let us propose four plus one more difficult level to differentiate achievement.

TOPIC: Multiplication of numbers raised to powers.
(1)   Can give 5 examples of numbers raised to a power
(2)   Can complete 5 statements of form $a^p \times a^q =$

(3)   Can complete 5 statements of the form $a^u \times b^u =$
(4)   Can complete 5 statements of the form $(a^p)^q =$
(5)   Can show that $a^o = 1$

Now it is by no means certain that these criteria would be accepted by maths teachers as valid or in this order but this is not our point. Where a target can be stated in terms of performance levels the possibility of a self assessment which can be checked by teachers is indicated. Explicit statements of cognitive performance (whether or not organized in levels) constitute 'can do' statements of criteria analogous to the recorded 'have done' statements of personal experience. The potential for this form of self assessment seems limited to those areas of the curriculum for which 'pupil-friendly' criteria can be stated. These are easier to set up in maths, science and modern languages than in those subjects where specification of what pupils should be able to do are far more contentious.

Some writers have argued for self assessment of competences which 'cut across' the curriculum. 'Abilities to read and follow instructions'; 'ability to present a coherent argument' are examples but they tend to be so general and content-free that teachers who have tried to help children apply them have reported difficulties of many kinds (PRAISE, 1987). It could be argued that these non-specific attributes which can, however, be demonstrated in many specific contexts, are among the more important aims for education and that failure to tackle their assessment by teacher or pupil may lead to their demotion in the priorities of teachers especially in the light of what seems certain to be a predominantly subject-based national curriculum.

Some schemes have tried to elicit cross-curricular or global assessments among older pupils. In London schools, for example, 'investigative skills', 'motivation' and 'communication skills' are held as highly desirable profile components. The important issue, however, is not whether pupils are prepared to undertake such assessments but with what degree of reliability and validity they can be helped to do so. Since many factors may contribute to uneven demonstration of general skills across subject areas high reliability will almost certainly be extraordinarily difficult to attain. Perhaps the best way of dealing with assessment of cross-curricular attributes would be to invite pupils to comment on their features within subject areas and then to aggregate their responses across areas where common features may be observed. Thus if 'motivation' is to be assessed within, say, four subject areas the best estimate of 'cross-curricular motivation' would be the aggregation of ratings in those areas.

(c)   If self assessment of cognitive aspects of learning is proving more difficult for pupils, then self assessment of 'personal qualities' is proving the most controversial. One of the superficially attractive reasons for the assessment of personal qualities is that they are of great interest to potential employers yet remain unassessed by current examination procedures. Although a number of pilot schemes have been initiated little consensus has been reached as to which qualities it is desirable or possible to assess (whether by teacher, pupil or both). The discussion is clarified by listing those qualities most frequently mentioned in pilot schemes. They come from a number of sources: contemporary models of responsible and 'mature' behaviours; socially defined 'ideal' human beings'; teacher preferences for 'well-behaved' pupils; employers' statements about the kind of young people they seek. Of course, these qualities are highly value-laden and culturally influenced. Those most commonly cited include (in no particular order) reliability, initiative, politeness, consideration for others, sociability, cooperation, courtesy, self discipline, independence, tidiness, personal appearance and grooming, determination, punctuality.
      Whilst a case could be made that many of these qualities are influenced by schools, those which specify aspects of personality may be less susceptible to school pressures. Some may be relatively stable and consistent, others are obviously indicative of responses to particular social groups or situations. The implication in summative assessment is that such qualities observed in school are predictive of future behaviour outside school – a highly doubtful proposition in very many cases.

Enough has been written to question the desirability of attempting an 'agreed' list of qualities. It is by no means clear that teachers – let alone pupils – have the detailed knowledge necessary to assess personal qualities though they may not hesitate to formulate their opinion if asked to do so.

Several methods for the self assessment of personal qualities have been attempted. Some schools have provided little structure beyond an open-ended invitation to respond. Results have often been highly correlated with the pupils' verbal abilities. Some teachers have found a need to give greater guidance by providing headings of selected qualities. Others have gone further and have compiled computer banks of descriptions which may be chosen for use in 'references' written in continuous prose. However, few have considered the implications of the concepts of reliability and validity to the results. One thing is clear: a considerable amount of time is needed by pupils to complete such assessment, and it has sometimes been relegated to the status of 'time-filler' in pastoral periods in secondary schools. For self assessment to be of value in the formative sense teachers have had to find additional time in which to discuss the results, confidentially, with their authors. Sometimes pupils have been helped to achieve insights (Geddes, 1982) and teachers have been made aware of hitherto hidden pupil feelings of self worth and self efficacy. However, self assessment of personal qualities remains notoriously difficult and contentious. One is tempted to hazard the prediction that self assessment will have, at most, a minor role within the national curriculum and will gain credibility only where corroborative evidence is provided to indicate the dependability of the result.

Teachers' or Pupils' Criteria for Self Assessment?

The answer to this question appears to lie in the nature of the attribute being assessed. Suppose a pupil is trying to solve a mathematics problem. Here the criteria of an acceptable solution are unlikely to be left to the choice of the learner himself (unless of course he is in advance of his teacher in subject matter knowledge). However, if a group of children is working to produce, say, a wind generator, the criteria of success appear to be the performance of the generator in producing an electric current and the question which arises is whether output matches a target wattage whose prior specification may have been reached through teacher–pupil discussion. Other pieces of work may be regarded as more personal, as in the case of a painting in which criteria may be modified and the emerging product constantly reassessed as the artist examines the results of his processes. Not all teachers accept the pre-specification of criteria as desirable, however. Pre-specification, it can be argued, can impose entirely unacceptable constraints on learning, to the detriment of the activity of self-discovery or where individual responses are sought: poetry appreciation and writing, and drama are examples where 'personal' criteria would be encouraged.

Interim evaluation of self assessment procedures suggests, as might be expected, that 'less able' pupils find particular difficulty in setting criteria (PRAISE, 1987). Some find little to say and resort to making unfavourable comparisons with their more able peers whilst remaining unable to handle the abstract concepts so freely used by teachers: 'personal reliability' and even 'achievement' have presented considerable difficulty, for example. More able pupils have been reported as reticent when assessing their own achievements and this has been attributed to a 'prevailing culture which frowns on self-promotion' (p. 90). Some success has been claimed by teachers who have discussed suitable criteria for pupils to apply to their products at the beginning of group and individual work. As with so many educational innovations the success of such schemes depends as much on teacher commitment, managerial support and available time as on the pupils themselves. Not all pupils 'take' to such practices: one report (Geddes, 1982) collected pupil comments varying from the enthusiastic ('it has opened my eyes to my problems and made me think of ways to overcome them') to the abusive ('I think it is pathetic, stupid, twitish (*sic*) flipping rubbish thing I have ever wasted time on'). Whilst one acknowledges the theoretical advantages of incorporating self assessment into records, pupils will continue to look to teachers as authorities in relation to at least some of the aspects of learning undertaken. Specified goals help pupils in self assessment whether these are supplied by teacher or teacher with pupil. Where pupils lack frames of reference they are likely to experience difficulty in assessment. To throw children back exclusively on to their own criteria for assessment may increase feelings of insecurity among some. In these circumstances one of the potential advantages of self assessment is thereby lost, for instead of identifying the degree of correspondence of their work with the criterion and thus what

must be done if it is not attained, they place themselves relative to
the distribution of all children working towards similar criteria and
resort to comparative judgement. Indeed, to remove all externally
administered criteria for assessment is to deny the importance of
reinforcement theory in showing the importance of extrinsic rewards in strengthening newly acquired capacities and dispositions.
When asked as an adult what it was like to have Piaget as a father,
Laurent (one of the most famous children in the entire literature of
child development) is reported to have replied: 'How would you
like it? He would only ever ask me what I thought.'

We suggest that teachers continue to experiment and document
the results of pupil self assessment using mixed criteria (that is
those supplied by teachers working with pupils) because purely
'self-made' criteria – though appropriate in areas like art and
drama – are likely to lack credibility, especially if they are highly
idiosyncratic. The educational value of setting criteria for self
assessment may lie as much in the process as in the product by
requiring pupils to become much more aware, at an explicitly
conscious level, of the features of their own learning (Bowen,
1988).

The Format for Self Assessment

Because the processes have been the subject of trial and experiment in many schools, a considerable variation exists in the kinds
of instrument and record for self assessment. As with other
methods of assessment there is simply no 'one way' of doing it: we
must continually ask pertinent questions about the reliability and
validity of self assessment as of any other type, although our
conceptions of these terms may have to be modified to incorporate
a wider variety of purpose than has been true of more traditional
forms. Above all, in deciding what to record and in what form, we
must demand of the outcome that it provides information relevant
to formative evaluation (that is, to inform teaching and learning
while they are taking place) and, if it is to be incorporated into
summative data, that its properties be defensible by those who
wish to interpret its meaning for other users of the assessment at a
later date. This requires a clear understanding by pupil and
teacher of the purpose of the assessment: an informal self criticism
may well serve an invaluable formative function yet because of its
informality and transience have no part to play in summative

statements. Given that no large-scale evaluation of the processes and recording of self assessment (which is not bound up with broader issues of profiling and records of achievement) has yet been undertaken, it is possible only to call the attention of the reader to what is regarded as 'good practice' by many commentators. (Bear in mind that 'good practices' are often little more than those urged upon teachers by people whose motives have been developed elsewhere than at the 'chalk-face'.)

We have already indicated in the previous discussion that pupils are likely to find the appraisal of out-of-school activities and some personal qualities far easier than when assessing subject-specific achievement or the even more elusive 'cross-curricular competences'. Written comments prompted by a series of questions have been found to elicit self assessment from average and able pupils. These have the merit of being open-ended and permit formulation of outcomes and comments 'closed down' by check lists of descriptors which some teachers and pupils prefer. The latter permit speedier compilation of the assessment by less able pupils but are objected to by some in that they curtail the range of comment found necessary. In the purely formative context, there is no reason why the results of such self assessment should be written down. Oral self assessment, which forms such a central part of the personal presentations beloved of management in industry, commerce and the civil service, may have an informal counterpart in the ordinary life of schools whenever pupils are asked to reflect over or pass judgement on their work. Where recording is necessary this can be done on tape, or in written form as where diaries of the pupils' interests and activities undertaken may be stored. What seems to be required in this case is a decision by pupils and teachers what to record and some (preferably attractive) form or folder in which to accumulate the assessment. They can range from headings requiring free comment to prescribed lists of 'has done' statements to be initialled by pupils and teachers as evidence.

Greater difficulty is encountered, however, when recording the results of self assessment of subject-specific achievement. Let us assume that the teaching–learning programme can be divided into discrete chunks corresponding with units of study (roughly thought of as topics which have a beginning, middle and end). Informal self assessments may well be encouraged throughout a unit but, if all were recorded, would yield an unwieldy mass of information. In these circumstances we will assume one set of self assessments per unit for recording and, possibly, later incorporation into summative records. It is probably useful to consider the objectives for the unit (even if these remain inplicit) as falling under major headings: knowledge, skills and processes, understanding, effort and interest. Not all will necessarily be applicable to all units, of course. Teachers need to consider which of these are accessible to self assessment and the extent to which 'assessment tasks' (or tests) can be set in advance for each unit. To take as a concrete example, a unit concerned with 'measurement' for use with pupils age 11–12 years. Suppose the materials consisted of eight pieces of wood labelled A to H and two rulers, one short and one long, and the demands on the children were expressed as follows:

Using the short rule provided, measure pieces A to D in millimetres. Write your answers on your answer sheet. Now use the longer rule to measure pieces E to H. This time measure them *in centimetres and millimetres* expressing them in the form 12cm 8mm.

Now take the metre ruler and measure the following objects *to the nearest whole centimetre*:

1. Width of a floor tile
2. Width of the table top
3. Width of door
4. Length of red chalk line on blackboard
5. Length of table top

Following this task, the child may be requested to assess his own performance. (This may be followed by teacher assessment of accuracy to show the reliability of the record made by the pupil.) The task is one in which the possession of measurement skills is being evaluated; hence self assessment would be restricted to this aspect, as in the following questions:

Your skills   When measuring the lengths E to H did you:

(1)   Choose the correct scale on the ruler (centimetres, not inches)?

(2)   Take care to place the origin (beginning) of the scale exactly against the left-hand end of the wood?

(3)   Keep the ruler parallel to the edge of the wood or exactly on top of it whilst measuring?

(4)   Read from left to right noting the whole number nearest but to the left of the end?

(5)   Count the number of millimetres upwards from the whole number to the end and note the nearest millimetre?

(6)   Write your answer in centimetres and millimetres?

(7)   Check your answer carefully?

Now compare your answer with the correct answer. Were you correct?

If you got a wrong answer how much was your answer in error?

Why do you think you were wrong?

This brief document, when completed, provides formative information on the content of the child's skill and diagnostic information in the event of error. If preserved, the document can provide – together with others in the series on measurement – summative information for inclusion in a skills profile. This simple method can be applied in principle to any objective for learning a skill or algorithmic solution process, for example when multiplying decimals.

If the nature of the learning is more open-ended pupils can participate in the process by negotiating short-term objectives with their teacher. It might be of mutual benefit to draw up a set of questions by which the success or otherwise in reaching those goals can be assessed. (This approach owes much to the American system of negotiated contracts of work.) Pupils may supply self assessment by answering these questions. As an example, consider two children who have set themselves the goal of constructing say, a bird cage. Teacher–pupil discussion would lead to the setting up of a set of specifications for such a cage (volume; height; width between the bars, etc.). When plans had been drawn up, a check list of specifications would be used to evaluate success of the design. This would provide formative and corrective feedback. Pupils would again assess their finished product against the check list.

Far greater difficulties for self assessment would be experienced by pupils where the activity was essentially one of 'self discovery' where no specification could be stated in advance of the attempt to perform. An example can be drawn from the realm of creative dance where pupils might be set the task of developing an express-ive response to a stimulus. Here the assessment would be *post facto* and probably in consultation with a trusted observer. The point here is not that self assessment could not be undertaken but that it would be futile to suggest a form or format in which it would take place before the processes of activity are begun. Perhaps a video of the 'polished' performance would be presented as part of a record of personal achievement together with a written commen-tary based on the subjectivity of the performer by way of self assessment.

Some indication has already been given earlier in the chapter as to how self assessment of intellectual performance may be under-taken, provided 'can do' criteria agreed by teacher and pupil can be set up. If the teacher can decide upon the core units making up the study of a subject area and similar criteria can be written for each, these can provide the check list for formative and be collected for summative self assessment. There is always considerable diffi-culty in deciding which areas of a subject constitute its core as distinct from other activities that may be peripheral to them. However, teachers are strongly recommended to establish which units or sections of units are going to be reserved for records of self assessment. Perhaps the national curriculum may provide some guidance as to which these units are to be, that is, those which provide a field in which the study of the 'attainment targets' can be undertaken. Nevertheless, it is highly unlikely that pupils can or even should be required to record self assessments of all their activities and pieces of work for the process can well become mechanical and boring. Judicious oral and informal assessments may be required as part of normal teacher–pupil interactions while the written records are reserved for those activities which are to form part of a summative statement or record of achievement agreed within the school or LEA, or on a wider scale if standardized records are recommended by groups currently researching their place in the national curriculum.

SELF ASSESSMENT OF EFFORT, INTEREST AND PERSONAL QUALITIES

These are usually seen by teachers as less problematic than assessment of intellectual characteristics. Indeed, several schools which report the use of self assessment restrict it to these domains (Geddes, 1982). However, there are problems!

If self assessment of interests consists merely of records of experiences gained, clubs attended, awards received (all of which are connected with school life) then few, if any, problems are raised since written statements seem all that are required. Some schools provide pupils with the open-ended opportunity to state their personal qualities whilst others provide guidance in the form of a list of attributes (reliability, consideration for others, politeness, etc.) which undoubtedly alert pupils to the kinds of characteristic which may be looked for by future employers. If such a list is deemed desirable, pupils may supply written statements on each or, in some cases, avail themselves of ratings ('like me'; 'unsure'; 'unlike me', for example). These and other personal qualities may be of interest to employers though ethical objections may be offered in asking pupils to comment on them. Moreover, it is not always clear to pupils whether such qualities are to be assessed as 'generally true' of them, or related to specified contexts in which teachers and others may have an opportunity to reach their own assessments for later comparison with those of pupils. One recommendation implicit in PRAISE (1987) is that a distinction be drawn between qualities over which schooling may have little or no effect ('basic' personality characteristics such as sense of humour, warmth, sociability) and those which more specifically reflect a pupil's response to school (e.g. punctuality). While it may be of interest to many to require pupils to build up such assessments these are unlikely to have much credibility in summative reports unless corroborated from a perspective other than the pupil's. Teachers can formulate opinions only from in-school activities or those which they may otherwise observe and there is no particular reason to suppose that teachers possess the necessary skills and insights to carry out such an assessment. The value of such self assessment, however, appears to lie in its potential for helping pupils reach a state of self awareness or self knowledge usually thought to be characteristic of the more mature adult. Social psychology is full of studies of the ways in which young people develop a sense of identity through interaction with others and seeing the reactions they provoke in their peers. To this extent informal self assessment is embedded in social interaction but may be formalized in some of the ways described above.

Many teachers have sought to extract assessments of specific effort from pupils; that is, tied to the particular topic, unit or task being undertaken in the belief that pupils know best 'how hard they have tried'. A list of questions with or without descriptions is adequate here, but again, reserved for core units of study. These take the brief form of:

How would you rate your interest in this unit using this scale:

1	2	3	4	5
Not at all interesting	Of little interest	Neutral	Quite interesting	Very interesting indeed

or, in its open-ended version:

Describe your interest in this unit...........

Similar statements could be provided for 'effort' although interest and effort assessments are correlated.

It is important to emphasize that such statements are of no use in summative comparisons between students since each pupil will have his own conception of what constitutes 'working hard' and his assessment will be ipsative (i.e. relative to his generalized or average effort in school work).

ISSUES OF RELIABILITY AND VALIDITY

Recall that where the result of an assessment is expressed as a score the essence of reliability is to estimate the size of the associated error of measurement. Error is a technical term and may be estimated by the appropriate method already described in chapter 7. The aim is to attach limits around the obtained score within which the 'true score' is likely to lie. If the outcome of an assessment is not expressed as a score other (weaker) conceptions of reliability (for example, the degree of agreement or concordance between judges) must be adopted. Criterion-referenced tests present special problems when estimating reliability and probably the only method within the scope of the teacher is to study the consistency with which equivalent test items which define a criterion classify a group of children as 'masters' (reached the criterion) and 'non-masters' (failed to reach the criterion) on the occasion of administration.

Reliability of self assessment can be interpreted in terms of measurement error only in those rare instances where children 'score' their own products according to marking schemes. In other cases, where grades or descriptors are provided, the degree of agreement between teacher and pupils may be calculated. Low agreement fulfils the formative function of initiating teacher–pupil discussion – it is the starting point for a 'negotiation'. But since the calculation of a coefficient of reliability entails many pairs of teacher–pupil assessments, this is providing redundant information for that particular purpose. Lack of explicit demonstration of reliability, then, is not serious where informed discussion follows the assessment, in a purely formative setting. When self assessment is seen as an aspect of personal recording, technical reliability is an irrelevant issue. Indeed, many advocates of personal records see them as involving no assessment, still less as a component of an examination. However, if some of the outcomes were to be used as components of summative records of achievement and, further, major discussions were in some way contingent upon them, then important reliability issues would be involved. Nuttall and Goldstein (1986) have pointed out some of these in the context of 'profiles' and 'graded tests' where, in the absence of high reliability, an apparent difference between scores or grades within and between profiles may be attributable entirely to measurement error, that is to factors other than 'real' differences between the scores or grades. Until studies are performed on self assessment, profiles, records of achievement and graded tests a strong suspicion that the elements are assessed with far lower reliability than is at present the case in public examinations will remain. Many formidable problems of reliability in new types of assessment (where errors will arise from many sources) may gradually be solved as greater rigour is applied to their development. Nevertheless, in the meantime, and all other things being equal, lack of reliability data will weaken the confidence with which assessments can be interpreted.

The validity of an assessment has two major aspects: establishing just what it 'is' which is being assessed, and demonstrating that the assessment and the inference which can be drawn from it fulfil the purpose for which it was undertaken. The following questions must be asked as appropriate:

(a)   Does the experience as recorded accurately reflect what has been done?

(b)   Does the recorded achievement accurately reflect the attainment of competences fostered by the curriculum that has been taught?

These correspond to the establishment of content validity.

(c)   Do the components of assessment reflect what it is they claim to reflect? (for example, if the assessment is of the pupils' 'initiative' what evidence corroborates the claim that this has been assessed).

(d)   Can the information provided be used in contexts for which it has been obtained? (for example, at least in informing teaching and learning, or diagnostic in revealing weaknesses for remedial action).

(e) Does the assessment yield credible and dependable state-ments to inform parents and, where relevant, future em-ployers?

These last two correspond to criterion-related validity.

So far as can be inferred from the literature, and in keeping with the ideology of self assessment, many teachers have been convinced of the validity in respect of the use of information in formative and diagnostic functions. Preliminary work has been undertaken in some areas to establish the content validity of records. For example, one LEA sends representatives to schools to corroborate content and units successfully completed.

Of course, validity of an assessment is not established by a single act of corroboration or testimony as to the usefulness of the information it provides. Systematic studies of, for example, the predictive validity of attributes exhibited in school settings for later life have not yet been undertaken. Given that well-tried traditional methods of assessment have had little success ('A level' grade in the prediction of university degree level obtained is an example) the difficulties are clear. Standardized tests, too, fare no better. In addition, the extent to which self assessment can com-plement teacher judgement and traditional – even if enlightened – examination techniques in reaching a useful appraisal of young people has yet to be realized, and is certain to remain a matter of debate for some time to come. Its place in a national curriculum, if any, needs consideration, and the task of convincing employers that self assessment is an acceptable alternative or complement to external or internal teacher assessment on a large scale remains. That introducing self assessment has proved valuable in enabling older pupils to develop reflective attitudes and in encouraging self direction is undeniable when the practices are guided by teacher commitment to the value of the exercise. However, many teachers believe that comparatively few pupils seem to study for the sake of it or for the joy in learning, preferring instead to place an instru-mental value on education. One consequence of these attitudes has been that many pupils seek external authentication of their attainments and see self assessment as of little value in compari-son. However, the last five years have witnessed many and varied changes in assessment practices which have to a considerable extent forced changes on the curriculum (e.g. the GCSE). More empirical evidence – as distinct from the intuitions of teachers – is needed to show whether the high face validity of the techniques is borne out, for if self assessment is to become more than the latest 'fashion' in education it needs clearer definition and more extensive evaluation than has so far been the case.

Diagnostic Assessment

FORMAL AND INFORMAL DIAGNOSIS

The chief purpose of diagnostic assessment is, of course, the identification of underlying learning problems or difficulties (often called 'learning disabilities') from the features of a child's performance. Generally speaking there are two main approaches:

(1) to locate the relative weaknesses or 'malfunctioning' of the child's perceptual or intellectual processes; and
(2) to infer the nature of intellectual processes hidden from view to the outside observer.

At first sight there may appear to be little difference between these approaches but the distinction can be illustrated with reference to the diagnosis of reading disability. One test which has been extensively used for this purpose is the Illinois test of psycholinguistic abilities (ITPA). The rationale of this test is to 'dissect' language ability into a number of 'subskills' or pre-requisites and to present subtests which correspond to them. The 'subskills' evaluated include:

(1) auditory reception (the ability to comprehend the spoken word);
(2) auditory closure (the ability to complete a whole word when only part of it is heard);
(3) auditory sequential memory (the ability to reproduce a sequence of auditory symbols); and
(4) sound blending (the ability to synthesize separate phonemes and to integrate them into a whole word).

In all, twelve such subskills are investigated.

Readers will appreciate that this test is a sophisticated one; despite this Newcomer and Hammill (1975) reviewed a number of studies but were unable to conclude that its validity for diagnosis had been satisfactorily demonstrated. The important point for our purposes, however, is to note that the test embodies a *formal analysis* of the target ability (reading) and thereby directs the search for specific strengths and weaknesses. Scoring helps the user depict these by means of a profile and enables the teacher to prescribe a set of remedial activities appropriate to the deficits identified.

The second type of diagnosis is less formal but leaves more scope for the teacher's ability to intuit the nature of the underlying problem. In it, no particularly structured analysis of what is involved in the target activity is used. Instead, close observation of the child's performance on the actual task (reading) is undertaken and his or her attempts examined, through which the kinds of processes 'going on' are then inferred. This approach is exemplified by the work of Goodman (1970) who studied the errors (or 'miscues') made by children in oral reading and tried to suggest the processes that operate when the syntactical and semantic information extracted from the passage interacts with what the child already knows. As a result, Goodman conceived of reading as being a 'psycholinguistic guessing game' in which the child guesses from the context, and from what he or she already knows, the words he or she is finding difficulty in reading. This conception has led Goodman to argue that miscues are worthy of the teacher's serious attention only when the meaning of what is written is altered. Unlike the ITPA, the diagnostic information provided by this approach is not a set of scores on component skills in reading but a qualitative and quantitative analysis of the miscues themselves. To this end, *Reading miscues inventory* (Goodman and Burke, 1972) has been published.

These two approaches to diagnosis – illustrated by reference to reading ability – are not, of course, mutually exclusive but complementary. Whereas the former depends on a formal structural analysis of the task itself, the latter relies on naturalistic observations, i.e. those occurring during the performance itself. We shall refer to these as *formal-structural diagnosis* and *informal-heuristic diagnosis* respectively. ('Heuristic', by the way, means discovering by one's own efforts.) As is obvious, the latter can subsequently lead to the later development of a formal-structural model of the learning task.

STAGES IN THE PROCESSES OF DIAGNOSIS AND REMEDIATION

Classroom teachers are chiefly interested in diagnostic assessment insofar as the information acquired can lead to the development of remedial programmes, or indicate where further teaching is required. Criterion-referenced assessment is capable of identifying what the child has and has not learned, of course, but diagnostic assessment is concerned with a closer examination of failure in an attempt to find reasons for it. The purpose of diagnostic assessment is, therefore, different from criterion-referenced assessment but the latter often constitutes the 'warning signs' that more extensive diagnostic assessment is required.

Although there will be variations in approach to diagnosis according to the time and facilities available in schools the sequence shown in figure 12.1 represents a very common type of model.

We are not suggesting that classroom teachers will have a great deal of time in which to conduct diagnostic assessment separately from their normal classroom activities. Nor will it be possible to cope effectively with the most intractable problems of educational or mental deficiency. In extreme cases, referral to the educational psychologist may be the only course of action left open. The most serious learning deficiencies are likely to be 'picked up' quite early in schooling and children who are clearly unable to cope with normal classrooms identified for possible treatment in special schools. Even so, a large number of pupils in ordinary schools were judged by the Warnock Report (DES, 1978) to be in need of special help, and psychologists in the Schools Psychological Services are overwhelmed with 'cases' referred for their attention.

Very many books are now available on the diagnosis of a wide range of disabilities and it is clearly beyond the scope of a chapter of this kind to examine how all specific abilities can be studied. Instead, the general principles of the stages in figure 12.1 will be described and brief summaries of the methods by which performance in basic skills may be studied will be discussed. This, it is

Figure 12.1   Stages in a diagnostic–remedial assessment.

hoped, will encourage classroom teachers to develop assessment procedures suited to their own environment and needs, derived from a few basic principles.

Stage 1: Screening

Using standardized or published tests

Screening can be accomplished in a number of curriculum areas by use of group-administered standardized tests. These enable teachers to identify those children whose level of functioning is 'well below' the mean. The comparison of pupil performance with the new national curriculum attainment targets (using standardized assessment tasks) should also help to identify those who need further diagnosis. In any large group of children teachers may expect to find a number of children whose performance is poor. On the assumption of a normal distribution of the ability or performance examined, one expects to find roughly 16% of children whose scores on the day are lower than one standard deviation below the mean. Just where the 'line is to be drawn' for a child to be deemed in need of diagnostic assessment will probably depend as much upon the facilities available as on the needs of the child. If the test used is one which, for example, expresses the child's performance in terms of a reading age, rules-of-thumb for labelling those in need of diagnosis have tended to be used. Moseley (1976) has suggested that a child whose reading age score is lower than 80% of the score expected of a boy or girl of the same chronological age is described as 'backward' and, presumably, may be helped if teachers have time to diagnose the nature of the problem faced. In practice, many teachers have adopted a criterion of one year's retardation as indicative of backwardness in reading, but this seems far too stringent a criterion. (A pupil of 15 who is reading at the level of a 13 year old is certainly functional in reading.) Since reading deficit tends to be cumulative more children in secondary than in junior school will be classified as 'backward' by this method. It does not mean that their actual reading skills are 'getting worse', of course. Similarly, the Department of Education and Science has provided guidelines for the cut-off score on intelligence tests below which children are described as 'subnormal'. Very low performance on an intelligence test has traditionally been regarded as indicative of low all-round learning potential although many have criticized the wisdom of this interpretation. The difference between classifying children as 'backward' using the reading age criterion from that using a standardized score is obviously that the latter yields a predictable proportion of backward pupils, which is likely to remain consistent over time, whereas the former cannot accomplish this. For this reason it is inadvisable to rely on a single source of information as to what kind of diagnosis is necessary. Instead, teachers will study pupils' performance in standardized tests, standard assessment tasks and formative classroom observation using oral as well as written modes of response. Tests which claim to provide 'arithmetic ages' have never been as popular as those which supply a summary 'reading age'. Although teachers may believe that the 'age' is more easily understood than a standardized score, the former does present quite considerable difficulties and may even be misleading. If reading ability is the object of the screening then several group-administered tests yielding standardized scores are now available. (The books by Vincent and Cresswell (1976) and Pumfrey (1977) provide extremely valuable sources of tests for all ages and stages in reading.)

We have already implied a distinction between the types of disability identified by the use of an intelligence test on the one hand from tests of specific abilities (reading, mathematics, etc.) on the other. Low scores on the former are often held to indicate children who are in need of special educational treatment 'across the curriculum', as it were. Low scores on the latter are taken to show poor progress in a specific area of educational attainment. Sometimes a diagnosis is attempted using both types of test. The most frequently encountered instances of this practice concern backward readers who may have to take an intelligence test when a reading score has been found to be low. This is often done to distinguish between two types of children which make up the group whose poor reading proficiency is giving cause for concern. Typically, some psychologists have claimed that this method separates 'underachievers' from 'slow learners'. The concept of 'underachiever' is applied to children whose reading is below average but whose intelligence test score is average or even higher. Basic to this labelling is the assumption that the intelligence test measures the child's potential for learning, the achievement test the actual level of functioning. Thus a child who has a high or average IQ but whose level of reading is below average is assumed to be able to do better and an explanation often sought in terms of social, cultural and emotional factors (Vincent and Cresswell, 1976). The idea of the underachiever accords with common sense but, in fact, the concept is a confused one (Thorndike, 1967). For although some children inevitably have an IQ which is higher than their standardized reading score there are others for whom the reverse is true. These, presumably, are 'overachievers'; those who are doing better than they ought to! One might have expected that the existence of these pupils would lead to a widespread mistrust of the intelligence test as a measure of potential, but the labelling continues. Nevertheless, although the concept is confused, knowledge that a child has an average or high IQ in spite of low achievement can be useful in alerting the teacher to look for possible causal factors in the child's environment.

It is probably better for a child in school to be thought of as an underachiever than as a 'slow learner', however! These latter are those children whose standardized test scores in school subjects are low and whose intelligence test scores are also below average. These are children who are thought of as 'doing as well as can be expected'. They may well be screened as in need of diagnostic assessment but there is a clear implication that no matter how skilled the remedial teaching high expectations are unrealistic. Now this will indeed be the case for those whose IQ is very low (say less than 70–75) but above this no such inference is warranted. The correlations between the intelligence test scores and school progress are far too low to posit a straightforward inference of the above type for any given child.

Although screening may appear to be a comparatively simple task some of the difficulties involved have been described. As we said in the chapter on reliability (chapter 7), however, even the best tests are less than perfect and children's scores vary from day to day. The use of a single test on a single occasion by which to decide whether diagnostic assessment is required is, therefore, indefensible in theory and practice. It seems desirable that a variety of sources of information including test scores, and if possible, the opinions of more than one teacher who has taught a pupil, be integrated into the decision making process.

At least two more sources of information may be available: the results of 'readiness tests' and the teachers' own observations.

Using 'readiness tests'
These are familiar to teachers of young children in the assessment of 'readiness for reading'. They are chiefly formal-structural in

intention. Such tests attempt to diagnose the competence of children in those intellectual and perceptual skills held by psychological and educational theory to be determinants of subsequent success, in particular to judge whether the child possesses those attributes on which the skill to be taught seems to depend. Unfortunately, the concept, though a common sense one, is fraught with problems. Readers interested in the concept can find a useful discussion in Downing and Thackray (1971). Although use of such tests may be able to identify those children who are 'more ready' than others, no precise cut-off point can ever be determined. Moreover, pupils have been known to read before they have been adjudged 'ready' to do so! (Vincent and Cresswell, 1976) and Ausubel's advice (1958) to teach first and then to infer readiness from those who do profit from the teaching seems sensible, if somewhat circular.

Although tests and check lists have been published by which, it is claimed, young children's readiness for reading can be assessed, their use as a screening device is probably to be recommended only with individual children as they are too time-consuming to be adopted on a large scale and are probably more correctly thought of as part of an attempt to prevent later failure than as a help in 'curing' a disability. Intelligence tests are of little use for this purpose with young children but tests which include aspects of visual and verbal functioning have achieved some success in the prediction of the ability to profit from reading teaching once this has been taking place for about a year (Feschbach et al., 1974). By and large, however, once schooling has well and truly begun (in middle and secondary schools) the best predictors of ability to profit from the next stage of teaching and learning are performances in earlier stages (Ausubel et al., 1978).

Using teachers' observations
Understandably, the bulk of tests useful for screening purposes has been composed of tests in basic subjects of the curriculum. Those for reading skills probably predominate. But the more formal-structural approach that such tests represent by no means exhausts the methods available. Indeed, in secondary schools (except perhaps in the first year in reading skills) very little formal screening occurs. In other areas of the curriculum and with older age groups, observations of children learning whatever it is they

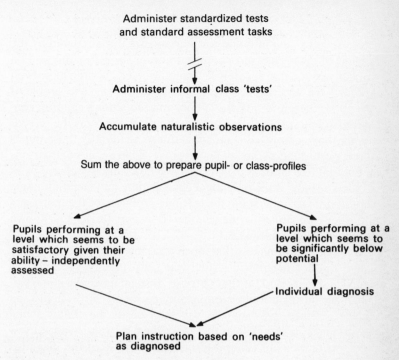

Figure 12.2   A model of screening and diagnosis.
Source: Ripley and Blair (1979, 94)

are being taught are the chief source of screening information. Generally speaking, as specialization occurs, no teacher worries over-much if a pupil's performance is poor in particular subjects other than those which are basic. Only where the pupil is low in attainment on account of a non-specific learning disability or because he or she has failed to master the basic subjects to a level where he or she can profit from teaching is diagnosis indicated. Possibly the administration of a published test provides the context in which teachers form their own judgements as to a child's need for diagnostic assessment with the score a mere by-product of little interest. (Vincent and Cresswell (1976) suggest that this is probably the only justification for the longevity of the Schonell graded word reading test; one which they rightly describe as 'antiquated'.)

In conclusion, the processes involved in screening and later diagnosis are as shown in figure 12.2.

Stages 2 and 3: Describing and Analysing the Problem

These stages shade into one another and are differentiated by the amount of detail they incorporate. In order to discuss this section we shall assume that severely learning-disabled children have been screened for and are receiving special attention. The problems described, therefore, are those encountered among children considered able to profit from normal schooling. Whereas the screening may have employed standardized tests to identify those pupils whose performances are below average, interest in comparisons among children stops at the stage of diagnosis and is replaced by as detailed a study of the individual child as time and facilities allow. This attempt to understand the learning problems of the individual in his/her own situation unencumbered by comparisons, is known as 'idiographic' assessment.

It is extremely unlikely that much time will be set aside in a busy school day for diagnostic testing using instruments specially designed and marketed for that purpose. Instead much diagnosis will take place during normal learning and teaching. This is, in fact, an advantage since the diagnosis will then be of the child's actual performance in the skill itself rather than in some artificial test item or situation. In general terms, the purpose of the diagnosis will be to find out the relatively broad area of the curriculum where learning difficulties occur and the type of skill in which the child is judged to be less than satisfactory (description), followed by a much closer study of the child's behaviour in order to determine the precise nature of the difficulty experienced (analysis). There is no particular mystery about the process: informal but systematic observation can go a long way in diagnosis. Such observation can take one of a mixture of three main forms:

(1)   the use of check lists based on task analysis;
(2)   skill analysis during the performance; and
(3)   case-study analysis.

We shall attempt to describe each of these in turn in relation to skills other than reading since extremely valuable sets of procedures for the diagnosis of reading disability have been described in numerous publications; chapter 8 in Vincent and Cresswell (1976) is a particularly helpful one in this connection.

Task analysis

This is probably the most formal of these informal procedures! Here a specific task is broken down into its successively smaller components. In other words, it is a formal analysis of the final performance in terms of subskills which are incorporated into it and which are assumed to be pre-requisite to overall satisfactory performance. To accomplish this quite difficult task the 'task analyser' begins with a description of the final performance and 'works downwards' to the most elementary skills involved. Each of these is then made an item in a check list and the child's performance assessed on each. This device is then assumed to indicate precisely at what element or combination of elements the child's overall performance is 'breaking down'.

As an example of a learning hierarchy, consider figure 12.3 which shows one model of the structure of the task: 'The pupil will be able to determine the work done when lifting a physical object through a specified height.'

The teacher who wishes to diagnose the learning problem presented by this task can prepare a quick check list as follows:

(1)   Can read unit scales.
(2)   Can recall that weight is the vertical force on a mass resulting from effects of gravitation.
(3)   Can measure force (wt) using a standard instrument.
(4)   Can measure distance using a standard instrument.
(5)   Can use standard instruments to determine 'error-free' values for f and d.
(6)   Can recall formula $w = f \times d$.
(7)   Can substitute values obtained from (5) into formula $w = f \times d$.
(8)   Can multiply real numbers to obtain product.
(9)   Can solve linear equations of the general form $a = b \times c$.
(10)   Can solve for the specific values of f and d.
(11)   Can name units for the answer.

Now it is conceivable that the pupil may fail to obtain an answer to the physical work problems presented because of errors at one or a combination of 'positions' in the hierarchy. Indeed, failure may even occur in an element which the teacher has not included in the check list because it is even lower in the hierarchy than the

Figure 12.3   Learning hierarchy for work problem
Source: *The conditions of learning*, 2nd edn, R. M. Gagné (1970). Adapted by arrangement with Holt, Rinehart and Winston.

level where it was assumed all pupils had the requisite competence. Recognition of the numerals nought to nine is a pre-requisite for the task, but a failure at this level would suggest that the topic was wholly inappropriate for the pupil in question! In other words, although the task could be successively analysed into smaller and more elementary components, a teacher will have to make certain assumptions as to how much competence can be taken for granted before a topic is begun. Quite obviously, certain kinds of task are very much easier to analyse in this way than others. For this reason one finds many more examples in mathematics and science than in arts subjects. Nevertheless, attempting to write a task analysis (or learning hierarchy) and thereby identifying pre-requisites is salutary for the teachers of all subjects and an invaluable aid to diagnosis. This method can, therefore, be classified as a formal-structural method.

Skill analysis (an example of an informal-heuristic approach)
Teachers are likely to find skill analysis much easier to perform than task analysis since it is not necessary to build a model of structure to carry it out. It is really little more than a systematic analysis of a homogeneous set of performance items (e.g. a number of similar arithmetic problems; several written paragraphs; a set of comprehension exercises) in order to detect errors. Those which occur frequently are held to be more relevant to the diagnosis than those which seem to be 'careless slips'. As an example, consider the performance on an informal test of subtraction administered to a group of seven year olds. The teacher has marked all those items where a particular pupil has made mistakes and has concluded, after study of the performance and questioning, that the child has been confused by the presence of noughts. In particular he seems to have multiplied by nought in some cases (figure 12.4). Similarly, at a more advanced level, an older pupil has reached a wrong answer when simplifying an algebraic expression which involves factors and fractions (figure 12.5). Here the teacher observes that an error has been made when factorizing the expression $a^2 + bc + d$. If this type of error were to be repeated in similar items a clear diagnosis with implied remediation would be made. At this stage, source of difficulty rather than interpretation of the problem is the goal of the analysis.

Skill analysis can be carried out most easily in school subjects where criteria of 'correct/incorrect' can be applied or where the performance varies along a continuum of 'good to poor'. Too often, teachers have little time to go beyond the correction of errors in children's work and, if the work has then to be covered in red ink (or its equivalent) this can be very depressing. Nevertheless, the principal purpose of this kind of analysis is to discover learning problems followed by constructive attempts to remediate performance, not to 'grind the pupil down'. So there is no real need to cover the pupil's work with actual 'corrections' to fulfil the aim of the analysis. Notice that it is not the purpose at this stage to offer explanation of the learning problems nor to suggest possible remediation.

Name: ..*John*......

```
  67        39        28        75        88
 -43       -20       -15       -40       -45
 ───       ───       ───       ───       ───
  24       (0)        13       3(0)       43


 347       182       883       975       578
-101      - 90      -570      -622      -220
 ───       ───       ───       ───       ───
2(0)6      9(0)       313       343      35(0)


 513       654       845       497       260
-206      -352      -203      - 82      -109
 ───       ───       ───       ───       ───
 307      (2)02     (6)02      415      1(00)
                                        │
                              '*Careless slips*'
```

Figure 12.4   Skill analysis of subtraction performance.

Note also, in passing, that criterion-referenced assessment is a form of diagnostic assessment when it is used to examine performance rather than to classify as master/non-master. Thus criterion-referenced assessment can serve the functions both of assessing progress and diagnosing learning failure, if not learning disability.

Case-study analysis

Much of the teachers' informal diagnostic assessment will be of the skill analysis type, but occasionally it will be necessary for several members of staff who teach a pupil to pool their knowledge in a detailed study of his or her performance and general school adjustment. Case studies are an attempt to integrate information from all possible sources in trying to evaluate and understand the problem faced by a child which transcends his or her learning of the specific subject or skill. The types of assessment which are relevant will go beyond the kinds of information with which this book has been principally concerned, to include classroom observations, performance data, general data about school adjustment and, perhaps, health and home records (used with caution!).

$$\frac{2}{x+4} - \frac{x-5}{x^2 + 7x + 12}$$

$$= \frac{2}{x+4} - \frac{x-5}{(x-4)(x-3)} \qquad LCM = (x-4)(x-3)$$

Incorrect Signs

$$= \frac{2(x-3)-(x-5)}{(x-4)(x-3)}$$

$$= \frac{2x-6-x-5}{(x-4)(x-3)}$$

$$= \frac{x-11}{(x-4)(x-3)}$$

Figure 12.5   Skill analysis of simplifying task.

Remedial teachers in schools will be particularly anxious to understand as many facets of the child's adjustment to school as can be evaluated by whatever assessments have been made in the (correct) belief that the more intractable learning problems are influenced in a complex way by many overlapping factors. But this is an extremely time-consuming task, and case-study analysis will probably be undertaken only where children who exhibit the most severe learning difficulties in the normal school are identified.

The following guidelines may be helpful in standardizing the case-study report which can then be discussed with parents. The full report cannot be written until stages 4, 5 and 6 shown in figure 12.1 have been conducted, of course:

(1) Include only that information which is likely to be of value in working with pupils.
(2) Distinguish impression judgements, opinions and objective information.

(3) List specific performance data (test scores, grades) making sure that the name of the test is included where relevant.
(4) List the specific basic skills where the child is judged to require remedial teaching.
(5) List specific remedial teaching – if tried – and evaluate outcome in terms of pupil progress (stages 4 and 5).
(6) Make specific suggestions for further remediation (stage 4).
(7) Include possible causal interpretations but avoid the types of explanation which 'blame' parents, since they are unlikely to be conducive to the establishment of productive home/school relationships.

Stages 4 and 5: Hypothesizing and Planning

We shall deal only very briefly with this since the task of diagnosing the underlying causes of learning disability is a complex one and conclusions are, at best, extremely tentative even when conducted by experts. Therefore the purpose of the hypothesis is not so much to construct a theory of explanation of the phenomena as it is to erect hunches as to the most appropriate educational actions to take.

It is assumed that by this stage the teacher or teachers involved will have identified in fairly precise terms the target weaknesses in performance. If teachers other than those who made the diagnosis are to be involved, the weaknesses will have to be spelt out with some precision if time is not to be wasted nor effort duplicated. Generally speaking, no matter what the performance to be 'remediated' three chief kinds of factors must be assessed (and action designed in stage 5). These factors are (Ripley and Blair, 1979):

(1) *learner-style* variables;
(2) *task* variables; and
(3) *resource* variables.

Decisions may be made by considering some important questions.

Learner-style variables
(a) Has the child shown any marked preference for working alone or in groups and how much anxiety or need for reassurance has he/she shown in previous work? Is a systematic

attempt to improve the child's self-concept indicated as a pre-requisite for or concomitant of remedial work (for example, through counselling)?

(b)   Is the child able to work at a single activity for a stretch of time or is he/she able, at present, only to concentrate for short periods?

(c)   In what type of structure does the child work most effectively? For example, is it to be strictly controlled or loosely disciplined: structured formally around tight objectives or largely informal with emphasis on a discovery approach?

(d)   Do attempts need to be made to change the attitudes of the child to work as a pre-requisite for remedial teaching?

(e)   If the child has reacted to failure defensively or by withdrawal, what steps can be taken to change this approach?

(f)   What kind of reward structure seems likely to provide the most appropriate incentives to effort? For example, does the child respond best to praise, to the intrinsic satisfaction of success or may it even be necessary to employ sanctions in the event of 'inadequate' motivation? Is it necessary to work out a systematic reward schedule for the pupil?

(g)   What are the existing *strengths* in the child's approach to tasks which can be built upon in the remedial work (for example, special ability at drawing; comparative efficiency in dealing with practical problems)?

Task variables

(a)   Given that the child has been diagnosed on account of performances which have failed to match certain basic objectives, which instructional objectives will be retained for the child, unmodified or modified? There is no particular justification for maintaining an objective for a pupil who, in spite of the best teaching available, has failed to learn it. A tactical withdrawal to an objective at a lower level of performance may be indicated. Alternatively, a new objective may be set following negotiations with the learner.

(b)   How can the task be presented so as to minimize the probability of a child's continued failure?

(c)   How far can tasks taken from the child's everyday experience be utilized to provide a context for the remedial work?

For example, can advantage be taken of the child's spontaneous interests as raw material for the development of the deficient skill?

(d)   Can the remedial requirements be incorporated into the existing class organization or to what extent will modifications have to be made to accommodate the difficulties? For example, is it desirable or possible to withdraw the child into a separate group if small group teaching is indicated? (Small group teaching would be considered a 'task' rather than a 'resource' variable if it was designed to permit certain forms of interaction among learners having similar difficulties.)

(e)   Is remediation of the skill required to be confined within a subject, or can opportunities be taken or provided across the curriculum? If, for example, the remedial work is required in a rather specific topic in mathematics, opportunities in other subjects are likely to be limited. If the language behaviour of the child is in question then all subjects are potentially capable of providing remedial contexts or tasks. Teacher cooperation is a pre-requisite for this type of task setting, of course.

(f)   Are existing structured remedial programmes suited to the learner's requirements? None of the published remedial schemes is a panacea, of course. Nevertheless, it is worthwhile consulting specific books on remedial teaching, liaising with other teachers who have faced similar problems, etc., to see whether existing tasks and processes serve the needs of the child and teacher. The best examples are found in reading remediation, notably American. Ripley and Blair (1979) for example, list a number of commercially available programmes for remediating basic skills in reading. Local Authority advisers in remedial work are usually able to help teachers find materials which may save considerable time and effort in devising remedial tasks.

Resource variables

It would be silly to construct a remedial programme which demands resources far in excess of the possible. So the question of resource allocation is designed to match the conclusions reached from assessments of learner-style and those relating to task analysis. Indirectly this serves as an assessment of the extent to which the school or teacher is able to meet remedial needs, with possible corrective effect. The most crucial questions concern the allocation of resources of time and effort:

(a) If the remedial task demands substantial individual teaching, how can this be accomplished without detriment to the progress of the average and most able members of the class? Are self-teaching devices available which minimize the dependency of the slow-learner on the types of immediate or personalized enforcement which can only be supplied by the teacher?

(b) Can a more efficient use of time and effort be achieved by grouping pupils with similar problems?

(c) What instructional materials (filmstrips, etc.) and approaches (remedial 'games') are already available? Can any be constructed to meet specific needs?

(d) Does the teacher have the skills necessary to promote the kind of improvement in performance that is required? Does the local teachers' centre, university school of education or similar institution provide courses which are of value in strengthening the teacher's competence?

No doubt, practising teachers will be able to supply many more questions than the above. Nevertheless, posing such problems will, it is hoped, enable teachers to hypothesize the forms of educational intervention which offer a reasoned basis for planning remedial work outside the context of the specialized remedial centres. The advice has been intended to generalize no matter what area of intellectual functioning is held to be deficient. It has, of course, excluded reference to the subnormal whose problems are generally too severe to be accommodated within normal schooling, at least given our present state of medical and psychological knowledge.

Stage 6: Assessing and Evaluating the Effectiveness

We shall concentrate chiefly on how progress in the skill remediated can be assessed although there may be many other aspects by which remedial teaching can be justified, even where little or no measurable progress can be demonstrated. (For example, caring for the individual learner and demonstrating concern for his or her problems may in indirect ways have an even more profound effect on children's learning than moral exhortation to behave well towards others.) Similarly, progress in the skill may be minimal but be accompanied, nevertheless, by progress in the development of attitudes or other affective components of learning (for example, increased enjoyment or interest).

There is an important difference between finding out whether the pupil has made progress *following* remedial teaching and finding out whether that progress (if made) is the *result* of remedial teaching. The former – though not without its difficulties – is relatively straightforward in theory, the latter much more difficult to carry out in practice.

It will simplify matters if we deal with these issues separately although both are subject to common but major difficulties which must be discussed. No matter how carefully the measurement is conducted there will always be a difference between the scores obtained on two occasions (i.e. before remedial teaching and after remedial teaching) even if there is no difference in the underlying ability being assessed, because of the presence of measurement error in the scores. This concept was dealt with quite fully in chapter 7 where reliability was discussed. The effect of the presence of measurement error is neatly and clearly described by Vincent and Cresswell (1976, appendix A). Briefly, if we assume a normal distribution of scores of a group of children on the first occasion the differences between the scores on the two occasions will themselves be normally distributed but with a standard deviation which is equal to the product of the standard error of the test and the square root of two (i.e. $SD_{diff} = SE_x \sqrt{2}$). Thus any group of pupils assessed on two occasions using a test with a standard error of six will yield 'gains' or 'losses' of about 17 points (that is, 2 × 8.48) to 5% of pupils whilst 68% of pupils will receive 'gains' or 'losses' within 8.5 points of the mean of the new distribution. This fact enables the statistically minded reader to compare the actual difference in score (second testing occasion minus first testing occasion) obtained, with what is to be expected from the known unreliability of the test, as indicated by the size of the standard error.

A second difficulty relates very closely to this. When the scores on two test occasions are imperfectly correlated (i.e. always!) the errors which cause test scores to vary are most 'influential' amongst the highest and lowest score bands in the group. Because of this, the average scores of pupils who are 'high' or 'low' on the first occasion are less extreme on the second. This phenomenon is called 'regression to the mean' and is a statistical artefact. Its importance for the assessment of remedial teaching is clear: some of the apparent change in remedial pupils (those who by definition scored substantially lower than average on the first test) is attributable to the regression of the scores rather than to improvement. Nevertheless, if the results of the standardized testings have been used to measure progress over a long period of time, and are backed up by criterion-referenced evidence of qualitative improvement in the actual features of the performance itself, the ubiquitous effects of regression may be assumed to be comparatively negligible, thus strengthening the belief that progress has been made.

There is one further source of potential error when interpreting difference scores (second testing minus first testing) as indexes of progress. Some of the improvements may well result from practice on the test items themselves with no improvement in the underlying ability being assessed. This is especially likely to happen where the same test is used on a number of occasions and can be overcome to a limited extent if parallel forms of the test (chapter 7) are used.

This has necessarily been a brief and inadequate account of some fairly tricky statistical problems in the interpretation of 'progress' (gain or loss) scores. The dangers are worth reiterating. When using a test on two occasions to assess progress remember:

(1) Part of the differences between scores will be attributable to the presence of measurement error. Actual differences between scores, therefore, should be compared with those expected from measurement error to see if progress has been made.

(2) Any group of children who are relatively extreme on the first testing occasion (for example, pupils given remedial help because of low scores on a standardized test) will tend to receive a mean score on the second occasion which is nearer to the overall mean of the second testing. Thus results from two testings will be subject to regression to the mean which

confuses the interpretation of progress. As Vincent and Cresswell (1976, 88) remark: 'the pupil who does really badly on a test could hardly do worse on a second occasion'. The reverse applies to a pupil or groups of pupils who are outstandingly good on the first occasion, of course. Teachers must be aware of claiming 'progress' using measurement of this kind.

(3) Test scores can also 'improve' because of the practice effects where the same or parallel forms of a test are taken on more than one occasion.

(4) Indexes of progress derived from the difference between scores on tests taken on two occasions should always be interpreted with great caution because some change in score is inevitable. Where possible, progress should be assessed using a combination of evidence, such as where the results of standardized tests can be supplemented by qualitative assessment of changes in actual performance as are obtained from the administration of criterion-referenced tests or provided by the processes of skill analysis described in this chapter.

(5) In subjects or areas of skill or knowledge where no standardized tests exist, progress is best assessed by an examination of actual performance. Many teachers might, in view of the difficulties described above, prefer to emphasize the qualitative aspects of progress rather than risk the difficult interpretation of test scores. In any event, if progress is to be reported, more information is potentially contained in a skill analysis than in a standardized score.

We have seen some of the problems in an attempt to assess progress following remedial teaching. It is very unlikely that teachers will have the time or resources to research whether the progress is *attributable* to the remedial programme, but it is useful to be aware of some of the difficulties. It has already been shown how changes in scores will result whether or not there has been 'real' progress. The problem of demonstrating that it is the remedial programme which is responsible for the changes and not the multitude of other factors known to affect performance requires, at very least, a comparison between two groups, 'identical' at the start of the enquiry, but only one of which receives the remedial teaching. This, of course, is the classic two-group (one-control) design which is itself barely adequate even though difficult to carry out in the practical setting of schools. Many complex experimental designs exist by which to tease out what is known as the 'treatment effects' and the reader interested in them could consult the book by Campbell and Stanley (1966). Without some sort of check provided by the control group progress could well be erroneously attributed to the remedial work when it belongs properly to the normal maturational effects or even to some extraneous external influence such as a relevant television programme! Ethical difficulties also arise, of course. Is a teacher justified in the deliberate withholding of a programme which it is hoped and believed will have beneficial effects in order to set up a control group?

In order to justify the remedial programme, then, teachers may assemble a variety of supporting evidence. They may point to the improved 'work-tone' of the class, to clear acquisitions of skill brought into view by qualitative descriptions of performance and to improved adjustment and attitudes on the part of individuals. Teachers are certainly not going to be able to show beyond doubt that these attributes would not have come about had remedial teaching not taken place (a roundabout way of arguing that remedial teaching 'works'!). Nevertheless, continuous monitoring and the use of a number of test scores and other types of evidence will provide some of the feedback necessary if the remedial teachers are to sustain their own motivation.

Because of an increase in awareness of the principle of accountability coupled with the impositions of increasing limitations on expenditure, one might anticipate the cost-effectiveness of remedial teaching to come under much closer scrutiny than has been the case to date. Perhaps the most useful type of evidence that teachers can offer in support of their work is qualitative descriptions of the features of improved performance where criterion-referenced assessment has been practised. If standardized tests are used (either the same test over time or parallel forms with an interval between) a rule-of-thumb can be given (Vincent and Cresswell, 1976). Those gains in score which are more than twice as large as standard error of the test may reasonably be used to claim that the improvement has been a 'real' one as distinct from one that could have arisen easily by chance. In case the reader's grasp of chapter 7 has proved somewhat tenuous, a reminder of the procedure may be in order. If the reliability, r_{tt}, of test whose standard deviation, σ_x, is 15 is 0.96, then the standard error of the measurement is given (formula [7.14]) by

$$
\begin{aligned}
SE_m &= \sigma_x \sqrt{1 - r_{tt}} \\
&= 15\sqrt{1 - 0.96} \\
&= 3
\end{aligned}
$$

Any increase in score which is greater than six points on the standardized test, then, probably indicates a real improvement.

Guide to Further Reading

Readers will appreciate that the references in this book can provide only an introduction to what is by now a vast field of study. In anticipation that some readers will wish to follow up some of the more important implications of the study of assessment for schools and teachers, a limited guide to the field is offered here. Full details are given only when a work does not appear in the reference list below.

Those who wish to make fuller study of the technical aspects of test design, construction and validation are recommended to consult the excellent source on these topics edited by Robert L. Thorndike (1971). If you wish to examine test items of a high standard of construction in most areas of the curriculum refer to the handbook by Benjamin Bloom, J. Thomas Hastings and George Madaus (1971).

For a sociological critique of the often covert effects of assessment on children and society read Patricia Broadfoot (1979). Many of the problems and dilemmas in assessment practices, especially with older pupils, are frankly discussed by Derek Rowntree (1977), and for an extreme attack on its worst effects look at Hoffman (1962). If, after this, you are convinced that assessment is indefensible and would like to see what teaching in an assessment-free environment might be like, study the work of Marshall (1968).

Readers who would like an introductory survey of psychological tests might start with Anne Anastasi (1982). A reasonably up-to-date critique of intelligence testing is provided by Kamin (1974) and, as an example of the kinds of re-appraisal currently going on in the area of the psychological assessment of children (especially if you are knowledgeable about the work of the schools' psychological services), the book edited by Bill Gilham (1978) is a provocative starting point. Finally, if you have a head for formulae and wish to study the theory of mental measurement try Frederick Lord and Melvin Novick (1968). For up-to-date developments, two journals

– *Journal of Educational Measurement* and *Educational and Psychological Measurement* – are worth consulting if you can get near the library of a university school of education, or other reference library.

Attention will continue to be paid to issues in the introduction of *Records of Achievement*. The recent appearance of the Report of the National Steering Committee (DES, 1989) will add impetus to the discussion, especially the recommendations it contains and its interesting suggestions for further research. Readers could study this publication alongside the carefully considered views of Burgess and Adams (1985). Given that these and other proposed innovations are often seen as contentious, a provocative set of opinions as to the need to reconstruct educational assessment can be examined in the essays edited by Nuttall (1986). For policy issues, see Broadfoot (1988).

The Schools Examinations and Assessment Council (SEAC) was set up under the Education Reform Act of 1988. Among other responsibilities of SEAC is that of developing the national assessment system in accordance with the parental expectation that pupils' achievements will be 'accurately measured' (DES, 1988d). Readers should keep a look out for future reports from SEAC, TGAT and the curriculum working parties for the national curriculum recommendations. These are published by the DES and usually announced in the educational press. SEAC has already arranged contracts with outside funded bodies (such as the National Foundation for Educational Research) for the production of standard assessment tasks (see Glossary) and those items designed for use in primary schools are eagerly awaited by teachers and assessment theorists alike.

Interest will continue to grow in the development of the GCSE and in the methods of assessment to be adopted for pupils at age 16 – both internal and external. Selkirk (1988) has presented an excellent series of readings on this topic and the books by Roy (1986), North (1987) and Gorman (1988) can be recommended as offering important perspectives on the new practices.

Finally, teachers continue to find the general text of assessment techniques by Frith and Macintosh (1984) a valuable resource. While its treatment of the issues in assessment is somewhat brief, it is full of helpful examples of test items of most kinds, and as such it can be thoroughly recommended.

References

Alkin, M. 1970: Evaluating net cost-effectiveness of instructional programs. In M. C. Wittrock and D. E. Wiley (eds) *The Evaluation of instruction: issues and problems*. New York: Holt, Rinehart and Winston.

American Psychological Association 1974: *Standard for educational and psychological tests*. American Psychological Association.

Anastasi, A. 1982: *Psychological testing*. 5th edn. New York: Macmillan.

Anderson, S. B., Ball, S. and Murphy, R. T. 1975: *Encyclopaedia of Educational Evaluation*. San Francisco: Jossey-Bass.

Ausubel, D. P. 1958: *Theory and problems of child development*. New York: Grune and Stratton.

Ausubel, D. P., Novak, J. D. and Hanesian, H. 1978: *Educational psychology: a cognitive view*. New York: Holt, Rinehart and Winston.

Balogh, J. 1982: *Profile reports for school leavers*. London: Longman for the Schools Council.

Bar-Tal, D. 1978: Attributional analysis of achievement-related behaviour. *Review of Educational Research*, 48, 259–71.

Berk, R. A. (ed) 1980: *Criterion-referenced measurement*. Baltimore: Johns Hopkins University Press.

Black, H. 1962: *They shall not pass*. New York: William Morrow.

Black, H. D. and Dockrell, W. B. 1984: *Criterion referenced assessment in the classroom*. Edinburgh: Scottish Council for Research in Education.

Block, J. H. 1972: Student evaluation: toward the setting of mastery performance standards. Paper presented at annual meeting of American Educational Research Association, April 1972, Chicago.

Block, N. J. and Dworkin, G. 1976: *The IQ controversy*. New York: Pantheon.

Bloom, B. S., Engelhart, M. A., Furst, E. J., Hill, W. H. and Krathwohl, D. R. 1956: *Taxonomy of educational objectives. Handbook I: Cognitive domain*. London: Longman.

Bloom, B. S., Hastings, J. T. and Madaus, G. F. 1971: *Handbook on formative and summative evaluation of student learning*. New York: McGraw Hill.

Bowen, J. 1988: Student self assessment. In Brown, S. (ed) *Assessment: a changing practice*. Edinburgh: Scottish Academic Press.

Bowles, S. and Gintis, H. 1976: *Schooling in capitalist America*. London: Routledge and Kegan Paul.

Bray, E. 1986: Profiling. In Lloyd-Jones, R. and Bray, E. (eds) *Assessment: from principles to action*. Basingstoke: Macmillan.

Broadfoot, P. 1979: *Assessment, schools and society*. London: Methuen.

Broadfoot, P. (ed) 1986: *Profiles and records of achievement: a review of issues and practice*. London: Holt.

Broadfoot, P. 1987a: *Introducing profiling: a practical manual*. Basingstoke: Macmillan Educational.

Broadfoot, P. 1987b: *Profiles in context*. London: DES, Further Education Unit.

Broadfoot, P. 1988: Research and policy-making in assessment: some unanswered questions. In Black, H. D. and Dockrell, W. B. (eds) *New developments in educational assessment*. Edinburgh: Scottish Academic Press, *British Journal of Educational Psychology*. Monograph Series No. 3.

Brown, S. and Black H. 1988: Profiles and records of achievement. In Brown, S. (ed) *Assessment: a changing practice*. Edinburgh: Scottish Academic Press.

Buber, M. 1958: *I and thou*. New York: Charles Scribner.

Burgess, T. and Adams, E. 1985: *Records of achievement at 16*. Windsor: NFER-Nelson.

Burt, C. 1955: The evidence for the concept of intelligence. *British Journal of Educational Psychology*, 25, 158–77.

Burton, N. W. 1978: Societal standards. *Journal of Educational Measurement*, 15, 263–71.

Campbell, D. T. and Stanley, J. C. 1966: *Experimental and quasi-experimental designs for research*. American Educational Research Association.

Cast, B. M. P. 1940: The efficiency of different methods of marking English compositions. *British Journal of Educational Psychology*, 10, 49–60.

Cattell, R. B. 1973: *Personality and mood by questionnaire*. New York: Jossey-Bass.

Child, D. 1970: *The essentials of factor analysis*. London: Holt, Rinehart and Winston.

Child, D. 1977: *Psychology and the teacher*, 2nd edn. London: Holt, Rinehart and Winston.

Child, D. 1986a: *Psychology and the teacher*, 4th edn. London: Cassell.

Child, D. 1986b: *Applications of psychology for the teacher*. London: Cassell.

Cleary, T. A., Humphreys, L. G., Kendrick, S. A. and Wesman, A. 1975: Educational use of tests with disadvantaged students. *American Psychologist*, 30, 15–41.

Clough, E. E., Davis, P. and Sumner, R. 1984: *Assessing pupils*. Windsor: NFER-Nelson.

Cronbach, L. J. 1961: *Essentials of psychological testing*, 2nd edn. New York: Harper and Row.

Cronbach, L. J. 1971: Test validation. In R. L. Thorndike (ed) *Educational Measurement*, 2nd edn. Washington, D. C.: American Council on Education.

Cronbach, L. J. 1975: Five decades of public controversy over mental testing. *American Psychologist*, 30, 1–14.

Cronbach, L. J., Gleser, G. C., Nanda, H. and Rajaratnam, N. 1972: *The dependability of behavioral measurement*. New York: Wiley.

Cronbach, L. J. and Meehl, P. E. 1966: Construct validity in psychological tests. In C. I. Chase and H. L. Ludlow (eds) *Readings in educational and psychological measurement*. Boston: Houghton Mifflin.

Cureton, E. E. 1966: Kuder–Richardson reliabilities of classroom tests. *Educational and Psychological Measurement*, 26, 13-14.

Dearden, R. 1968: *The philosophy of primary education*. London: Routledge and Kegan Paul.

Department of Education and Science 1978: Report of the Committee of Enquiry into the education of handicapped and young persons (The Warnock Report). London: HMSO.

Department of Education and Science 1978: *Monitoring mathematics*. London: DES.

Department of Education and Science 1984: *Records of achievement: a statement of policy*. London: HMSO.

Department of Education and Science 1987a: *Records of achievement: an interim report*. London: HMSO.

Department of Education and Science 1987b: *Task group on assessment and testing*. A report. London: HSMO.

Department of Education and Science 1988a: *Mathematics for ages 5 to 16*. London: HMSO.

Department of Education and Science 1988b: *Report of the Committee of inquiry into the teaching of the English language* (Kingman Report). London: HMSO.

Department of Education and Science 1988c: *Science for ages 5 to 16*. London: HMSO.

Department of Education and Science 1988d: *News Bulletin*, 279/88. London: HMSO.

Department of Education and Science 1989: *Records of achievement: Report of the Records of Achievement National Steering Committee*. London: HMSO.

Donaldson, M. 1978: *Children's minds*. Glasgow: Fontana.

Downing, J. and Thackray, D. 1971: *Reading readiness*. London: University of London Press.

Dunstan, M. 1959: Examining in English at the matriculation level. Unpublished M.Ed. thesis, University of Sydney.

Ebel, R. L. 1972: *Essentials of educational measurement*. Englewood Cliffs, N.J.: Prentice Hall.

Erikson, K. T. 1962: Notes on the sociology of deviance. *Social Problems*, 9, 307–14.

Feschbach, S., Adelman, H. and Fuller, W. W. 1974: Early identification of children with high risk of reading failure. *Journal of Learning Disabilities*, 7, 639–44.

Finlayson, D. S. 1951: The reliability of the marking essays. *British Journal of Educational Psychology*, 21, 216–34.

Flanagan, J. C. 1955: The development of an index of examinee motivation. *Educational and Psychological Measurement*, 15, 144–51.

Flanders, N. A. 1970: *Analyzing teacher behavior*. New York: Addison-Wesley.

Foster, J. 1972: *Recording individual progress*. London: Macmillan.

Fraenkel, J. R. 1969: Value education in the social studies. *Phi Delta Kappan*, 50, 457–61.

Frith, D. S. and Macintosh, H. G. 1984: *A teacher's guide to assessment*. Cheltenham: Stanley Thornes.

Gagné, R. M. 1970: *The conditions of learning*. 2nd edn. London: Holt, Rinehart and Winston.

Gagné, R. M. 1974: *Essentials of learning for instruction*. Hinsdale, Ill.: Dryden Press.

Garforth, D. and Mackintosh, H. 1986: *Profiling: a user's manual*. Cheltenham: Stanley Thornes.

Gaudry, E. and Spielberger, C. D. 1974: *Anxiety and educational achievement*. New York: Wiley.

Geddes, B. 1982: Pupil self assessment: theoretical and practical issues. Unpublished MEd thesis, University of Bristol.

Gerberich, J. R. 1956: *Specimen objective test items*: A guide to achievement test construction. New York: Longmans.

Gilham, B. (ed) 1978: *Reconstructing educational psychology*. London: Croom Helm.

Glaser, R. 1968: Adapting the elementary school curriculum to individual performance. *Proceedings of the 1967 Conference on Testing Problems*. Princeton, N. J.: Educational Testing Service.

Glass, G. V. 1978: Standards and criteria. *Journal of Educational Measurement*, 15, 237–61.

Goacher, B. 1983: *Reading achievement at 16+*. London: Longmans for the Schools Council.

Goldman, L. 1971: *Using tests in counseling*, 2nd edn. Calif.: Goodyear.

Goldstein, H. and Nutall, D. 1986: Can graded assessments, records of achievement and modular assessment co-exist with GCSE? In Gipps,

C. V. (ed) *The GCSE: an uncommon exam.* Bedford Way Papers, London Insitute of Education.

Goodman, K. S. 1970: Reading: a psycholinguistic guessing game. In H. Singer and R. Ruddell (eds) *Theoretical models and processes of reading.* Newark, Del.: International Reading Association.

Goodman, Y. and Burke, C. 1972: *Reading miscues inventory.* New York: Macmillan.

Gorman, G. 1988: *GCSE: A guide for parents, employers and candidates.* London: Kogan Page.

Gosling, G. W. H. 1966: *Marking English compositions.* Australian Council for Educational Research.

Green, B. F. 1970: Comments on tailored testing. In I. Holtzman (ed) *Computer assisted instruction, testing and guidance.* New York: Harper and Row.

Gronlund, N. E. 1971: *Measurement and evaluation in teaching,* 2nd edn. New York: Macmillan.

Guilford, J. P. and Fruchter, B. 1973: *Fundamental statistics in psychology and education,* 5th edn. Tokyo: McGraw Hill.

Hambleton, R. K. 1980: Test score validity and standard-setting methods. In Berk, R. A. (ed) *Criterion-referenced measurement: the state of the art.* Baltimore: Johns Hopkins University Press.

Hargreaves, A., Baglin, E., Henderson, P., Leeson, P. and Tossell, T. 1988: *Personal and social education.* Oxford: Basil Blackwell.

Hargreaves, D. H. 1967: *Social relations in a secondary school.* London: Routledge and Kegan Paul.

Hartog, P. 1941: *The marking of English essays.* London: Macmillan.

Hartog, P. and Rhodes, E. C. 1936: *The marks of examiners.* London: Macmillan.

Head, J. J. 1966: Multiple marking of an essay item in experimental O-level Nuffield biology examination. *Educational Research,* 19, 65–71.

Henrysson, S. 1971: Gathering, analyzing and using data on test items. In R. L. Thorndike (ed) *Educational Measurement.* Washington, D. C.: American Council on Education.

Hitchcock, G. 1986: *Profiles and profiling: a practical introduction.* Harlow: Longmans.

Hoffman, B. 1962: *The tyranny of testing.* New York: Crowell-Collier Press.

Hunter, I. M. L. 1962: An exceptional talent for calculative thinking. *British Journal of Psychology* 53, 243–58.

Jacobs, P. I. 1966: Effects of coaching on the college-board English composition test. *Educational and Psychological Measurement,* 26, 55–67.

Jencks, C. et al. 1973: *Inequality: a reassessment of the effect of family and schooling in America.* London: Allen Lane.

Jensen, A. R. 1972: *Genetics and education*. New York: Harper and Row.

Jewett, A. and Bish, C. E. (eds) 1965: *Improving English composition*. Washington: National Education Association.

Kamin, L. J. 1974: *The science and politics of IQ*. New York: Wiley.

Karmel, L. J. and Karmel, M. O. 1978: *Measurement and evaluation in the schools*, 2nd edn. New York: Macmillan.

Klausmeier, H. J. and Ripple, R. E. 1971: *Learning and human abilities*, 3rd edn. New York: Harper and Row.

Krathwohl, D. R., Bloom, B. S. and Masia, B. B. 1964: *Taxonomy of educational objectives. Handbook II: The affective domain*. New York: McKay.

Lien, A. J. 1976: *Measurement and evaluation of learning*. Dubuque, Iowa: Wm C. Brown.

Livingston, S. A. 1972: Criterion-referenced applications of classical test theory. *Journal of Educational Measurement*, 9, 13–26.

Lloyd-Jones, R. and Bray, E. (eds) 1986: *Assessment: from principles to action*. Basingstoke: Macmillan.

Lord, F. M. 1957: Do tests of the same length have the same standard error of measurement? *Educational and Psychological Measurement*, 17, 510–21.

Lord, F. M. and Novick, M. 1968: *Statistical theories of mental test scores*. Reading, Mass.: Addison-Wesley.

Lucas, A. M. 1971: Multiple marking of a matriculation biology essay question. *British Journal of Educational Psychology*, 41, 78–84.

Marshall, M. S. 1968: *Teaching without grades*. Corrallis, Oregon: Oregon State University Press.

Markle, S. M. and Tiemann, P. W. 1973: Behavioural analysis of cognitive content. In Thornberg, H. (ed) *School learning and instruction*. Monterey: Brooks Cole.

Medley, D., Schluck, C. and Ames, N. 1969: Assessing the learning enviroment in the classroom. *A manual for users of OSCAR 5*. Princeton, N. J.: Educational Testing Service.

Mehrens, W. A. and Lehmann, I. J. 1978: *Measurement and evaluation in education and psychology*, 2nd edn. New York: Holt, Rinehart and Winston.

Merton, R. K. 1957: *Social theory and social structure*. Glencoe: The Free Press.

Meskauskas, J. A. and Webster, G. W. 1975: The American Board of Internal Medicine recertification examination process and results. *Annals of Internal Medicine*, 82, 577–81.

Messick, S. 1965: Personality measurement and the ethics of assessment. *American Psychologist*, 20, 136–42.

Metfessel, W. S., Michael, W. B. and Kirsner, D. A. 1969: Instrumentation of Bloom's and Krathwohl's taxonomies for the writing of behavioral objectives. *Psychology in the Schools*, 6, 227–31.

Miller, G. E. 1976: Continuous assessment. *Medical Education*, 10, 81–6.

Moseley, D. 1976: *Helping with learning difficulties*. Milton Keynes: Open University Press.

McClelland, D. C. 1966: The measurement of human motivation: an experimental approach. In A. Anastasi (ed) *Testing problems in perspective*. Washington, D. C.: American Council on Education.

Newcomer, P. L. and Hammill, D. D. 1975: ITPA and academic achievement: a survey. *Reading Teacher*, 28, 731–41.

Nisbet, J. D. 1955: English composition in secondary school selection. *British Journal of Educational Psychology*, 35, 51–4.

North, J. 1987: *The GCSE: An examination*. London: Claridge Press.

Nuttall, D. (ed) 1986: *Assessing educational achievement*. London: Falmer Press.

Nuttall, D. and Goldstein, H. 1986: Profiles and graded tests: the technical issues. In Broadfoot, P. (ed) *Profiles and records of achievement*. London: Holt.

Payne, D. A. 1974: *The assessment of learning*. Lexington, Mass.: D. C. Heath and Co.

Phillips, G. E. 1948: The marking of children's essays. *Forum of Education*, 7, 19–29.

Pipho, G. (ed) 1978: Minimum competency testing. *Phi Delta Kappan*, 59, 585–629.

PRAISE, 1987: *Pilot records of achievement in schools evaluation: an interim report*. Open University and University of Bristol Schools of Education.

Pumfrey, P. D. 1977: *Measuring reading abilities*. London: Hodder and Stoughton.

Ripley, W. H. and Blair, T. R. 1979: *Reading diagnosis and remediation*. Chicago: Rand McNally.

Rosenthal, R. R. and Jacobson, L. 1968: *Pygmalion in the classroom*. New York: Holt.

Rowley, G. L. 1974: Which examinees are most favoured by the use of multiple-choice tests? *Journal of Educational Measurement*, 11, 15–23.

Rowntree, D. 1977: *Assessing students: How shall we know them?* London: Harper and Row.

Roy, W. 1986: *The new examination system – GCSE*. London: Croom Helm.

Royd, G. H. and Haladyna, T. M. 1982: *A technology for test item writing*. New York: Academic Press.

Satterly, D. J. and Brimer, M. A. 1971: Cognitive styles and school learning. *British Journal of Educational Psychology*, 41, 294–303.

Schmuck, R. A. and Schmuck, P. A. 1974: *A humanistic psychology of education*. Palo Alto, Calif.: National Press Books.

Seashore, H. G. and Ricks, J. H. 1950: Norms must be relevant. *Test Service Bulletin 39*. New York: The Psychological Corporation.

Selkirk, K. (ed) 1988: *Assessment at 16*. London: Routledge.

Sperry, L. (ed) 1972: *Learning performance and individual differences: Essays and readings*. Glenview, Ill.: Scott Foresman.

Stalnaker, J. M. 1934: The validity of the University of Chicago qualifying examination. *English Journal (Coll. Ed.)*, 23, 384–8.

Stansbury, D. 1984: *Principles of personal recording*. Totnes: Springline Trust.

Start, K. B. and Wells, B. K. 1972: *The trend of reading standards*. Windsor: NFER Publishing Co. Ltd.

Stevens, S. S. 1946: On the theory of scales of measurement. *Science*, 103, 677–80.

Stones, E. 1979: *Psychopedagogy: psychological theory and the practice of teaching*. London: Methuen.

Stratton, N. 1986: Recording achievement: The City and Guilds experience. In Broadfoot, P. (ed) *Profiles and records of achievement: a review of issues and practice*. London: Holt.

Thorndike, R. L. 1967: 'Overachievement' and 'underachievement' as psychological concepts. In B. P. Komisar and C. J. B. Macmillan (eds) *Psychological concepts in education*. Chicago: Rand McNally.

Thorndike, R. L. 1968: A review of Pygmalion in the classroom. *American Educational Research Journal*, 5, 708–11.

Thorndike, R. L. (ed) 1971: *Educational measurement*, 2nd edn. Washington, D. C.: American Council on Education.

Tinkelman, S. N. 1971: Planning the objective test. In R. L. Thorndike (ed) *Educational measurement*, 2nd edn. Washington, D. C.: American Council on Education.

Vernon, P. E. 1979: Intelligence testing and the nature/nurture debate 1928–1978: What next? *British Journal of Educational Psychology*, 49, 1–14.

Vernon, P. E. and Millican, G. D. 1954: A further study of the reliability of English essays. *British Journal of Statistical Psychology*, 7, 65–74.

Vincent, D. and Cresswell, M. 1976: *Reading tests in the classroom*. Windsor: NFER Publishing Co. Ltd.

Weiner, B. 1980: *Human motivation*. New York: Holt, Rinehart and Winston.

Wertheimer, M. 1945: *Productive thinking*. New York: Harper.

Wesman, A. G. 1971: Writing the test item. In R. L. Thorndike (ed) *Educational measurement*, 2nd edn. Washington, D. C.: American Council on Education.

Wesman, A. G. 1972: Testing and counseling: fact and fancy. *Measurement and evaluation in guidance*, 5, 397–402.

Weston, P. and Evans, A. 1988: *Changing approaches to achievement and assessment in England*. A study for the Commission of European Communities. Slough: National Foundation for Educational Research.

Whitehead, A. N. 1950: *The aims of education and other essays*. London: Williams and Norgate.

Wood, R. and Napthali, W. A. 1975: Assessment in the classroom: what do teachers look for? *Educational Studies*, 1, 151–61.

Appendix

z-scores (column 1) and areas from mean to z-score in curve of normal distribution (column 2). Reproduced by arrangement with Holt, Rinehart and Winston – New York, from *Experimental design in psychological research*, 3rd edn by A. L. Edwards, 1968.

1	2	1	2	1	2	1	2	1	2
0.00	0.0000	0.70	0.2580	1.40	0.4192	2.10	0.4821	2.75	0.4870
0.01	0.0040	0.71	0.2611	1.41	0.4207	2.11	0.4826	2.76	0.4971
0.02	0.0080	0.72	0.2642	1.42	0.4222	2.12	0.4830	2.77	0.4972
0.03	0.0120	0.73	0.2673	1.43	0.4236	2.13	0.4834	2.78	0.4973
0.04	0.0160	0.74	0.2704	1.44	0.4251	2.14	0.4838	2.79	0.4974
0.05	0.0199	0.75	0.2734	1.45	0.4265	2.15	0.4842	2.80	0.4974
0.06	0.0239	0.76	0.2764	1.46	0.4279	2.16	0.4846	2.81	0.4975
0.07	0.0279	0.77	0.2794	1.47	0.4292	2.17	0.4850	2.82	0.4976
0.08	0.0319	0.78	0.2823	1.48	0.4306	2.18	0.4854	2.83	0.4977
0.09	0.0359	0.79	0.2852	1.49	0.4319	2.19	0.4857	2.84	0.4977
0.10	0.0398	0.80	0.2881	1.50	0.4332	2.20	0.4861	2.85	0.4978
0.11	0.0438	0.81	0.2910	1.51	0.4345	2.21	0.4864	2.86	0.4979
0.12	0.0478	0.82	0.2939	1.52	0.4357	2.22	0.4868	2.87	0.4979
0.13	0.0517	0.83	0.2967	1.53	0.4370	2.23	0.4871	2.88	0.4980
0.14	0.0557	0.84	0.2995	1.54	0.4382	2.24	0.4875	2.89	0.4981
0.15	0.0596	0.85	0.3023	1.55	0.4394	2.25	0.4878	2.90	0.4981
0.16	0.0636	0.86	0.3051	1.56	0.4406	2.26	0.4881	2.91	0.4982
0.17	0.0675	0.87	0.3078	1.57	0.4418	2.27	0.4884	2.92	0.4982
0.18	0.0714	0.88	0.3106	1.57	0.4429	2.28	0.4887	2.93	0.4983
0.19	0.0753	0.89	0.3133	1.59	0.4441	2.29	0.4890	2.94	0.4984
0.20	0.0793	0.90	0.3159	1.60	0.4452	2.30	0.4893	2.95	0.4984
0.21	0.0832	0.91	0.3186	1.61	0.4463	2.31	0.4896	2.96	0.4985
0.22	0.0871	0.92	0.3212	1.61	0.4474	2.32	0.4898	2.97	0.4985
0.23	0.0910	0.93	0.3238	1.63	0.4484	2.33	0.4901	2.98	0.4986
0.24	0.0948	0.94	0.3264	1.64	0.4495	2.34	0.4904	2.99	0.4986
0.25	0.0987	0.95	0.3289	1.65	0.4505	2.35	0.4906	3.00	0.4987
0.26	0.1026	0.96	0.3315	1.66	0.4515	2.36	0.4909	3.01	0.4987
0.27	0.1064	0.97	0.3340	1.67	0.4525	2.37	0.4911	3.02	0.4987
0.28	0.1103	0.98	0.3365	1.68	0.4535	2.38	0.4913	3.03	0.4988
0.29	0.1141	0.99	0.3389	1.69	0.4545	2.39	0.4916	3.04	0.4988
0.30	0.1179	1.00	0.3413	1.70	0.4554	2.40	0.4918	3.05	0.4989
0.31	0.1217	1.01	0.3438	1.71	0.4564	2.41	0.4920	3.06	0.4989
0.32	0.1255	1.02	0.3461	1.72	0.4573	2.42	0.4922	3.07	0.4989
0.33	0.1293	1.03	0.3485	1.73	0.4582	2.43	0.4925	3.08	0.4990
0.34	0.1331	1.04	0.3508	1.74	0.4591	2.44	0.4927	3.09	0.4990
0.35	0.1368	1.05	0.3531	1.75	0.4599	2.45	0.4929	3.10	0.4990
0.36	0.1406	1.06	0.3554	1.76	0.4608	2.46	0.4931	3.11	0.4991
0.37	0.1443	1.07	0.3577	1.77	0.4616	2.47	0.4932	3.12	0.4991
0.38	0.1408	1.08	0.3599	1.78	0.4625	2.48	0.4934	3.13	0.4991
0.39	0.1517	1.09	0.3621	1.79	0.4633	2.49	0.4936	3.14	0.4992
0.40	0.1554	1.10	0.3643	1.80	0.4641	2.50	0.4938	3.15	0.4992
0.41	0.1591	1.11	0.3665	1.81	0.4649	2.51	0.4940	3.16	0.4992
0.42	0.1628	1.12	0.3686	1.82	0.4656	2.52	0.4941	3.17	0.4992
0.43	0.1664	1.13	0.3708	1.83	0.4664	2.53	0.4943	3.18	0.4993
0.44	0.1700	1.14	0.3729	1.84	0.4671	2.54	0.4945	3.19	0.4993
0.45	0.1736	1.15	0.3749	1.85	0.4678	2.55	0.4946	3.20	0.4993
0.46	0.1772	1.16	0.3770	1.86	0.4686	2.56	0.4948	3.21	0.4993
0.47	0.1808	1.17	0.3790	1.87	0.4693	2.57	0.4949	3.22	0.4994
0.48	0.1844	1.18	0.3810	1.88	0.4699	2.58	0.4951	3.23	0.4994
0.49	0.1879	1.19	0.3830	1.89	0.4706	2.59	0.4952	3.24	0.4994
0.50	0.1915	1.20	0.3849	1.90	0.4713	2.60	0.4953	3.30	0.4995
0.51	0.1950	1.21	0.3869	1.91	0.4719	2.61	0.4955	3.40	0.4997
0.52	0.1985	1.22	0.3888	1.92	0.4726	2.62	0.4956	3.50	0.4998
0.53	0.2019	1.23	0.3907	1.93	0.4732	2.63	0.4957	3.60	0.4998
0.54	0.2054	1.24	0.3925	1.94	0.4738	2.64	0.4959	3.70	0.4999
0.55	0.2088	1.25	0.3944	1.95	0.4744	2.65	0.4960		
0.56	0.2123	1.26	0.3962	1.96	0.4750	2.66	0.4961		
0.57	0.2157	1.27	0.3980	1.97	0.4756	2.67	0.4962		
0.58	0.2190	1.28	0.3997	1.98	0.4761	2.68	0.4963		
0.59	0.2224	1.29	0.4015	1.99	0.4767	2.69	0.4964		
0.60	0.2257	1.30	0.4032	2.00	0.4772	2.70	0.4965		
0.61	0.2291	1.31	0.4049	2.01	0.4778	2.71	0.4966		
0.62	0.2324	1.32	0.4066	2.02	0.4783	2.72	0.4967		
0.63	0.2357	1.33	0.4082	2.03	0.4788	2.73	0.4968		
0.64	0.2389	1.34	0.4099	2.04	0.4793	2.74	0.4969		
0.65	0.2422	1.35	0.4115	2.05	0.4798				
0.66	0.2454	1.36	0.4131	2.06	0.4803				
0.67	0.2496	1.37	0.4147	2.07	0.4808				
0.68	0.2517	1.38	0.4162	2.08	0.4812				
0.69	0.2549	1.39	0.4177	2.09	0.4817				

Glossary of Assessment Terms[4]

Academic aptitude. A combination of abilities and skills, whatever their origin, on which learning in school depends. An *aptitude test* is one made up of items which predict success in later academic work but are minimally dependent, if at all, on the effects of instruction. Thus such tests attempt to measure the elusive property of potential for learning.

Accountability (in education). An explicit or implicit responsibility on the part of schools for bringing about certain educational objectives in a cost-effective way. The processes by which schools and local authorities justify the expenditure to the taxpayer.

Achievement test. A test which is designed to measure how much a child has acquired as the result of specific teaching. The acquisitions are usually of information, knowledge or skills which schools have made a deliberate intention to teach.

Affective test. A test of non-cognitive classroom characteristics of pupils, such as motivation, interests, attitudes and aesthetic awareness.

Age-equivalent score. The average score of a group of children of specified age. This average is usually obtained either by direct observation or estimated using other tests (singly or in combination) which are known to correlate with the score in question.

Age norms. Sets of average scores for successive age groups.

Aggregated assessment. An assessment in which scores or grades on a number of components are combined into a single grade or mark.

---

[4] Some definitions are based on *A glossary of measurement terms* published by CTB/McGraw-Hill, Monterey, California 93940. Reproduced by permission of the publisher. Copyright © 1959 by McGraw-Hill, Inc. All rights reserved. Printed in the United States of America.

Arithmetic mean. Usually abbreviated to 'mean' it is the value obtained when the sum of a set of scores is divided by the number of scores. Mathematically it is that value about which the sum of the deviations (q.v.) is zero.

Assessment task. Any task or problem considered worthwhile in itself in which the desired performance of an individual or group may be observed and assessed (see *standard assessment task*).

Average. A vague way usually of specifying the arithmetic mean but sometimes loosely employed to indicate the median (q.v.) or the mode (q.v.).

Baseline measures. Measurements obtained to indicate levels of performance before the intervention of an educational or other programme against which to assess change (compare *pre-test*).

Bivariate chart (sometimes called a 'scatter diagram'). A diagram defined by two axes (*x* and *y*) in which tally marks are made to show the scores of a group or individual, on two tests. A useful device for checking on the shape of the relationship between two tests prior to the calculation of a correlation coefficient (q.v.).

Ceiling. The top score or upper limit of ability or achievement that can be measured by a test. A test is said to have a 'low ceiling' if it fails to differentiate a group of children whose overall performance exceeds or reaches the highest level at which it can discriminate.

Central tendency. A single score or value which provides a suitable summary of the properties of the complete set of scores. The three most commonly used are the mean (q.v.), median (q.v.), and mode (q.v.). For some sets of scores one or other of these may not provide a meaningful index of central tendency: for example, in a distribution of scores where each score occurs the same number of times.

Certification. The use of assessment data to make a formal attestation to a learner's competence or performance, especially the level of success in an examination or as a licence to practise a profession or trade or to gain entry to it.

Check list. A list of behaviours or characteristics of children's work drawn up to aid systematic observation. The rater responds by ticking 'yes' when he or she has decided that the characteristic in question has occurred to his or her satisfaction but leaves the item blank or records otherwise in the absence of this.

Class interval. The size of the divisions of a frequency distribution bounded by upper and lower score values. For example, a test of 100 items where the scores are cast into divisions which correspond to 40–4, 45–9, 50–4, etc. has a class interval of five.

Completion item. A type of test question which requires the respondent to complete a phrase or sentence where one or more gaps have been left.

Composite score. A score which is obtained by the combination of several other scores. This is usually done by addition though different weights are often applied to the contributing scores to increase or decrease their contributions to the whole.

Concurrent validity. The strength of the relationship – usually expressed as a correlation coefficient (q.v.) between scores on a given test and another criterion of the same ability or characteristic obtained at or near the same time. For example, scores on a test of personality with estimates of adjustment, or scores on an end-of-term test with teacher ratings of achievement.

Construct validity. The extent to which a test measures an underlying, usually abstract, psychological trait. For example, the extent to which a test of verbal ability correlates with the property common to other verbal tests identified through factor analysis (q.v.)

Content validity. The extent to which a test represents a balanced sample of the outcomes the programme of teaching or instruction was designed to achieve: for example, a test would have poor content validity for a course in *mathematics* if it consisted solely of problems in arithmetic. The balance is best achieved by using a specification table (q.v.).

Continuous assessment. Where all learning activities or assignments (or a selected combination of these) taken throughout the course provide the only data for certification (see *terminal assessment*).

Control group. A group of children who do not receive an educational programme that an investigator wishes to evaluate, as contrasted with an experimental group who do.

Correction for guessing. A device for reducing scores in tests where right answers can be obtained by chance. In a true/false question a formula sometimes used is $(R - W)$, but all are based on the assumption that guessing in an objective test will yield a number of wrong answers that is proportional to the number of alternative responses to each item. The usefulness of this device is, however, questionable.

Correlation. A general term which refers to the relationship between two sets of scores or measures. The fact that high scorers on one test achieve high scores on the other (and vice versa) does not necessarily indicate a causal relationship between the abilities measured.

Correlation coefficient. A precise mathematical index of the strength of the relationship between two sets of scores which can range from $+1.0$ (perfect positive agreement) to -1.0 (perfect negative agreement) with zero indicating a complete lack of relationship. The most common type of coefficient is the Pearson product–moment correlation (symbolized r) but other types are often calculated.

Covariance. The average of the product of the deviations of separate pairs of scores from their respective means. Thus if the deviation of an x score for a child is $(x - \bar{x})$ and the y score for that same child is $(y - \bar{y})$, then $\Sigma(x - \bar{x})(y - \bar{y})/n$ is said to be the covariance of x and y (where $\Sigma =$ the sum of).

Criterion-referenced test. A test used to ascertain the degree of correspondence between the performance or learning by an individual and a precise definition of the behaviour exhibited by a 'successful' learner of a well-defined objective for learning. Most commonly, such tests cover relatively small units of content and the scores are interpreted as showing *what* the individual learner can do rather than as a comparison with other individuals (contrast standardized tests). See also *mastery test*.

Cross-sectional data. Results of assessments made on representative samples of children chosen from age groups which span a number of years. Often adopted as an economical substitute for longitudinal data (q.v.).

Culture-fair test. A test which is said to provide an equal opportunity of success to all respondents irrespective of culture and experiential background. Its content must, therefore, contain only that material which is common to all cultures – probably an impossibility to attain in practice – or material which is equally novel for all cultures.

Culture-free test. A test which is said to be free from the effects of cultural experience and reflects only that part of ability which is hereditary. Such claims are seldom if ever made for contemporary tests.

Decile. An example of a quantile (q.v.). One of the nine score points which divides a distribution into ten equal parts.

Deviation (d). The difference between any one score and a reference score. Most frequently a deviation score is the amount by which the score x_{ij} differs from the mean of the group of scores to which it belongs ($\bar{x}$). Thus $d = (x_{ij} - \bar{x})$. Deviation scores can also be found from the median or mode (q.v.) of a group of scores.

Deviation IQ. An index of general mental ability most commonly used in the Wechsler tests of intelligence. It is based upon the deviation of a person's score from the typical or average score for persons of the same chronological age. Deviation IQs are usually standard scores with the mean of 100 and standard deviation 16.

Diagnostic test. A test which analyses an individual's performance in order to locate its strengths or (more commonly) its weaknesses. Wherever possible diagnostic tests suggest the cause of the difficulties either by providing subscores on components identified by a formal analysis of the intellectual skill (e.g. reading) or, less formally, by discovering the nature of the difficulty during ordinary classroom performance.

Differentiation by outcome. An approach to assessment in which no attempt is made to match item or task difficulty to individual differences but where all pupils of a given age are presented with the same task and where different degrees of success may be observed.

Difficulty index. The difficulty of a test item measured by the proportion (or percentage) of children in a given age group who answer that item correctly.

Difficulty value. The difficulty of a test item as measured by the Rasch method of objective measurement.

Discrimination index. An index which expresses the effectiveness of a single item to differentiate children who are high scorers from those who are low scorers on the overall test result. Most commonly it is obtained by finding the number who 'pass' the item in the highest 27% of scorers and in the lowest 27% of scorers and taking the difference between them.

Distracter. One of the plausible but incorrect options in a multiple choice test.

Distribution. A table of scores showing the number of children who obtain each score or have a score within each score interval.

Domain-referenced test. A test which consists of a representative set of items drawn from a clearly defined area of knowledge or competence. For example, a test consisting of 50 items measuring knowledge (recall) of chemical symbols drawn at random from the domain of chemical elements, listed in the Periodic Table.

Equivalent scores. Where there are two or more forms of a test each measuring the same ability, equivalent scores are a means of translating the scores on one form into units on the other form.

Error of measurement. One of a number of statistical devices for estimating the size of the error present in a given score (see *standard error*).

Evaluation. Using assessment data to arrive at a judgement of the value or effectiveness of something. For example, the scores obtained by children to decide whether or not a programme of instruction has been 'successful'.

Expectancy table. A two- or multi-way table which shows the relationship between scores on a predictive test and a criterion: for example, one which compares scores on a criterion-referenced test with a second judgement of mastery of a given skill.

Face validity. A weak form of validity in which a test 'appears to measure' what it claims to measure but in the absence of any evidence beyond that appearance.

Factor. A hypothetical trait which is assumed to underlie and affect performance on two or more (usually mental) tests. Thus a factor is the theoretical construct responsible for correlations between tests. It is identified by factor analysis (q.v.).

Factor analysis. A family of statistical methods for isolating a more parsimonious number of underlying traits by which to account for the overlap (correlations) among a number of mental tests. It shows how much of the variance (q.v.) in the original tests is associated with each factor.

Flotation technique. A method of reaching an assessment in which the teacher is recommended to record the most salient characteristics of a child, that is those which 'float to the top' of the teacher's recollections. Recommended by Marshall (1968) as an alternative to the use of check lists or any other set of criteria presented in advance and of universal application.

Formal assessment. Assessment conducted in situations which have been set up solely for that purpose (see *informal assessment*) usually using well-validated tests or other instruments.

Formative evaluation. The use of assessment data by which to obtain knowledge of the effects of teaching and learning during its development. The general aim is to provide information to modify a programme of education (contrast *summative evaluation*).

Frequency polygon. A line graph joining the number of individuals who obtain each score, or who occur within a given score interval.

Goal card. Charts showing the objectives of learning, the criteria of passing those objectives and incorporating a space for self-recording of progress. Useful in individually guided learning.

Graded test. A test in which a number of defined standards of performance can be set at progressively higher levels and where progress to the next level depends upon success at the previous level.

Group test. A test designed to be taken by a number of individuals simultaneously and administered by a single examiner.

Idiographic assessment. Assessment designed to understand the individual in his own right without comparison with others.

Individual test. A test designed to be administered to one person at a time.

Informal assessment. Assessment conducted while pupils are carrying on with normal classroom activities (see *formal assessment*).

Intelligence quotient (IQ). Originally the ratio of a person's mental age (q.v.) to his chronological age expressed as a percentage but now replaced by a standardized score (q.v.) which takes the individual's raw score and age into account. The mean IQ for a group is 100 with a standard deviation (q.v) of 15 or 16. The IQ is often interpreted as a general measure of a person's 'brightness'.

Item. A single question or exercise in a test.

Item analysis. A set of methods for examining an item to determine its difficulty, discrimination and validity.

Item bank. A collection of items classified by content and level of difficulty for purposes of test construction.

Item (or matrix) sampling. A method used in test construction in which subgroups of respondents take subgroups of items thus avoiding the need for all pupils to take all items.

Kuder–Richardson formulae. A family of formulae for estimating reliability (q.v.) by studying the internal consistency of a test.

Leptokurtic curve. A distribution of scores which rises more steeply to a peak than a normal, or mesokurtic, curve (contrast *platykurtic*).

Longitudinal data. Results of repeated assessment of the same children, usually over a considerable period of time (contrast *cross-sectional data*).

Mastery test. A test designed to determine whether a pupil has mastered a given objective of instruction or a unit of knowledge or skill. Differs from criterion-referenced testing (q.v.) in its goal, which is to label pupils as master/non-master of any objective which needs to be attacked before more difficult work can be undertaken.

Matrix sampling. A method of dividing a long test into shorter subtests and of administering each subtest to samples of children chosen by random from a population. If properly carried out, reliable estimates of total scores can be obtained, thus saving time in administration and scoring.

Mean. See *arithmetic mean.*

Measurement. Assigning numbers to objects or characteristics.

Median. The 50th percentile (q.v.) or middle score in a group which divides the distribution into two equal parts such that half the scores are above and half below the median.

Mental age. The age for which a given score in a test of mental ability or intelligence is average. Thus if the average score of a large group of children aged seven years nine months is 65 then any child receiving that score is said to have that mental age irrespective of his chronological age. Mental ages are especially difficult to interpret among children older than about 11 years of age.

Mesokurtic curve. A distribution of scores which is normal or near normal.

Mode. The score which occurs most frequently in a distribution. Any distribution may have more than one mode.

Monitoring. Regular and systematic assessment of basic attainments of representative groups of children to establish changes in typical performance over a period of time (e.g. in the maintenance of standards).

Multiple choice test. A test composed of items in which the task is to select one or more correct answers from a number of options.

Negotiated assessment. An assessment in which the learner and his or her teacher collaborate (on 'equal terms') to reach an agreed description, mark or grade, and report. It often follows agreement on the nature of the task to be undertaken and the criteria to be applied.

Nomothetic assessment. Assessment of individuals with a view to making comparisons among them or to generalize to larger populations.

Normal distribution. A distribution in which scores are symmetrically distributed about the mean with most scores concentrated near it but decreasing in frequency with increasing distance from it as described by a particular mathematical function. In a normal distribution (sometimes called a Gaussian curve) mean, median and mode coincide. The assumption that psychological, educational and other phenomena are normally distributed is a widely accepted model in the statistical description and interpretation of scores.

Normalized standardized scores. Scores manipulated to conform to the normal curve having a known mean and standard deviation. (For example, *T*-scores have a mean of 50 and SD of ten.)

Norms. Tables of scores describing the average performance of large, often representative, groups of children to provide an interpretive frame of reference by which to give meaning to the scores of individuals. The most common norms in education are IQ and verbal reasoning in standardized score form, percentile ranks and stanines. Norms represent only average, not desirable, performance and to be of value should have been obtained from groups similar to those to whom interpretation is to be extended.

Norm-referenced test. A test explicitly designed to be used to make comparison among individuals (contrast *criterion-referenced test*) with norms (q.v.) for interpretation.

Objectives. Narrow definitions of children's behaviour or performance which are indicative of the goals of teaching (see *goal cards*).

Objective measurement. A term applied to the approach developed by Rasch. The scale of difficulty values is independent of the sample on which the items have been scored and the ability measures are on a scale which expresses the odds of a respondent's success on items of known difficulty.

Objective test. One whose scoring is unaffected by the opinions of different scorers. Thus criteria of 'correctness' are set up in advance and consistently applied by a number of markers.

Percentiles. An example of quantiles (q.v.). The division of a ranked distribution into 99 groups each composed of the same percentage of scores. Thus the 40th percentile (P_{40}) is the score which separates the 'top' 60% from the 'bottom' 40% of scores.

Platykurtic curve. A distribution of scores which is flatter than that of a normal or mesokurtic curve (contrast *leptokurtic*).

Placement. Using assessment data to classify an individual for the purposes of matching him with one of an alternative number of educational programmes either as an individual or member of a group.

Post-test. A test administered at the end of an educational programme designed to evaluate the effectiveness of that programme by comparison with the pre-test (q.v.).

Power test. A test designed to be taken with no time limit, or a very generous one to measure ability or performance unconstrained by the demand of quick responding.

Practice effect. The effect of a previous experience with a test on a later administration of the same or similar test.

Predictive validity. The claim that a test is valid based on its correlation between it and scores on a criterion at a later time.

Pre-test. A test designed to obtain information about children before a programme which is to be evaluated is administered (contrast *post-test*).

Product–moment correlation. See *correlation coefficient*.

Profile. An array of assessments – usually of a broad range of a pupil's characteristics using a variety of methods – designed to report his or her attainments under a number of headings. Each heading represents an important aspect of the pupil's performance or curriculum.

Profile component. Any of the agreed categories or headings which collectively define the profile (q.v.). These can be aspects of the pupil or of the way the subject of study is held to be organized. For example, the recommendation by the National Curriculum mathematics group that attainment be reported under three components: knowledge, skills and understanding in number, algebra and measures; knowledge skills and understanding in shape, in space and data handling; practical application of mathematics.

Profiling. Any of the processes which are involved in the development of profiles, and in the recording of the results of assessments that contribute to an individual's profile.

Protocol. A record of the actual words used by a child when answering questions during problem solving or learning. The protocol is usually transcribed and later analysed for its significance in providing information about the processess of thought involved, e.g. for research or diagnostic purposes.

Questionnaire. A set of printed questions designed to elicit information from respondents by self report.

Quantiles. A family of techniques for dividing a distribution of scores into equal groups (e.g. quartiles, deciles, percentiles).

Quartile. One of three points which divide a distribution into four equal-sized groups. Thus Q_1 separates the 'lowest' quarter of the group from the top three quarters.

Random sample. A set of individuals (or items on a test) drawn from the population in such a way that every member of that population has an equal chance of being selected. The sample is drawn in such a way as to preclude bias and so that certain statistical techniques for estimating population values are appropriate. Sometimes the population is divided into special subgroups before random selection from within them: this is *stratified random sampling*.

Range. The difference between highest and lowest raw score on a test.

Raw score. The actual scores obtained on a test (in education usually the 'number right').

Readiness test. A test which claims to measure the extent to which an individual has acquired the skills or knowledge required to learn some new task successfully.

Recall item. An item which requires the respondent to supply the correct answer from his memory.

Recognition item. A test item which requires the respondent to recognize or select the correct answer from among two or more alternatives.

Record of achievement. Sometimes used synonymously with 'profile', but usually the document which records the positive achievements and experiences of pupils in and out of school as evidence of the pupil's curriculum during the years of secondary schooling.

Regression effect (regression to the mean). A consequence of imperfect correlation, it is the tendency of a predicted score to be nearer the mean of the predicted scores than was the score from which it was predicted from the mean of its series. Thus children who are very high scorers on the predictor, though above the mean on the criterion or on a second administration of the same test, are nevertheless nearer the mean on the latter. The converse is true of very low scorers on the predictor.

Reliability. The extent to which a test is consistent or dependable in measuring whatever it is that it measures.

Reliability coefficient. The coefficient of correlation between two forms of a test, between scores on two administrations of the same test taken a week or so apart or between halves of the same test after Spearman–Brown correction (q.v.). An alternative type of reliability coefficient is provided by the Kuder–Richardson formulae (q.v.).

Representative sample. A sample which accurately reflects the population from which it was drawn with respect to certain defined characteristics.

Response set. A habit or temporary disposition that causes a person to respond to test items in a particular manner.

Self assessment. Any process or product of self evaluation by the pupil of his or her learning outcomes, experiences or personal characteristics.

Side-effects (of assessment). The unintended (positive or negative) results of assessment.

Simulation. An attempt to set up conditions that represent 'real life' in order to make an assessment of behaviour or performance.

Skewed distribution. A distribution of scores which departs from symmetry or balance around the mean. A distribution for which the average of the z-scores (q.v.) raised to the third power (i.e. z^3/n) is negative is said to have 'negative skew', one in which z^3/n is positive has 'positive skew'.

Sociometry. Measuring aspects of the inter-personal relationships among members of a group, usually the patterns of friendship, by asking respondents to identify the individuals they would be most likely to choose in a variety of social settings.

Spearman–Brown formula. A formula most commonly used to estimate the reliability of an entire test from a correlation between the two halves. Generally it expresses the relationship between the reliability of a test and its length.

Speed test. A test where performance is measured by the number of items correctly 'passed' in a given time. Items are usually on a similar level of difficulty within the test.

Specification table. A two-way grid (or table) summarizing the objectives of teaching and the content of the course. Entries in the grid specify the importance of the various topics and the relative importance to be alloted to them in the construction of the achievement test.

Split-half reliability coefficient. The estimate of reliability obtained by correlating scores for a given group of respondents obtained on the two halves of a test corrected by application of the Spearman–Brown formula. Comparable halves are commonly obtained by splitting the test into totals on odd- and even-numbered items. This type of coefficient is sometimes referred to as an internal consistency coefficient.

Standard. Level of requirement, degree of excellence or attainment set as a goal for pupil effort.

Standard assessment task. An assessment task, for all pupils of a given age cohort and represented under standardized conditions to assess the attainment of targets making up the national curriculum.

Standard deviation. A linear measure of the dispersion or 'scatter' of scores in a distribution, obtained by finding the square root of the size of the average squared deviation from the mean. In a normal distribution approximately two-thirds (68.3%) of the scores occur within the range from one standard deviation below the mean to one standard deviation above the mean.

Standard error of estimate. An estimate of the error inherent in predicting a criterion score from a test with which it is correlated (a predictor). It is the standard deviation of the criterion times the square root of one minus the square of the correlation coefficient.

Standard error of measurement. A statistic applied to a single obtained score to estimate the amount by which that score differs from the hypothetical 'true score' (q.v.). The larger the standard error the greater the amount of error contained in the score. The standard error of measurement is the standard deviation of the test times the square root of one minus the reliability coefficient.

Standard score. A general term describing a variety of scores transformed to make them comparable. The simplest kind is the 'z-score' in which each is the ratio of the difference between the raw score and the mean to the standard deviation of the score: $z = (x_{ij} - \bar{x})/\sigma_x$. Since these scores range from positive to negative formulae are sometimes used to remove this undesirable feature (see *T-scores*).

Standardization sample. The sample of individuals or schools selected in order to provide norms for the interpretation of test scores.

Standardized test. A test containing a balanced set of items designed to be taken under prescribed conditions, scored objectively and interpreted in norm-referenced terms. A commercially published standardized test should present details of item analysis, reliability, validity and the nature of the standardization sample on which the norms are based.

Stanine (short for standard-nine). Usually normalized standardized scores, stanines have values from one to nine with a mean of five and standard deviations of two. Stanines two to eight inclusive have a width of half a standard deviation.

Statistical significance. A score or a result of an analysis which is unlikely to have occurred by chance. Thus 'significant at the 0.05 level' means it has been calculated that the obtained result could have occurred by chance five times (or less) in 100.

Summative evaluation. Use of assessment data to determine the effectiveness of a learning episode, unit of study, course or programme at its completion.

T-scores. A normalized, standardized set of scores constructed to have mean 50 and standard deviation ten.

Taxonomy. A principle for the classification of educational objectives.

Terminal assessment. Where assessment of work done throughout the course is not taken into account but is subordinated to the results of assessment (usually examinations or tests) taken at the end of a course or school career (see *continuous assessment*).

Test–retest reliability coefficient. A type of reliability coefficient which measures the stability of a test by correlating scores obtained by the same sample of children on two administrations of the test.

Test-wiseness. A state of readiness by a respondent to profit from previous experience of similar tests. Differential test-wiseness within a group of children is a source of invalidity in scores.

True score. Hypothetical but average score that would be expected if a child took the same test on a large number of occasions (assuming no practice effect or change in the ability being measured).

Unobtrussive assessment. Observations made with little or no awareness on the part of the assessed, usually during normal classroom practice.

Validity. A general term which describes the extent to which a test performs the function claimed for it (see *content, concurrent* and *predictive validity*).

Variance. The average of the squared deviations from the mean: the square of the standard deviation.

z-score. A type of standard score formed by dividing the deviation by the standard deviation (i.e. $z = (x_i - \bar{x})/\sigma_x$). Thus z-scores have a mean of zero and standard deviation of one.

Index